ZIONISM AND MELANCHOLY

NEW JEWISH PHILOSOPHY AND THOUGHT

Zachary J. Braiterman

ZIONISM AND MELANCHOLY

The Short Life of Israel Zarchi

Nitzan Lebovic

INDIANA UNIVERSITY PRESS

This book is a publication of

Indiana University Press
Office of Scholarly Publishing
Herman B Wells Library 350
1320 East 10th Street
Bloomington, Indiana 47405 USA

iupress.indiana.edu

Manufactured in the United States of America

Cataloging information is available from the Library of Congress.

ISBN 978-0-253-04181-4 (hardback)
ISBN 978-0-253-04182-1 (paperback)
ISBN 978-0-253-04185-2 (ebook)

1 2 3 4   24 23 22 21 20 19

To my parents, with love.

CONTENTS

ISRAEL ZARCHI'S WORKS
UNDER DISCUSSION

The works below are ones discussed within this book. Dates are original publication dates. Occasionally my discussion of Zarchi's works uses later editions of his novels or stories, and I indicate that within the text or its notes.

I followed the exact transliteration, when available. If unavailable, I tried to keep as close as possible to the Hebrew.

"The Leader of Israel," unpublished
Alumim (Youth), 1933
Yamim Yechefim (Naked days), 1935
Ha'Neft Zorem La'Yam Ha'Tikhon (And the oil flows to the Mediterranean), 1937
Massa Le'Lo Tz'ror (Traveling without luggage), 1938
"Shimshon Mi'Shuk Habsamim" (Samson from the perfume market), 1939
Har HaTzofim (Mount Scopus), 1940
"Reichaim shel Ruach" (Millstones of the wind), 1940/3
Iturei Yerushalaim (Jerusalem's ornaments), 1942
Malon Orchim (The guesthouse), 1942
Nachalat Avot (Land of our fathers), 1946
"Sambatyon," 1947
Eretz Lo Zru'a (Unsown land), 1947
Kfar HaShiloah (Shiloh village), 1948

PREFACE

A S A RESPONSE TO WALTER BENJAMIN'S PLEA FOR a history of *acedia*, sadness, and the defeated, *Zionism and Melancholy* examines the history of critical Jewish melancholy in the first half of the twentieth century, preceding Israeli statehood in 1948. It does so by charting the career of Israel Zarchi (1909–1947), an unjustly forgotten author who lived in Palestine during the 1930s and 1940s, and his series of melancholic tales of Zionist pioneers.

Based on newly unearthed and previously unpublished documents discovered in a Tel Aviv literary archive, the book casts new light on the early history of modern Hebrew literature and the cultural history of pre-Israel Zionism. Among Zarchi's close interlocutors one finds well-known authors and cultural figures such as the national poet H. N. Bialik, the Nobel Prize winner S. Y. Agnon, and the father of the Jewish history of literature, Joseph Klausner. Zarchi shared with all of them his innovative understanding of melancholy. Discussing these writers' lives as they intersected with Zarchi, *Zionism and Melancholy* thus offers both a microhistory of Hebrew literature and a case study assessing the relevance of melancholy as a critical paradigm in both psychoanalytical and political terms—with Zarchi's life and work as the golden thread. My reading of melancholy as a political or affective mode departs from the distinction between radical forms of melancholy and what Walter Benjamin—and, following him, Wendy Brown, Rebecca Comay, Judith Butler, Roberto Esposito, Enzo Traverso, and others—saw as a "left-wing melancholy." For an alternative and a radical form of melancholy, I argue, we need to think about it in the minor key, as a counternarrative, and from the perspective of the forgotten, who challenge consensual norms and ideology.

Israel Zarchi (1909–1947), who emigrated from Poland to Palestine in 1929, saw himself as a Zionist pioneer but quickly found that he lacked the physical strength and mental toughness needed to work the land or build roads. His mental life was dominated by the European literature and philosophy of the previous century. Following the path of beloved figures such as Goethe, Heine, Rilke, Dostoyevsky, and Tolstoy, he sank into a melancholy that became a clinical depression. Despite Zarchi's early death at age thirty-eight, he published six novels, several collections of short stories, and classic translations of Heinrich von Kleist (from German), Joseph Conrad and W. Somerset Maugham (from English), and Janusz Korczak (from Polish). Yet his remarkable production failed to move his critics, and his name was erased from the pages of Hebrew literature; his sort of melancholy was not in tune with the contemporaneous understanding of melancholy as an empowering force of settlement. Zarchi's books, therefore, offer an alternative to the usual history of Hebrew literature, to the politics and discourse of Zionist idealism, and to the politics of melancholy.

Zarchi's story is far more than the story of a melancholic intellectual during the early years of community builders; it is a narrative of grand historical movements, warring philosophical principles, and practical politics. At the heart of this story is melancholy, an ancient Greek idea connected to black bile, mad dogs, and long nights—hopelessness in every context, from the biographical to the political, the literary to the historical. As demonstrated in this book, melancholy—in its modern Zionist garb—is a dark manifestation of internal conflicts, a gap between the Zionist language of fulfillment and the failure to realize that ideal. Melancholy, in other words, is a personal and a psychological reaction to an oppressive political discourse that does not allow the individual to express frustration freely.

Zarchi's melancholy was born at the time of return (to Zion) and therefore undermined the idealist (European) discourse at its first moment of engagement with reality (in Palestine). On the face of it, there is nothing unique about the failure to realize a utopian ideal, but Zarchi was able to make this failure a general literary theme, a counternarrative that mirrored the growing distance between the lost past of the Zionist pioneers and their radically different present. On stepping off their ships at Jaffa harbor, those hopeful women and men discovered that they were expected to invest all their physical and mental power in a new community, without a glance backward. Freud's characterization of melancholy as a double loss—the loss of an object and of its very memory—applies perfectly to the demand that these settlers give up their European past and culture in favor of a new communal life in the sands and swamps of Palestine.

Zarchi was a self-proclaimed admirer of "Rabbi Freud," as he called him in his diaries, quoting often from Sigmund Freud's works and testing his ideas. He identified those works with an immanent openness to the other, the foreigner, the exile, the Arab, the woman—with both friends and political adversaries. Yet Zarchi's critical attitude toward the Zionist project was accompanied by keen support for the idea of return and the revival of the Hebrew language. He wished to offer an alternative from within, rather than an open and an explicit critique from the outside. For Zarchi, melancholy demonstrated how the Zionist project of colonizing the land sacrificed the individual—be it the Ashkenazi intellectual or the Arab-Jewish dreamer. Yet he never intended to criticize the Zionist project as a whole. In that respect, he was a man of his time: a romantic, an Orientalist, an avid idealist, a true believer, a "left-wing melancholist," and diagnostician of "left-wing melancholia." This book depicts him as both a cipher and a symptom of his time.

Zarchi was not the only writer to depict the melancholy of Zion. Indeed, other and better-known authors of his time—for example, Bialik, Agnon, or the father of modern Hebrew prose, Y. H. Brenner—conveyed similar forms of melancholy and described a similar gap between promise and realization. Zarchi's more consistent and focused perspective, however, sheds light on a broader rhetorical phenomenon. In short, the story of Zarchi is that of a tormented individual whose "purer" form of melancholy challenged both his own generation and the later native-born sabras.[1]

As I argue in this book, left-wing melancholy lies at the heart of my generation of Israelis. Melancholy is the heritage of the European-born Jews—my grandparents on both sides among them—whether they are eastern European refugees of pogroms or German-speaking Holocaust survivors. Theirs was the generation that established the political institutions of the *yishuv* and the state, on the basis of socialist and social-democratic ideals. But this first generation of pioneers, idealist fighters, and administrators ignored the fact that their idealism and their politics were based on the idea of an empty land awaiting a revival, when it was in fact already inhabited and living. Negation of both the presence of Arabs and their own past united the personal and the collective voice in Zionism. This negation required the erasure of individual traumas and exilic memory and led, often unintentionally, to the exclusion of those who did not belong to the myth of revival, specifically, the Arab population already living on the land and "latecomers," such as Mizrachi Jews, who did not belong to the European, social-democratic, story. With all these negations and blind spots, it is not surprising to find a fundamental sense of loss supporting the Israeli identity, as well as an inability to mourn the lost past. In place of this lost past, melancholy became the marker of belonging. It is no mere coincidence that Israeli popular culture sings about itself at once in melancholic tones and in high idealistic terms (known as the shirei Eretz Israel hayafa, "Beautiful [land of] Israel songs"). It is equally unsurprising to find this melancholic voice turning into an obsession, a fetish, after the war of 1967.

By following the *effect* of Israel Zarchi's melancholy, I trace the evolution of "left-wing melancholy," from a symptomatic voice of the frustrated individual to the oppressive voice of an official narrative. The slogan "Shooting and Crying" of the post-1967 generation became identified with the melancholic expression of a political paradox: an expansionist-humanist voice, unwilling killing and merciful deportation, exclusive inclusion and included exclusion, the need to forget the past in order to reestablish the conditions for a bright new future.[2] Melancholy ensured that a growing militarization of the national ideology would not conflict with the supposedly humanistic, enlightened tone of Western identity. In short, a microhistory of Israel Zarchi is a microhistory of Zionist history (and nonhistory), and of my own sense of belonging (and nonbelonging). It is a history of left-wing melancholy as disciplinary mechanism.

Before I continue my narrative, however, I offer words of gratitude for those who accompanied this project along the way: to the editors at Indiana University Press, especially Dee Mortensen and Zachary Braiterman. To Reut Ben-Yaakov, Odelia Hitron, Yael Kenan, and Ronen Wodlinger, who helped with various parts of the research and warm advice. I owe more than I can express to Galili Shahar and Alys X George for their careful reading and commentary; their bright intellect and precision helped the framing of this project. I thank Michael Lesley and Joanne Hindman for their sharp eyes and exquisite editorial work, and to Nicholas Stark for his meticulous help with the bibliography. Uri S. Cohen, Michael Gluzman, Hagit Halpern, Avner Holtzman, and Dan Miron gave advice at crucial moments. Naama Rokem and Eugene Sheppard contributed wise comments to the final English manuscript. I owe a great debt to Nurit Zarchi, a rare literary mind, who conducted a series of conversations with me, encouraged me, and contributed many fascinating comments. I am grateful to the archivists at the Gnazim Literary Archive in Tel Aviv, who opened closed archives for me and helped me access previously unopened material, as well as the archivists at the Handwriting Section of the National Library in Jerusalem, the Central Zionist Archive, the staff archive at the Hebrew University, and the archivists and librarians at Lehigh University. I presented earlier versions of this research in different forums, including the Hebrew Literature Forum at Duke University, the German-Hebrew initiative at the University of Chicago, Jewish history at Indiana University and Jewish Thought at SUNY, Buffalo. I greatly benefited from the sophisticated commentary offered by students and faculty in those centers, especially by Shai Ginsburg, Na'ama Rokem, Noam Zadoff, and Noam Pines. I owe much to the warm and generous support I received from my dear friend Edurne Portela, and my colleagues and friends at Lehigh University: William Bulman, Chad Kautzer, Seth Moglen, Tamara Myers, John Savage, and the late and much missed John Pettegrew. I thank the Berman Center for Jewish Studies and its director Hartley Lachter, and the Humanities Center and its director Suzanne Edwards for helping to bring this project one step closer to the finish line; their generous support facilitated large parts of the research and writing of this book. Last but not least, this book, as everything else, owes its heart to my parents, Ilana, Raphael and Hava, and to my spouse and children, Avigail, Asaf, and Yael. This book was written with the hope of imagining a better, nonmelancholic future that is all yours.

INTRODUCTION

I N A TELEPHONE CONVERSATION IN 2011, THE AUTHOR and poet Nurit Zar-chi told me that her father's writings had been ignored for many years. "I think he was misunderstood," she said. After a short exchange about his books, I asked whether there was much unpublished material. "I had a suit-case with many papers and some letters for many years," she told me. "I usually kept them under my bed, but the suitcase started to rot. My mother told me to turn it over to the archive, but I didn't want to. It was hard for me to separate from it, I guess. This was the last thing I had from him, from my father." Then Nurit told me a story that sounded as if it had been taken from one of her books and, in fact, was later printed in her autobiographical novel, *In the Shadow of Our Lady*:

> The municipality did not sit idly, and seeing the cracks in the wall, which were growing and growing, took out a demolition order for our block. I browsed through the accumulation of mail. The date for the demolition was marked in red. I took a day off from school; . . . the suitcase alone was left lying at the center of the house. . . . Tomorrow, before they come to destroy the house, we will take it to the designated location.
>
> Morning, the sky is still low. Our Lady [i.e., Nurit's mother] and I exit the new house and take the old route in order to pick up the suitcase. . . . As we approach the neighborhood, the morning birdsong increases. The neighbor's chicken coop was destroyed last week. But where is our house? The eye loses its anchor point. Frozen in place, Our Lady looks at me and I look back at her. The pile of rocks where our house used to be brings us back to reality. We can't hear what the other is saying because of the ruckus of the bulldozers. The air above our heads is completely white. What is this? Egrets? Snow? The bulldoz-ers have come a day early. In front of my face swirls a whirlwind of my dad's pages. I run with my arms extended. I rise on my toes, trying to grasp the tips of the floating pages. My hands come back empty, as if I were trying to grasp snowflakes. As if I were chasing after the dead.[3]

"That was the end of what was left of my father," she concluded, without clarifying if she meant the lost papers or her memory of running with ex-tended arms, clasping nothing in the air.[4]

My conversation with Nurit—winner of the Prime-Minister Prize for Literature—did not lead to the discovery of new archival material beyond what I had already found at the archive, but it did offer me the framework for the story I want to tell, a story within a story. Nurit's "chasing after the dead" in the form of the lost memories of her father extends her own life story to the story of a whole generation, as well as the generations that followed. It is a story about negation, suppression, and remains, or what the German-Jewish thinker Walter Benjamin once called "that *acedia* which despairs of appropriating the genuine historical image as it briefly flashes up. . . . The nature of this sadness becomes clearer if we ask: With whom does historicism actually sympathize? The answer is inevitable: With the Victor."[5] The story I tell in this book is the story of the defeated and the forgotten, the one untold by history and the agents of triumphant memory. It is another story, a wider one, about flying papers and memories and about lost opportunities. It is a biographical story within a story of Zionist melancholy, or a story about Israel Zarchi within a story about how he was forgotten, how his unique melancholic interpretation vanished from the history of Israeli culture as a whole and the history of Hebrew literature in particular. In biographical and psychological terms, it is a tale about the image of "snapped roots" (from *The Guesthouse*, 1942) that preoccupies the heart of Zarchi's own novellas, and "a plant in a pot, whose root does not reach the soil" (from "Sambatyon," 1947), images that convey the same sense of loss as his daughter's description, set down many years later, of scattered papers flying in the air.[6] Both images suggest a failure to move from the possible to the practical, the ideal to reality, the potential to realization. The lost papers will never be read, and the plant will never grow. Israel Zarchi's life and writing exemplify this gap between promise and its materialization. The story I tell here examines this failed movement in the context of the early Zionist settlement of Palestine. Like Nurit Zarchi's tale, it tells a retrospective story about lost opportunities, oblivion, and what remains.

During the 1930s and 1940s, Zarchi wrote six novels and several collections of short stories. All of them revolved around the central themes of his life: uprooting, melancholy, and missed opportunities. Near the end of his short life, already mortally sick, he offered a sketchy autobiography in a letter to a friend. In the first section below, he provides a glimpse of the primary aspects of his writings that I will discuss:

> I was born on the seventh day of Sukkot [October 6, 1909] in the city of Jędrzejów, Poland. I received a liberal education; my language was Polish (by the time I learned Yiddish, I was already a big fellow). At first I went to a public Polish school, and later to a Jewish school. That school also offered courses in the Hebrew language, but since I excelled in all subjects (except Hebrew), I was

exempted from all classes related to Judaism, and for years I did not speak our language. At the age of fifteen and sixteen I spent time in northern Italy (in Tyrol), and I learned German because I was staying with an Ashkenazi Jewish family from Vienna. From Tyrol I came back to Poland and was awakened to the study of Hebrew. . . . In 1929 I came to *eretz Israel* [the land of Israel] as a *halutz* [pioneer]. At first I lived in the pioneers' huts . . . and worked paving the new road. For personal reasons I moved to the Giva'at HaShelosha Kibbutz, where I stayed for over a year. There I worked mostly in the orchards and with livestock. I prepared the land managed by the painter Reuven and his brother; they were going to plant citrus trees. One day I learned that the first seedling had been planted at a gala event by [the celebrated poet H. N.] Bialik. I was not present at this gathering because who was I, just a working boy taking care of the livestock. I only found out the next day, when I came to work in the orchard, and my heart ached with regret.[7]

Even in this short sketch Zarchi's perspective moves between two parallel registers, both typical of this early period of modern Jewish settlement in Palestine—what is known as the *yishuv*. The two voices are idealism and melancholy, the major and the minor keys. Here idealism is secular, utopian, enlightened, European, and nationalist—yet it is built on a foundation of melancholic loss and lost opportunities: "Who was I?" Zarchi asks rhetorically.

Zarchi's melancholic voice echoes the language of his time but also explores its implications; that is, the Zionist pioneers who spoke the new idealistic language—the sociologist Oz Almog characterized them as obsessed with "the different forms of *hagshama* [realization, consummation]" and "taken by an idealist euphoria"—had left their European roots behind.[8] For this generation of pioneers, idealism and melancholy were in wedlock, inseparable as it was from the beginning. After leaving Europe for the Middle East they hoped for a reunion of individual and community, of social classes, of tradition and political power, identity and territory, and, most important, for an end to their exilic existence and for the return, now secular and national, of Jews to Zion. Seeing immigration as a form of realization made the act a transcendental one: Immigrating to the land of Israel is called in modern Hebrew *aliyah*, literally "ascending," and the term is used to describe the collective waves of immigration of Jews from the Diaspora to Israel as a form of self-realization. The connotation was one of a militant male action; the pioneers devoted themselves to becoming what the Zionist thinker Max Nordau (1849–1923) called the "muscular" or "new" Jew.[9] Nordau, an Austro-Hungarian Jew who with Theodor Herzl cofounded the

World Zionist Organization, adopted a language suited to grappling with and subduing a "barren land."[10] As the historian David Biale explained it, "Nordau's Zionism reflects [his] diatribe against degeneration," which he identified with the psychology and physiology of the Jew in exile.[11] For Nordau, as well as for other nationalists of his time, there was no separation between the imaginary impregnation of the static, biblical geography of Zion and the evolutionary and biological function of the (male) body.[12] According to the late historian Boaz Neumann, in his discussion of Nordau and Yitzhak Tabenkin—the father of the socialist kibbutz movement—the Bible was "a kind of 'birth certificate' that helped remove the barrier between the pioneers and their land."[13] Hannan Hever argued that early Zionist Hebrew literature followed Nordau's discursive instruction and tried "[to] shape an authentic sense of reality that is nonliterary, in the service of the collective norms of the *halutz*, the new Jew, who tried to control his space using unmediate measures of control of the landscape and the nature of the land."[14] Indeed, Zarchi's narratives begin with the Zionist ideal, presented by a man (not a woman). His protagonist is usually committed to a physical and assertive existence, one in which biblical time has blotted out the pioneers' previous lives and induced a state of denial. In denying his own past, the pioneer also denied thousands of years of Jewish existence in exile, that is, everything since the completion of the Bible. Amnon Raz-Krakotzkin argued that the negation of exile is imbued with a messianic notion of a mythic return to the land.[15] The cultural historian Yael Zerubavel talked about "the symbolic bridge that makes it possible to 'weave' the ancient past into the modern National Revival, skipping over the discredited exilic past."[16]

During the latter half of the nineteenth century, European intellectuals—Christian and Jewish—united cultural and nationalistic ideals, tossing into the mix the linked pair, land and power, and reviving ancient myths and languages.[17] The new Zionist intellectuals wrote often about the revival of Hebrew, and the term for that revival, *tehia*, became the slogan for a whole generation.[18] The language of *tehia* proposed, next to the resettlement of the land, a stubborn plea for unity in collective and spatial terms, but also in temporal and symbolic terms. As Benjamin Harshav explained it: "The revival of [the] Hebrew language was not just the revival of a nice accent or of words 'that can already be said in Hebrew.' It was a revival not only of the Hebrew language but also of Hebrew culture and a Hebrew society. Moreover, the process was circular: the revival of Hebrew culture and of an ideological society brought about the revival of the language; and, reciprocally, the revival of the language enabled the growth of the culture and the new society."[19]

* * *

Melancholy was the deep, minor organ point sounding under the major and loud harmonies of idealism and *tehia*. As shown by the psychoanalytic studies discussed below, melancholy is the "reaction to the loss of a loved person, or to the loss of some abstraction which has taken the place of one, such as one's country, liberty, an idea, and so on."[20] In his essay "Mourning and Melancholy" from 1917, Freud noted that *melancholy* can be distinguished from *mourning* on the basis of its response to "'ideal' rather than 'real' forms of loss," its obsessive and unconscious nature, its prolonged temporality, and its reliance on narcissistic identification with the lost object.[21] In the context of the analysis of Zionist melancholy, the structure of double negation should be discussed more narrowly as an effect that exposes the gap between the utopian discourse of realization in Zion (the ideal) and the impossible demand that the pioneers who immigrated to Palestine erase their past and start anew (the lost object). Simply put, Zionist melancholy expresses a double loss: the loss of the (European) past and a demand that all feelings about that loss be suppressed in favor of an imagined ideal.

* * *

Literature offered an alternative to this ideological dead end: It adopted the terminology but refused to accept its semantic implications as given; by adopting the idealist language alongside its melancholic effect, literature proposed an alternative to the unitary vision of *tehia*. It focused and explored precisely the gap that opened between the utopian negation of the past—an ideological demand most authors of the Jewish yishuv accepted and agreed with—and the demand to suppress the individual mourning of it, a demand the more interesting of the yishuv *dis*agreed with and rebelled against. In this book I discuss the gap between the collective jargon and the individual or psychological effect in terms of a political-literary apparatus.[22] Zarchi's protagonists, much like the protagonists of classic works by Yosef Haim Brenner and Shmuel Yosef Agnon (known as Shai Agnon), wave a warning flag about the possible destructive effect such a linguistic apparatus might have for both the personal and the collective. Together with leading thinkers such as Gershom Scholem, they warn about the potential failure of the whole Zionist project, if this gap continued to widen.

In context, melancholy is the *differentia specifica* of literature: It exposes the weak heart of this circular process and discursive mechanism. The role of the melancholic protagonist is essential for the understanding of the interchange between politics, culture, society, psychology, and literature. Even when the Zionist melancholic agreed that personal or individual sacrifice was necessary, he or she dwelt inordinately on the accompanying pain. Loss and sadness, therefore, were the starting points for any discussion of revival. The melancholic mourned the loss of traditions, both European and Jewish, and even refused to disengage. In more general terms, the melancholic sign stands for the rupture in both literary time and literary space.

If melancholy holds the suffering protagonist in his misery, history enables him to explain the cost of his lost past and the effect it has on his present. For Zarchi, and his protagonists, the pain and effect translated to constant travels. In his autobiographical sketch to his friend, Zarchi continued to talk about his life and a melancholic search for meaning, specifically by describing his travels:

> At the end of this early period I wrote my first book, *Alumim* [Youth, 1932] and the manuscript followed me as I wandered about. I then moved to Tel Aviv and got a job helping build a house on Yehuda HaLevi Street, and whenever I pass it my heart misses a beat—to this day. In 1932, following a recommendation from Bialik, I started studying at the Hebrew University . . . [and] graduated in 1936. . . . In 1934 I went to Iraq, wandering the deserts and many remote places in the Near East. Consequently, I wrote *Ve'Haneft Zorem La'Yam Ha'Tichon* [And the oil flows to the Mediterranean, 1937]. In 1938 I traveled in Europe— Italy, France, and Belgium—but I spent most of my time in England. While at [the University of Cambridge], I took a course designed especially for academics from abroad. This journey was depicted in my book *Rishumei Masa* [Traveling without luggage, 1938]. The list of my travels would not be complete without a mention of something seemingly minor, whose effect on me was not less substantial than those "big" journeys. In the summer of 1940 I spent several weeks in the Old City of Jerusalem.[23]

The more time Zarchi spent in Palestine, the greater grew the distance between his early hopes for an idealist utopia and the personal search for meaning that came to preoccupy him. Jerusalem became for him a melancholic prototype, standing for the spatial or geopolitical inability to fuse the old Jewish world with the new Zionist utopia, or the personal past with the collective futurist ideal. In his writing, Jerusalem is a cracked and infertile city full of pits and empty wells, but its sadness enables the existence of strong women and of dreamy men; its imaginary and impossible geography reminds one of the ancient labyrinth.[24]

Neumann said about the early Zionist rhetoric that in it "the exile is a space of endless, purposeless movement."[25] For the pioneer, at least as an imaginary figure, as for the educated, "territory always has bodily form, and a body is always territorial."[26] For the melancholic intellectual, this sense of unity was lost. In his later stories Zarchi turned the theme of "purposeless movement," between the ideal and its failure, the body and its malfunction, to an explanatory mechanism and a political diagnosis of his time.

* * *

Let's zoom in and say more about Zarchi's own relation to such themes. The two voices are blended in Zarchi's writings (more so in the earlier texts), and the idealistic and the melancholic colors produce an intriguing picture. Both *Youth* (1933) and *And the Oil Flows* (1937) open with the more hopeful idealistic voice but gradually evolve into the melancholic, giving the narrative a multifaceted reading of simultaneous production and undermining of idealism, a quality found in no other writer of the day.

Zarchi's vocabulary was grounded in the discourse of the Zionist yishuv, and he was particularly beholden to a trinity of Zionists whom he mentioned in his diaries, letters, and fictions as among the most sainted fathers of Zionism. From Max Nordau he took the idea of the manly "new Jew" and altered it into a series of ill, dreamy, intellectual protagonists or strong-willed women. From Eliezer Ben-Yehuda he took the utopian terminology of a linguistic tehia (revival), which he quickly turned back to the old Midrashic Hebrew. And he borrowed the cultural messianism from Joseph Klausner, his academic mentor, and turned its militancy into a story about the nonarrival of a messianic sovereign. Nordau was the ideologue of the Zionist body; Ben-Yehuda (1858–1922) was considered responsible for the revival of Hebrew; and Klausner (1874–1958), who denied the possibility of a truly Jewish existence outside of Palestine, pioneered the re-creation of Hebrew as an exclusionary political movement. The historian of literature, Hannan Hever, identified this national literature of tehia with "a messianic political-theology."[27] All of the ideas these three held dearest—the new man, the utopian relation to language, and the denial of exilic life—were based on a negative relation to the past grounded in a sense of loss. Zarchi made those into allegorical (and sometimes literal, in the case of Ben-Yehuda) figures in his works. Melancholy exposed the inability to come to terms with their collective demands and pressure on homogenization.

Equally important to Zarchi was the poetics of the period, which often evinced a clear sense of melancholy. At times evoking travel literature,
at others romantic dramas, and even venturing into modes found in European folklore and the subversive voices of rebellious individuals, Zarchi sounded something like S. Ben-Zion (Simcha Alter Guttman), Yosef
Haim Brenner, Aaron Abraham Kabak, Haim Hazaz, Avigdor Hame'iri,
H. N. Bialik, and S. Y. Agnon, the leaders of the new Hebrew literature.
Their work reverberated with mournful laments of the loss of the old Jewish world, yet few treated the topic with the deep and consistent melancholy of Zarchi.

If other authors see melancholy as a necessary precondition to the Zionist tehia, in Zarchi, there is no escape from melancholy. For that reason,
any sign of idealist hope is embedded in melancholic tale. Both voices, the
idealist and the melancholic, appear in his stories, but he differs from other
memorialists of the yishuv because his protagonists—*all* of them, early *and*
late—give in to melancholy. The heavy melancholic burden borne by his
protagonists flattened their ideals. Obviously, his melancholic poetics had
a cost: As an outsider whose poetics subtly deviated from the norm, Zarchi
does not appear in the literary histories of the period.

Poetically and biographically, what started for Zarchi in aliyah and
Mikveh Israel, the agricultural education center for Zionist pioneers, ended
with destruction, personal failure, or, at best, dislocation. His early novels
Youth (1933) and *Naked Days* (1935) trace the shift from the promise that
attracted hopeful immigrants to the realization that something quite different was in store for them. They were forgotten almost as soon as they
were published. The later works won little, and usually negative, recognition. *And the Oil Flows to the Mediterranean* (1937), *The Guesthouse* (1942),
Unsown Land (1947), and *Shiloh Village* (1948) end with a transformation of
the idealistic voice of the European (Ashkenazi) Jewish settler into a mythic
apocalypse or a legendary Yemenite (Mizrachi) storyteller, a displacement
from Mikveh Israel to the Old City of Jerusalem, and from secularism to a
mythic, destructive, or mystical realization. In other words, the redemptive return to Zion is undermined, and redemption is revealed to be either
empty or a fable. In this sense, the literary use of melancholy enabled Zarchi
to expose the fundamental gaps of his world and re-universalize it, not on
the basis of ideological and territorial homogenization but on the basis of
a bringing together internal and external perspectives. As Raz-Krakotzkin
noted, "Any 'return to history' means a return to the history of salvation.

. . . The idea of returning to history, and the concomitant historiographi-cal 'return' of the Jews to the writing of history, follows a fundamentally Christian attitude concerning the Jews and their destiny."[28] Zarchi's return to history was an ambivalent one: In the context of his literary milieu, Zar-chi was a unique example of alluding to both the Christian and the Jewish corpus, to both Ashkenazi and Mizrachi Jewish settlers, Arab and Jewish workers of the land, women and men, Orthodox and secular. All of them presented one or another form of failure, defeat, illness, and despair.

* * *

Chronologically, Zarchi's novels work in temporal reverse: His last novel is his earliest in historical terms. His first novel, *Youth*, describes Zarchi's recent past and the reality of the early 1930s, yet *Unsown Land* and *Shiloh Village*, his last novels, written during the late 1940s, describe nineteenth-century Yemenites in Jerusalem. Reversals also occur in his plots, as stories generally terminate in a foretold failure, a defeat predicted by their hopeless tone. From the failure of the state of Israel's utopian ambition he traveled back to depict the newly arrived, homeless protagonist, and from the re-settlement of the second and third *aliyot* (immigration waves) to the first, going back from the 1930s and 1940s to the early 1900s.

This storytelling device was an alternative to other Zionist writings: Both Zarchi's life and his plots function as a form of *derealization*. The idealistic melancholy of his protagonists left them on the border between reality and imagination, unable to tell one from the other. (As will be shown later, this is an essential observation for the correct understand-ing of the Zionist phantasmagoria, identified with Palestine.) Equally sig-nificant, Zarchi's language moved away from a high modernist language to a more historically layered language rich in words of yesteryear and biblical references. As I will show, the feeling of instability typical of the early novels—arising from a mistrust of representation and a disjunction between individual hope and reality—turned in his later novels to a sense of tumult.

The themes of his novels were far from those that educated, idealis-tic, secular, social-democratic, and consensus-oriented Ashkenazis found agreeable. Even as early as the 1920s and 1930s topics such as ethnic dis-crimination, male chauvinism, the failure of the pioneers, and the insen-sitivity of the social and political yishuv crop up. During the 1940s new vocabulary and ideas creep into his books, among them apocalypse, anarchism, and messianism, which the nationalist-secularist yishuv could not comprehend. The reversal of time, diving deeper into the prehistory of the settlement of Palestine, marked a retreat from the language of Zionist realization. In contrast to Agnon's strong sense of belonging, or the messianic tone of Uri Zvi Greenberg, Zarchi's poetics neither shaped the consensus nor provoked much opposition. The idealist framework he created hid the melancholy from his confused critics, but the melancholy estranged and distanced the reader from his idealist and collectivist dream. Zarchi was forgotten because this discursive device was not consensual, but also was not provocative enough.[29]

* * *

I end this short introduction with a few words about the political implications of Zarchi's melancholy. The interpretation of his poetics requires a critical examination of his writing as a "symptom," which itself entails figuring out the reasons for his disappearance from literary history.

Zarchi's melancholy achieved radical aims within the confinement of his own narratives, yet Zarchi never made it into a demand for change in the world. In that, once again, he was an excellent representative of his, and the next, generation. Not long after Zarchi's death, melancholy became the most apparent tone of the Israeli left, specifically of the generation born in the late 1940s and early 1950s. It belonged to a hybrid discourse that fused militarism and progressivism, occupation and antiwar slogans, labeled during the 1960s as "combatants' discourse" (*siach lochamim*), later "shooting and crying." It eventually fueled demands for a formal separation of Israel from the Palestinians living in Gaza and the West Bank, either in the form of a liberal two-state solution or as a gradual annexation.[30]

Tempting as it is to cast Zarchi as a seer who prophesied the sorrowful dissatisfaction of the left, his vision was not uncritical—a "left-wing melancholy" who keeps mourning the lost cause rather than fighting for it—nor was it the open battle cry of the opponents of Zionism.[31] On the one hand, he did not subscribe to mainstream idealism; on the other hand, he shared its language of tehia even when undermining its effect. The stark juxtaposition of failed hopes and idealism was far from the decisiveness required for military action. For Zarchi's protagonists, the only possible path was a sort of passive idealization that supported a minor literary key and a self-destructive psychology. It is for that reason that his books stand at a forgotten crossroad, marking a path not taken. Indeed, his view of literature could serve both as a cipher and a symptom of his time.

Writing about melancholy, incompleteness, and liminality means visiting the no-man's-land of the past—the rootlessness that Zarchi portrayed and the oblivion that surrounded it. His melancholy was presented as part and parcel of the left-wing discourse during the time of the yishuv, but it did not answer the needs of the progressive left, nor did it suit the theopolitical and colonialist discourse of the right wing. The Palestinians are present mostly in their absence (he is more interested in Bedouins in Iraq), or—as I show in chapter 5—talked about with an idealist and an Orientalist tone. Zarchi's voice did not justify or ground the Jewish right to the land, but it did praise the Jewish return to Palestine and the inevitability of idealist loss. In what follows I use Israel Zarchi's private archive to trace the slow genesis of his poetics of melancholy during the late 1930s and early 1940s. I read the emotions running through his work as a road not taken in the period just before the creation of the state of Israel.

Under my study of Zarchi's works, a fissure opens in both literary and historical space-time: The close relationship between negative poetics, failed idealism, and forgetting. I also study the relation between alternate literary forms, political critique, and "the tradition of the oppressed," as Walter Benjamin characterized it in the eighth thesis of his *On the Concept of History* (1940).[32] As I will explain, this connection modifies our understanding of Zarchi's literature as a specific type of what the historian Enzo Traverso characterized, after Benjamin, as a left-wing melancholia, "an obstinate refusal of any compromise with domination" that "was always a hidden dimension of the left"; or what the theoreticians Deleuze and Guattari call, from a different methodological angle, "minor literature."[33] A series of close readings, supported by a detailed historical and philosophical analysis, may shed new light on the contemporary discussion of melancholy as a literary apparatus and a political effect.

Following the history of the forgotten and the lost cannot reverse time or gather the flying papers back into the suitcase, nor can it replant the snapped roots in the soil. What it could do is to remind us that part of our past, someone's past, is still floating there, unrecognized. It also reminds us that negligence and oblivion are products created by powerful forces. Melancholy serves as a gate for that particular history of the forgotten, the oppressed, and the minor.

Fig. 0.1 Israel Zarchi ca. 1947, the year of his death. © Israel Zarchi Archive, Gnazim Institute, Tel Aviv; used with permission.

Notes

1. According to Oz Almog, "the Sabra generation includes the Jews born in Palestine . . . and who were educated in social frameworks belonging, formally or informally, to the labor movement of the Yishuv, as well as immigrants who arrived in Palestine as youngsters and were assimilated into the same milieu." Oz Almog, *The Sabra: The Creation of the New Jew*, trans. Haim Watzman (Berkeley: University of California Press, 2000), 2.

2. A scene from Elia Suleiman's film *The Time That Remains* (2009) comes to mind. The children of an Arab school in Nazareth are required to welcome representatives from the Israeli Ministry of Education by waving little Israeli flags and singing Naomi Shemer's utopian-melancholic song "Tomorrow" without understanding the meaning of the words. The song concludes with the lines, "Then each man will use his own two hands / To build that of which he dreamed today."

3. Nurit Zarchi, *Be-tsel gevirtenu* [In the shadow of our lady] (Tel Aviv: Yedi'ot Aharonot: Sifre Hemed, 2013), 33–34 (my translation).

4. Ibid.

5. Walter Benjamin, "On the Concept of History," Thesis VII, in *Selected Writings*, vol. 4: *1938–1940*, trans. Edmund Jephcott et al. (Cambridge, MA: Harvard University Press, 2003), 391.

6. Israel Zarchi, "Sambatyon," in *Yalkut sipurim* [A collection of stories] (Tel Aviv: Yachdav, 1983), 99. For "The Guesthouse," see Israel Zarchi, *Bet Savta Shecharav: Sipurim* [The destroyed house of my grandmother] (Tel Aviv: Misrad Habitachon, 1988).

7. Israel Zarchi to Haim Toren, 7 May 1946, Israel Zarchi Archive, file 171, correspondence, section A: 69577–586, Gnazim Institute, Tel Aviv.

8. Oz Almog, *The Sabra: The Creation of the New Jew*, trans. Haim Watzman (Berkeley: University of California Press, 2000), 64.

9. Sander Gilman wrote about Nordau's depiction of the "new Jew," saying, "For Nordau, the reform of the Jew's body would reform his mind, and finally his discourse. Nordau's title recalls the 'Muscular Christianity' of the late nineteenth century, with its advocacy of regular exercise to improve the body and to control 'lascivious thinking.' Nordau's Zionism also shares with German nationalism the code of *mens sana in corpore sano*." Sander L. Gilman, *Franz Kafka, the Jewish Patient* (New York: Routledge, 1995), 106.

10. Nordau contrasted the term "barren land" to the civilized, counterdegenerative, fertile, and male occupier. This is an example of his general understanding of Western civilization and is apparent in his interpretation of Zionism in particular. For Nordau's "muscular Jew" metaphor, see Max Nordau, *The Conventional Lies of Our Civilization*, unknown translator (Chicago: L. Shick, 1884), 242. For an analysis of Nordau's images of the male body as an occupier of "barren land," see David Biale, *Eros and the Jews: From Biblical Israel to Contemporary America* (Berkeley: University of California Press, 1997).

11. Biale, *Eros and the Jews*, 178.

12. Leon Pinsker, the father of "auto-emancipation," preached in 1882, "The great ideas of the eighteenth and nineteenth centuries have not passed by our people without leaving a trace. We feel not only as Jews; we feel as men. As men, we, too, would fain live and be a nation like the others." Leon Pinsker, *Auto-Emancipation*, trans. D. S. Blodheim (New York: Maccabean, 1906), 12.

13. Boaz Neumann, *Land and Desire in Early Zionism*, trans. Haim Watzman (Waltham, MA: Brandeis University Press, 2011), 69.

14. Hannan Hever, *Lareshet et Haaretz, Lichbosh et haMerchav* [To inherit the land, to conquer the space] (Jerusalem: Mossad Bialik, 2015), 61.

15. According to Raz-Krakotzkin, the messianic model follows a Christian order of *historia sacra*. Amnon Raz-Krakotzkin, "Jewish Memory between Exile and History," *Jewish Quarterly Review* 97, no. 4 (2007): 536.

16. Yael Zerubavel, *Recovered Roots: Collective Memory and the Making of Israeli National Tradition* (Chicago: Chicago University Press, 1995), 33.

17. As Eric Hobsbawm noted, "Standard national languages, to be learned in schools and written, let alone spoken, by more than a smallish elite, are largely constructs of varying, but often brief, age." Hobsbawm describes here the imagined "historic continuities of Jews or Middle Eastern Muslims" or "mothers and grandmothers of Flanders" [who] spoke "only metaphorically but not literally a 'mother-tongue.'" Eric Hobsbawm, "Introduction," *The Invention of Tradition*, ed. Eric Hobsbawm and Terence Ranger (Cambridge: Cambridge University Press, 2012), 14. Benedict Anderson discussed a long list of modern national languages in that vein, partly revived from ancient or medieval sources, partly borrowed from different neighboring languages, but answering always a demand for primordiality. See Benedict Anderson, *Imagined Communities: Reflections on the Origin and Spread of Nationalism* (London: Verso, 2006), 77.

18. For a more comprehensive analysis, see Jeff Halper, *Between Redemption and Revival: The Jewish Yishuv of Jerusalem in the Nineteenth Century* (Boulder, CO: Westview Press, 1991).

19. Benjamin Harshav, *Language in Time of Revolution* (Stanford, CA: Stanford University Press, 1993), 92.

20. Sigmund Freud, "Mourning and Melancholy," *The Standard Edition of the Complete Psychological Works of Sigmund Freud*, trans. James Strachey (London: Hogarth Press, 1957), 14: 243.

21. I roughly rely here on the excellent and succinct summary of Seth Moglen, *Mourning Modernity: Literary Modernism and the Injuries of American Capitalism* (Stanford, CA: Stanford University Press, 2007), 13.

22. The historian Derek Penslar writes about "two forms of continuity": "One a transfer of ideas across space, the other a preservation of ideas across time, linked the settlement engineers with the European and Jewish environment in which they operated. The creation of a Jewish national economy in Palestine was conceived as a great reformist and developmental enterprise of the sort that dominated the landscape of the Western world during the last years of the epoch before World War I." Derek J. Penslar, *Zionism and Technocracy: The Engineering of Jewish Settlement in Palestine, 1870–1918* (Bloomington: Indiana University Press, 1991), 151

23. Zarchi to Toren, 7 May 1946, Zarchi Archive.

24. Like David Vogel (1891–1944), another experimental modernist writer of that generation who was forgotten for many years until new editions of his books appeared in the 1990s, Zarchi focused on weak men and failures. He wrote about strong, rebellious women, settlers who grew only thistles and thorns, and politicians driven by selfishness.

25. Neumann, *Land and Desire*, 76. Neumann confirms the imaginary figure of the pioneer with his desire and reality.

26. Ibid., 74. Neumann calls this phenomenon the "geo-body."

27. Hannan Hever, *Moledet Ha'mavet Yafah* [Beautiful motherland of death] (Tel Aviv: Am Oved, 2004), 18.

28. Raz-Krakotzkin, "Jewish Memory," 536. The melancholic often describes his experience in terms akin to the loss of telos, of unrealized eros, or the growing disconnect between heaven and earth—Benjamin called it "the rejection of eschatology . . . a rash flight into a nature deprived of grace"—the above and below. Walter Benjamin, *The Origins of German Tragic Drama*, trans. John Osborne (London: Verso, 1998), 81.

29. The linguistic rebellion of Yeshurun and Greenberg has been discussed more in the last few years than previously. I discuss at length in a later chapter Hannan Hever's analysis of Greenberg's poetics. A fascinating discussion of Yeshurun's rebellion can be read in Amos Noy, "Al ha'poS'Chim, yehandes lo lishkoach? Iyyun be'mila achat shel avot yeshurun" [Those who pass over: Do not forget Yahandes: An examination of a word from Avot Yeshurun's poetry], *Teoria U'vikoret* 41 (2013): 199–221.

30. See Alon Gan, "Ha'sufim ba'zariach ve'siach lochamim ke'zirei zehut mitpazlim" [Exposed in the tank turret and combatants' discourse as driving identities], *Israel* 13 (2008): 267–96. As Dan Laor showed recently, as early as the 1940s Nathan Alterman won more respect than any other literary figure in Palestine, mostly due to his ability to "separate between ethics and politics," or between Zionist ideology and the massacres that were carried out in its name. Dubbed the "national poet," Alterman supported David Ben Gurion's most militant line and the expansion of Jews in Palestine. In those places Israel had to withdraw, he supported scorched-earth tactics. Yet Alterman continued to argue in favor of a humanist Jewish ethics and criticized the actual murders carried out in K'far Kasem and other places. Dan Laor, *Alterman: Biographia* [Alterman: A biography] (Tel Aviv: Am Oved, 2013), 480–92.

31. For "left-wing melancholy," see Walter Benjamin, "Left-Wing Melancholy," in *Selected Writings*, ed. Michael W. Jennings, Howard Eiland, and Gary Smith (Cambridge, MA: Harvard University Press, 1999), 2: 424. I discuss this concept from Benjamin in more detail in chapter 4.

32. Walter Benjamin, "On the Concept of History," in *Selected Writings*, ed. Howard Eiland and Michael W. Jennings (Cambridge, MA: Harvard University Press, 2003), 4: 392.

33. Enzo Traverso, *Left-Wing Melancholia: Marxism, History, and Memory* (New York: Columbia University Press, 2016), 38, 45. Gilles Deleuze and Félix Guattari, *Kafka: Toward a Minor Literature*, trans. Dana Polan (Minneapolis: University of Minnesota Press, 1986).

ZIONISM AND MELANCHOLY

1

THE HISTORY OF A FAILURE

1. Background

Writing about the forgotten requires justification of either a long-lost history or of my own work in the present. Hebrew culture forgot Israel Zarchi and erased his name from its pages. The reason for this neglect was that his historical novels did not fit with "our customary mode of thought" and developed a "conception of history that avoids any complicity with the concept of history" to which later generations adhered.[1] Zarchi is mentioned very little in Hebrew literature, as revealed by a search from the early narratives of Avraham Shaanan, Shalom Kremer, Baruch Kurzweil, Dov Sadan, and Gershon Shaked through the corpus of Dan Miron's analyses and up to the essays of Avner Holtzman, Mikhal Dekel, Dan Laor, Nurit Govrin, Benjamin Harshav, Eric Zakim, and, most recently, Shai Ginsburg and Shachar Pinsker. Govrin is the only one who has discussed him in any way systematically, but even her short encyclopedic review presents Zarchi more as a representative of a certain cultural stance than as the creator of a significant body of work.[2] The root of the forgetfulness is embedded in the late 1940s context, and, beyond it, in the crystallization of a new discourse during the 1960s. Two landmark events in those decades—the war of independence (1948) and the Six Days War (1967)—shaped a narrative of redemption whose dark side swallowed Israel Zarchi.

Zarchi was lost in these historical narratives despite a relatively fertile body of work—six novels, a few collections of short stories, and three key translations (including a canonical rendering of Heinrich von Kleist's *Michael Kohlhaas*)—and close relationships with the best-known intellectuals of his generation: Shai Agnon, H. N. Bialik, Dov Sadan, Shin Shalom, Yaakov Fichman, Aaron Abraham Kabak, Yaakov Orland, Joseph Klausner, Asher Barash, and others. Yet his name is not mentioned in the social and intellectual histories of the yishuv written by Anita Shapira, Hillel Weiss, Shlomo Avineri, and Derek Penslar—to give just a few examples. He is not even mentioned in the counterhistories of Hannan Hever, Idith Zertal, Hamutal Tsamir, Yehouda Shenhav, and Michael Gluzman. Zarchi's name disappeared from the pages of history even though *Unsown Land*, his most celebrated novel, was a finalist for the Ussishkin Prize and won the prestigious Jerusalem Prize in 1947, the year of his death. The oblivion surrounding his name makes it difficult to analyze his appeal as a writer, yet it also opens up a new way of reading his works, of seeing them as examples of what I call here a Zionist melancholy of the left.

Zarchi was forgotten because his later writing, although better in literary terms, did not fit with the yishuv's idealist self-image nor with how the Israeli state would in due course want to remember the yishuv. The earlier writing, though, exhibited a style that was much closer to the language of the time in which it appeared. Before his immigration to Palestine, Zarchi wrote short stories that were dedicated to the Zionist dream, their tone passionate, idealistic, and explicitly messianic. In one story titled "The Leader of Israel," which Zarchi presented to a childhood friend named Yishayahu Graizer, he tells of young students at an Orthodox religious school who break away to join a group of secular students dreaming of a return to Zion and the revival of Hebrew, the ancient language of the Torah. Uniting students from different backgrounds is their shared hope for a messianic redemption in Palestine, led by the vision of Theodor Herzl—"our great leader," as the early Zionist activist is described in this story. From an Orthodox tract about abandoning the old messiah, the story shifts to the coming of the new messiah: "His name is Theodor Herzl, and he lives in Vienna. . . . We must also become worthy of our leader. We must revive the language of our forefathers."[3] The boys embark on a utopian mission: "Ideas had united them in an indissoluble chain. And so the boys began to study Hebrew, reading books about Zion. . . . They remained uniformly and unflinchingly faithful to their idea." The mission ends with the death of the great leader and the transformation of the messianic creed into a national, secularized promise: "Though our leader has died, our ideal remains eternal, and we will serve it. . . . Yes, we will serve our idea as long as we have strength." Such short stories did not amount to much in literary terms, and Zarchi never published them. Indeed, the published work drives the process of transformation in the exact opposite direction to this authoritative Zionist rhetoric. Yet a certain messianic thread survived in the later published work, in spite of its turnabout.

In Palestine, Zarchi took a job paving roads for the Zionist construction company Solel Boneh, then worked as a laborer in different settlements and at Kibbutz Giv'at HaShlosha. Paging through his diaries, one finds dried flowers he gathered alongside quotations from Fyodor Dostoyevsky, Leo Tolstoy, Gottfried Keller, Rainer Maria Rilke, Honoré de Balzac, Charles Dickens, and Joseph Conrad. He spoke a new language, one that undoubtedly drove his writing from a high European style to something far more modern. The change seems to have been carefully considered: Hebrew, as his early diaries show, felt like the language of the future; Arabic was ignored as if irrelevant, and it is only later, during the early 1940s, that an ancient and more traditional Hebraic formulation seeps into his writing. Reviving an old register of Yemenite traditional Hebrew questioned, in turn, the fundamental assumptions of Zarchi's early writing or the explicit Zionist tone of his texts. If the Zionist notion of "revival" required a movement from an ideal to realization, language to nation, Zarchi's end point questioned the very conditions of possibility required for the process; an old, Yemenite, traditionalist, mythical, allegorical Hebrew negated the secularist telos of Zionist claims and what Benjamin Harshav called "a revival not only of the Hebrew language but also of Hebrew culture and a Hebrew society."[4]

The shift in tone was not the only change reflected in the diaries. Early entries, like the story quoted above, describe a man constructing a world around the idea of a secularized and subjective redemption—the redemption of the land through work, the redemption of the soul through love, the redemption of mankind via a new anthropology. The "new men," the Zionist pioneers, reshaped their language to better describe their territory and a national collectivity while embracing a new subjectivity; they combined "knowledge of the land, a hatred of the Diaspora, a native sense of supremacy, a fierce Zionist idealism, and Hebrew as their mother language."[5] As Shai Ginsburg wrote recently, in a reflection on the modern and idealist style that Bialik—the national poet—introduced into Hebrew, "At the core of Bialik's [linguistic] transpositions lies a new aesthetics that aims to produce a new bodily experience and, more than that, a new subjectivity."[6] Zarchi's early novels built on Bialik's linguistic reforms, citing him and the other reformers of the Hebrew language while ignoring the telos of it all. Language and personality, text and character were the same for him; when Zarchi wanted to understand a person, he would sit at her side and question her without looking beyond her shoulder. When he wanted to write about a person, he considered himself his mouth and mind. Writing was a direct and unmediated act of sharing with his reader his own empathic impressions and those of his fictional creations, whom he often constructed from traits and linguistic formulations he heard around him and memorized or documented in his diaries. For example, his last novel, *Shiloh Village,* concerned the Yemenite emigration to Palestine, and his research for the novel included a series of interviews with the elders of this first aliyah; their voices and turns of phrase, recorded by Zarchi, emerge, often verbatim, from the lips of the book's fictional figures and contrast directly with the Zionist and secular story of national redemption or the "new man."[7]

Zarchi's strange fit with Zionist ideals and their realization can be seen in his relationship between labor and writing. Ironically, farming and other manual labor broke Zarchi's body.[8] Literature, as he reported, revived his body and soul even when it did not find an audience and even when the spiritual search ended in utter exhaustion and mental crisis. Long periods of asceticism appear in his journals, love and sex vanish from his life (at one point, for two years), and he pays little attention to what most consider necessities or the facts of life. His close friends described a man who was warm but difficult, and his correspondents complained time and again about his "absence," "distance," or "foggy look." The man, some of his lovers complained, was simply "not there."[9]

Zarchi's melancholic literature did not fit with the conventions of the time. As Mikhal Dekel showed, the literary conventions of the early yishuv were often those of tragedy rather than melancholy. The tragic mode fit the Zionist ideology of the time, lending it an identity both modern and premodern and ensuring that volunteerism remained ambiguous.[10] But Dekel's thesis—accurate in the context of the yishuv literature—applies poorly to Zarchi's melancholy. Although an avid reader of the tragic mode, Zarchi chose a noncathartic tone of ambivalence in his narratives, political affiliations, and personal life. After his immigration to Palestine, Zarchi never endorsed a political movement, party, or leader. In contrast to his friends—the poet Yaakov Orland comes to mind—or his teachers, such as Yosef Haim Brenner and Bialik, he was not looking for a way to integrate into the political or cultural elite, and his melancholy was not balanced by public action. In contrast to other writers, Zarchi did not endow his characters with tragic flaws, such as hubris. His characters do not rise and fall; they simply fall—from the very first sentence. Finally, also in contrast to

Agnon, he made no effort to find a midpoint between the old and the new yishuv, sticking with the presettlement period, before the yishuv achieved its more established form.[11]

2. The Idealist-Revolutionary Ethos

Zarchi identified with the ideological rhetoric of members of the second and third aliyah—the waves of immigration to Palestine that took place between 1904 and 1914 and between 1919 and 1924. Those immigrants arrived from eastern Europe with the idea of occupying the Holy Land, realizing the socialist ethos, and bringing about the revival of Hebrew. The idealist mission, as historians and linguists have shown, is tied inherently to the revolutionary German-Russian philosophy that the pioneers imported and integrated into revivalist literature and history.[12]

The arrivals from Europe reflected a cultural and a political transformation. As historian Anita Shapira wrote, at the end of the nineteenth and the beginning of the twentieth centuries, a change occurred; it was brought about by a new generation of young Zionist activists who reacted to the persecution of Jews in the Diaspora:

This [Zionist] leadership was not blessed with religious erudition, or economic status, or ties to the authorities, [but it possessed] remarkable language skills, saw itself as responsible for the fate of the nation, and produced a new ideology of change. It belonged to the lower middle class, a moderately educated group that maintained an affinity with traditional Jewish culture but added a worldview and mindset derived from nineteenth-century European thought. Such is a portrait of the leadership of the Hibat Zion movement. . . . To this was added a sense of injustice and the need to overcome it, which came naturally to those settlers. . . . Aspiring toward an exemplary society, based on the morals of the prophets and the leading European humanistic cultural values, was a dominant feature of the Zionist movement from its outset.[13]

The young Zionists were influenced by similar revolutionary movements in eastern and western Europe; young Jews answered the growing pressure of emancipation and secularization from the West as well as a push for collective and radical changes in the East. Shapira describes their "belief in the ability of activist minorities to expedite the dilatory course of history" in response to a growing sense "that something had gone wrong with history's inevitable course, that assistance was needed in propelling it forward—this was a central aspect of the Russian revolutionaries' motivation, and it was passed along to the Zionist socialists. This was also the source of the[ir] feelings of urgency and personal responsibility."[14]

Only the birth of modern Zionism, historian Shlomo Avineri wrote, "turned the land of Israel into the actual—and not only ideal or utopian—center point for the Jewish people."[15] In other words, the Zionist movement was able to realize its utopian revolutionary ideals. It did so by emphasizing terms such as "emergence," "urgency," and "an acceleration of history," as Shapira put it—that is, the urgent plea to hasten the necessary chain of events leading to the redemption of people and land. All of these were essential components of the second, third, and even fourth aliyah (1900–1930). Giving abstractions an immediate political or institutional shape meant turning to the old messianic rhetoric, and there was a real "impatience with the slow pace of the wheels of history and the impulse to take one's destiny in hand and serve as 'midwives' for history."[16]

The push for quick results was not without cost. Historian of psychology Eran Rolnik showed that between 1910 and 1923 "suicide reached epidemic proportions, making up some ten percent of all deaths among the pioneers."[17] An "instrumental relationship to the past" created a tension "between the cultural heritage and past of individual immigrants and Zionism's interest in constructing an imaginary collective Diasporic Jewish past that pointed teleologically toward a shared future in the Holy Land."[18] The result was melancholy and even depression. As I will show, Zarchi juxtaposed the theme of the redemptive acceleration of history with his conceptualization of melancholy. In his later writings, the two are strongly connected, especially where they collide and collapse into each other.

Dan Miron explained the ideological pressure the pioneers experienced by characterizing the aesthetic rhetoric of the aliyot. According to Miron, the third aliyah demanded expressionism and rejected mimetic description, the delicate rendering of sensual impressions, the search for the ineffable beauty and truth of the metaphysical symbol, and fidelity to rigorous and protracted psychological analysis.[19] He wrote of the pioneers of the third and fourth aliyot, Zarchi's class, that their enterprise was a way "to find redemption—*ge'ula*—personal, national, universal"; they created new forms of expression that concentrated on the "externalization of feeling."[20] In other words, the desperation that followed a wave of pogroms in eastern Europe and the rise of antisemitism in western Europe became a political force through the secular acceleration of history, the sense that the settlers were living in messianic days, and its agency. The affective transformation was also given a written form.

In contrast to Avineri's teleological argument, Miron's aesthetic reading assumes the possibility of diverse voices in a period of ideological strictness. Such a reading benefits from the reemergence of lost options. Yet Miron's stress on affect and rhetoric misses a crucial political-theological dimension: A critical reading of the militant idealistic discourse points to the divine legitimacy it utilized. Avineri's narrower and affirmative reading shows that the Zionist discourse of the early twentieth century "succeeded in creating a normative, communal and public focal point."[21] Zarchi's protagonists present an alternative to both Avineri's teleology and Miron's aestheticism. From the perspective of his literature, both Avineri's teleology and Miron's aestheticism fail to find a clear focal point, in either personal or collective terms. Zarchi's protagonists rebelled against the "sabra-centrism" (as Yitzhak Laor called it) and the stress on the male Zionist body, and they failed to reach a clear territorial sense of belonging, in spite of the idealistic terms they borrowed from the Zionist discourse.[22] The centrality of failure and melancholy enabled Zarchi, or his narrators, to offer the obsessive pursuit of beauty and truth as an alternative to a teleological political and ideological discourse, a struggle that forced them, in turn, to suppress and hide their feelings, if not their personal worldview.[23]

3. "Life Isn't an Incessant Hora"

In a diary entry from October 1933 Zarchi reflected about his sources of inspiration. He mentioned Shakespeare and Goethe, but in the same breath he noted the stories of "minor" authors such as the socialist Upton Sinclair (1878–1968), who wrote about the conditions of American workers.[24] Then he commented: "Those setting an example in these days of madness in the world—days of mass hunger and civil wars . . . these were not the canonical writers who mitigated the rulers' cruelty (save for many of the prophets, Euripides, etc.)."[25] In other words, in contrast to the fiercely nationalist writers of his time, Zarchi saw negative poetics as a means of exposure and critique.[26] If, as Na'ama Rokem wrote, "for both Herzl and Bialik . . . prose became a productive medium to work through what they perceived as a challenge of groundlessness," for Zarchi it was a way to expose the crisis as a given, without any aspiration of overcoming it.[27] As I will show, Zarchi asked questions, but unlike the leaders of Zionism, he was not looking for clear solutions, either political or literary. The authors he revered as role models were those who stylized the difficulties, not those who solved them.

Haim Toren characterized his close friend Zarchi's life and writing from that perspective: "He has had many times of crisis in his life, but he knew with great certainty that it is precisely in these times that a writer is measured."[28] According to Toren, "He was quite good at eradicating his sorrow and loneliness through strenuous and grueling work. He tried with all his might to distract himself in times of dreariness, but he was not always successful."[29] In spring 1931, while writing his novel *Youth*, Zarchi admitted in his diary, "There will be no hora dancing in my book, because life isn't an incessant hora."[30] The negative reference to the lighthearted circle folk dance popular with the pioneers suggested a real distance from the idealist and happy utopian spirit of the collective. Zarchi replaced the folkish with individual melancholy. In his second novel, *Naked Days*, Zarchi created a protagonist whose melancholy led to clinical depression: "He was in dire straits. His soul struggled, and he was fluttering in the clenching depths of despair. And despite his fierce and total determination, he did not dare to carry out the plan he had weighed and designed."[31] Melancholy was the apparatus that simultaneously constructed and deconstructed his stories and the ideological conditions supporting them.

Zarchi's melancholy was a reaction to his personal, historical, and sociopolitical context. But his literary means of expressing it was a response to a much wider discussion that had to do with the rise of melancholy during his lifetime. Hence, before pursuing Zarchi's story, I need to discuss the theory and history of melancholy, another motif of this book.

4. The History and Politics of Melancholy: Panofsky and Saxl, Benjamin, Agamben, and Esposito

To understand the importance and value of melancholy as a system of signification, one needs to consider its history and evolution. Where did the concept originate, and what is the source of its great impact on modernity? Before examining its political impact, most theoreticians and historians start their history of melancholy with ancient Greece. Tracing its lineage is something like dissecting Western culture from one end to another, in both historical and theoretical terms. We find melancholy in ancient Greek philosophy, in ancient Roman and early Christian texts, in Arabic astronomy during the Middle Ages, in the Renaissance, the Enlightenment, romanticism, and modernity. Its semantic transformation shifts, in crude terms, from the physical-psychological to the psychological-theological and finally to the psycho-cultural or psycho-political.[32] Indeed, melancholy is one of the first psychological concepts developed by Western culture, accounting for the connection between the basic organic functions (and dysfunctions) of the body and the negative ability of the spirit to reflect about an anthropocentric alienation from the environment—self-distancing from nature or the animalistic instinct—and it became a regular feature of medical and philosophical discourses across history.[33]

The philosopher Giorgio Agamben, a critic of contemporary biopolitics, pointed to the etymological roots of *melancholy,* which reside in the ancient Greek *melaina chole* (black bile), the "humor whose *disorders* are liable to produce the most *destructive* consequences."[34] In medieval humoral cosmology, he showed,

> Melancholy is traditionally associated with the earth, autumn (or winter), the dry element, cold, the north wind, the color black, old age (or maturity); its planet is Saturn among whose children the melancholic finds himself with the hanged man, the cripple, the peasant, the gambler. . . . The physiological syndrome of *abundantia melanchliae* (abundance of melancholy humor) includes darkening of the skin, blood, and urine, hardening of the pulse, burning in the gut, flatulence, avid burping, whistling in the left ear, constipation or excess of feces, and gloomy dreams; among the diseases it can include are hysteria, dementia, epilepsy, leprosy, hemorrhoids, scabies, and suicidal mania. . . . The melancholic is *pexime complexionatus* (worst complected), sad, envious, malevolent, avid, fraudulent, cowardly, and earthly.[35]

The typology and etymology of melancholy go back as far as Aristotle's analysis of it in relation to *eros.*[36] Agamben suggests "a dialectical limit tied to the erotic impulse to transgress, which transforms the contemplative intention into the 'concupiscence of the embrace.' That is, the incapacity of conceiving the incorporeal and the desire to make of it the object of an embrace. . . . The traditional contemplative vocation of the melancholic reveals itself vulnerable to a violent disturbance of desire menacing it from within."[37]

Agamben's analysis connects the ancient and the modern semantics of melancholy to its inherent dialectical inclination as well as to its inclination to transgress limits. How this dialectic relates to the metaphors discussed above, and the three kinds of obstacles—the creaturely, the spatial, and the temporal—Agamben leaves to a later discussion of modern melancholy after Freud. But before reaching the transhistorical axis that brings together the ancient black bile and the dialectical limit and transgression Agamben revives, let me say a few words about the early modern revival of melancholy as a popular theme of political and cosmological transgression, now attached to a new language of phantasmagoria.

To ground his argument, Agamben turned to the 1920s, drawing on the work of the cultural critic Walter Benjamin and a pair of art historians, filling in the missing links between the ancient and the modern perception of melancholy. According to Erwin Panofsky and Friedrich Saxl, who later became leading members of the Warburg school, the important element of Aristotle's analysis was the connection he supplied between melancholy and artistic genius. In *Saturn and Melancholy*—a book conceived in the early 1920s but published in 1964 with many additions from Raymond Klibansky—Panofsky and Saxl analyzed Albrecht Dürer's *Melencolia I* as an instance of a new language of images that evolved from the late Middle Ages through the Renaissance and ultimately assumed a new form in the seventeenth century. They followed the melancholic in art as it shifted from images conveying bile and the bodily to a rich cultural and sociopolitical language.

If during the Middle Ages the melancholic gaze was compared to "the look of a mad dog," usually black, and "the impression of the night," later it was psychologized and personified.[38] For example, during the fifteenth century the poet and writer Alain Chartier characterized melancholy as a form of weakness but also as a "figure" that enables us to help "the region of the imagination (called 'Phantasy' by some) open up and come into flux and movement."[39] In other words, melancholy facilitates conceptualization and aesthetic formations.

Panofsky and Saxl identified the late baroque period as a time when "divine madness," melancholy included, was re-theologized and secularized.[40] Melancholy became the signifier of the good sovereign, who embodied divine legitimacy while displaying a mastery of secular and psychological analytical tools and expressing dark thoughts. During the Enlightenment a new typology distinguished the normal and abnormal types of melancholy, in line with new concepts such as character and personality. Panofsky, Saxl, and, later, Klibansky saw this stage as a "poetic" period that emphasized "temporality." At the time they wrote, melancholy had come to mean a "temporary state of mind," which would not have been possible in previous centuries.[41]

The analysis of *Melencolia I* by Panofsky and Saxl, *Dürers 'Melencolia I':
Eine quellen- und typengeschichtliche Untersuchung* (1923), appeared, five
years later, in Walter Benjamin's failed habilitation, *The Origins of German
Tragic Drama* (1928).[42] His discussion emphasized the political aspects of
the melancholic plays of the baroque period and pointed out that while Panofsky and Saxl—two of the greatest historians of art—correctly traced the
medieval dualism of the concept, they missed its political implications. For
Benjamin, early forms of baroque melancholy suggest the line that passes
between the human and the animal, the sovereign and the creaturely—the
same line that rationalism and positivism tried to undermine. Melancholy,
in other words, is the liminal space between different zones of existence.
It was made to be transgressed. Benjamin showed that the paradigmatic
melancholic figure of the time was, for that very reason, the figure of the
prince, or, rather, a "beastly prince." In his words, "Nothing demonstrates
the frailty of the creaturely so drastically as the fact that even he is subject
to [melancholy]."[43] The palace's innermost sanctums echo with jeremiads
and sobs.[44] For Benjamin, Hamlet is the paradigmatic beastly prince, whose
words "contain both the philosophy of Wittenberg [i.e., Martin Luther] and
a protest against it"; in Shakespeare's play, "human actions were deprived
of all value" because "something new arose: an empty world."[45] Agamben
draws on Panofsky and Saxl's ideas via Benjamin's, and then expands on
them: "The lesson of melancholy is that only what is ungraspable can truly
be grasped; the melancholic alone is at his leisure among these ambiguous
emblematic spoils."[46]

The path leading to modernity passes through the nineteenth century's
emphasis on the creaturely. It is as if the nonhuman snuck between the
cracks of our human perception, or through the gap opening between our
great expectations and worldly realization. The crack, or gap, opens the
door to a different form of perception that was often interpreted not only
as subhuman, but also superhuman; as Eric Santner showed, while discussing the intellectual tradition that unites Panofsky and Saxl with Benjamin,
Freud, Sebald's *Rings of Saturn*, and Agamben's interpretation of the creaturely and the melancholic, "It is this peculiar and fragile tension and alliance between the melancholic immersion in creaturely life and the realm
of action and practice that defines Benjamin's thinking from beginning
to end. . . . Melancholy retards adaptation, attaches itself to loss; it says no! to
life without the object (or ideal) and thereby—so it claimed—holds open the
possibility of alternative frameworks of what counts as reality."[47] Indeed,

melancholy enables one to present alternatives to the normal or consensual. According to the romantic tradition—much in line with Aristotle's analysis—artistic genius depends on the creaturely human connection. In aesthetic terms, the romantic tendency to see the world via hyperbole and opposed pairs added a political aspect to the melancholic discourse. Benjamin demonstrated this by adding a political critique to Panofsky and Saxl's emphasis on Saturn, the star of melancholy: "The introspection of the melancholic man is understood with reference to Saturn, which 'as the highest planet and the one farthest from everyday life, the originator of all deep contemplation, calls the soul from externalities to the inner world, causes it to rise ever higher, finally endowing it with the utmost knowledge and with the gift of prophecy.'"[48] "Re-interpretations of this kind," Benjamin explained, "reveal a dialectical trait in the idea of Saturn, which corresponds astonishingly to the dialectic of the Greek conception of melancholy. In their discovery of this most vital function of the Saturn-image Panofsky and Saxl have, in their fine study, *Dürer's 'Melencolia I,'* completed and perfected the discoveries made by their predecessors. . . . Like melancholy, Saturn too, this spirit of contradictions, endows the soul, on the one hand, with sloth and dullness, on the other, with the power of intelligence and contemplation; like melancholy, Saturn also constantly threatens those who are subject to him."[49] As later sections of this book will show, Zarchi relied on many of the symbols of melancholy, including the figure of the black dog, Saturn, absolute emptiness, and the gift of prophecy, residing at the depths of his despair.

For Benjamin, a decade before Zarchi, politicizing Saturn and melancholy implied a transgression or at least a blurring of the line separating life and death and the line separating the normative perspective from the estranged or foreign view.[50] The prophetic ability mentioned in the passage must stand as the sign of a failure, then, not only as a political failure (of the prince, the sovereign), but also as the metaphysical failure to achieve redemption. Gershom Scholem characterized it, in a letter to Benjamin, as the "zero point" or the "nothingness of revelation."[51] Melancholy could predict only failure, not success—catastrophes, not revelations. Yet, in failure, melancholy provides the ability to transgress norms via negation, that is, the negation of the world: "For all the wisdom of the melancholic is subject to the nether world; it is secured by immersion in the life of creaturely things, and it hears nothing of the voice of revelation. Everything saturnine points down into the depths of the earth."[52]

The theorist Roberto Esposito, another leading exponent of biopolitical philosophy, connected the dots: "For much of the interpretative tradition . . . melancholic man has been defined precisely by his *opposition to communal life*. He has been defined insofar as he is not in common: sick, abnormal, even ingenious, but, because of this, outside of the community, if not against it. He may resemble a beast or a god . . . but resembles neither humankind in general nor the common generality of men."[53] In this presentation, the conventional exclusion of the melancholic as an outsider is itself a normative and a political division. The political history of such separations grows from the tradition that began with Hobbes's understanding of melancholy as (in Esposito's words) "one of the destructive passions that, if left unchecked, risks leading men into civil war. This is what defines melancholy, rather than as an individual pathology, as a sickness of the political body in its entirety."[54] From Hobbes, the topos of the melancholic outsider evolved and expanded from the individual to the collective and the universal, or, as Esposito explains, from Hobbes into Rousseau's "nostalgia for the absent community," Kant's notion of the "crooked timber of humanity," or the sublime with its "feeling of inadequateness when confronted with the imagination's task to adapt to reason," and finally back into the twentieth century's revival of ancient melancholy in Heidegger's work. "In *Being and Time*," writes Esposito, "Heidegger grasps both declinations of melancholy: the negative one, meaning *tristitia* or *acedia*, and the positive one, meaning the profound consciousness of finitude. . . . In the second case, melancholy is related to that *Angst* that suits not depression but the 'calm' and also the 'joy' of accepting the limit, or finitude as the condition that belongs most properly to us."[55] For Esposito, the post-Heideggerean lesson is that melancholy shapes "the only common place for which we've been destined, as the originary *munus* [task, duty, law] that unites us."[56] In a formulation that might have been inspired by both Benjamin and Heidegger, he concludes, "Melancholic thought touches a point beyond which we don't yet know where to go."[57] In another text he mentions the "fullness of a lost origin," any dream of realization as a phantasmagoria, and the melancholic *nothing-in-common* that turns into the very definition of "munus," or "the term *communas*, starting from the term *munus*, from which it derives."[58] Melancholy, in other words, comes very close to the point of utter destruction or absolute loss of orientation, but it is exactly its signifying and phantasmagoric value that allows it to avoid the collapse into chaos (and nihilism) and become instead the communal site of the nothing-in-common.

In short, melancholy exposes the negative, zero point of the common, and for that reason enables its transgression.

5. The Black Dog

Melancholy is a well-known theme in Hebrew literature, and some have used it to define the connections between that tradition and modern literature more generally.[59] It is this path that both Israel Zarchi and the retrospective view of his daughter—nearly a century later—chose in order to comprehend the melancholy of their time and its relation to Zionist ideology. Writing about melancholy implies the reconsideration of one's hidden hopes and wishes, spatial and temporal boundaries, and it also opens the gates to the path beyond them.

After describing her father shut up in his study, slaving day and night over his writing, Nurit Zarchi recalled what phantasm connected them, as well as her own sense of identity. Leaving the house after noticing her father's absorption in his work, she writes, "One day, during a game of hide-and-seek, I arrive at a part of the world beyond the world. My heart stops for a moment. Behind the house stands a huge black dog, just like the one I saw yesterday in a dream. A sort of primordial beast, above its eyes tightened brows, its extended tongue dangling from its mouth." She asks, "Is this really happening, or am I imagining it?" Immediately she replies: "The question is meaningless. It's no longer an accident; it's me."[60]

Standing up to the black dog—itself a historical symbol of the demonic or the creaturely—marked a negotiation with melancholy. The image parallels another recurrent image in the traditional literature about melancholy, that of the vast river or sea a protagonist attempts to cross, or the night that has to be followed to its end. As we shall see, in Hebrew literature after 1945 the black dog reappears as the representative of an encounter with absence and annihilation.

These metaphors present a series of struggles with three different types of obstacles: the necessity to come to terms with and overcome the creaturely, the necessity to overcome an obstacle in space, and the necessity to overcome an obstacle in time. I discuss these obstacles in the coming chapters, in the context of Benjamin's and others' historical analyses of melancholy as a creaturely force, in discussing Deleuze and Guattari's understanding of minor literature and deterritorialization as a melancholic topos, and as a form of suspense that encounters the Zionist acceleration of history in a critical way. Understanding melancholy enables the protagonist to comprehend the power structure that enables such obstacles and to expose it to a critical eye.

Zarchi, for his part, made a conscious attempt to expose the political ideals of Zionism; collective melancholy and individual suffering were his tools of diagnosis of his surrounding world, as well as his own psychological response. Zarchi was the subject and object of a "left-wing melancholy" that he used, and was captivated by, at the same time. When his three-year-old daughter Nurit fell sick, in 1944, Israel Zarchi wrote in his diary that suffering "expands one's access to profundity, as the Channel facilitates the passage from one country to another."[61]

Notes

1. Walter Benjamin, "On the Concept of History," in *Selected Writings*, ed. Howard Eiland and Michael W. Jennings (Cambridge, MA: Harvard University Press, 2003), 4: 393.

2. As I was completing this book, I had the opportunity to review a new book that, to my great surprise and delight, dedicated some fascinating pages to Zarchi as an example of the 1920s–1930s realism and "the tension between utopian aspiration and the lives of the workers." According to the author, who adopts a neo-Marxist lens to reconsider modern Hebrew literature, "Zarchi draws our attention to a common argument in the Marxist analysis of modernism, namely, that the feeling of alienation and loveliness so prevalent in modernist art . . . is not simply a matter of subjective artistic taste or personal belief. Rather these are aesthetic expressions of the increasing objective alienation of subjects from the forces that produce their world." See Oded Nir, *Signatures of Struggle: The Figuration of Collectivity in Israeli Fiction* (Albany: State University of New York Press, 2018). See also Nurit Govrin, "Ha-Nistarot ba-niglot: 'Al ha-shirah veha-prosah shel Asher Barash" [About the poetry and prose of Asher Barash], in *Keri'at ha-dorot: Sifrut 'ivrit be-ma'aglehah* (Tel Aviv: Gvanim and Tel Aviv University Press, 2002), 1: 259–80.

3. I am grateful to Oded Graizer for sending me this unknown and unpublished short story. The story is signed "Zerach ben Shimon, 1926," Zarchi's traditional name, which he adopted as a pseudonym for some of his earlier texts. Oded Graizer told me that he found the manuscript in a small wooden box his father kept until his death in 1973. The manuscript is handwritten in Polish. I am grateful also to Marysia Blackwood for her help in the translation from the Polish.

4. Benjamin Harshav, *Language in Time of Revolution* (Stanford, CA: Stanford University Press, 1993), 92.

5. Oz Almog, *The Sabra: The Creation of the New Jew*, trans. Haim Watzman (Berkeley: University of California Press, 2000), 7.

6. Shai Ginsburg, *Rhetoric and Nation: The Formation of Hebrew National Culture, 1880–1990* (Syracuse, NY: Syracuse University Press, 2014), 3.

7. Israel Zarchi Diary, 24 January 1945, Israel Zarchi Archive, file 171, K-3694, Gnazim Institute, Tel Aviv.

8. Zarchi reports on his mental crisis while still in Poland, during his training for the hard pioneer labor that awaits him in Palestine. He and other immigrants received training by the Zionist movement in special farms. See Diary, 28 July 1928, Zarchi Archive.

9. The quotes are taken from the eulogies written after his death. See, for example, Haim Toren, "Israel Zarchi," *Moznaim: Journal of the Hebrew Writers Association in Israel*, 25, December 1947, 157; Arie Lifshitz, "Achrei Mitato shel Israel Zarchi" [After the death of Israel Zarchi], *Gazit* 9 (May–June, 1947): 58; Joseph Klausner, "Lezichro shel Hasofer Israel Zarchi Z'L" [To the memory of Israel Zarchi], *Haolam*, August 28, 1947, 642; Ezra Menachem, "Al Israel Zarchi" [About Israel Zarchi], *Gilyonot* 21, nos. 1–2 (Summer 1947): 42. See also Haim Toren, *Iturim: Measef Sifruti Lezecher Israel Zarchi* [Ornaments: A literary collection to commemorate Israel Zarchi] (Jerusalem: Achiasaf, 1948), 82–83.

10. Mikhal Dekel, *Oedipus beKoshinev: Zionut, Sifrut, Tragedia* [Oedipus in Kishinev: Zionism, literature, tragedy], trans. Tal Hever-Hibovsky (Jerusalem: Mossad Bialik, 2014), 19.

11. As James Diamond explained, for the generation that fought in the independence war of 1948 "the war left not euphoria but a bitter taste and a profound emotional upheaval. For the first time many of them saw death and encountered the tragic dimension of life." James S. Diamond, *Homeland or Holyland? The "Canaanite" Critique of Israel* (Bloomington: Indiana University Press, 1986), 78.

12. Anita Shapira followed the impact of both literature and history on the creation of the national ethos in her *Land and Power: The Zionist Resort to Force, 1881–1948* (Stanford, CA: Stanford University Press, 1992).

13. Anita Shapira, *Ha'alicha al kav ha'ofek* [Visions in conflict] (Tel Aviv: Am Oved, 1997), 358–59.

14. Ibid., 361.

15. Shlomo Avineri, *The Making of Modern Zionism: Intellectual Origins of the Jewish State* (New York: Basic Books, 1981), 218.

16. Shapira, *Land and Power*, 151.

17. Eran Rolnik, *Freud in Zion: Psychoanalysis and the Making of Modern Jewish Identity*, trans. Haim Watzman (London: Karnak, 2012), 45.

18. Ibid., xxxi–xxxii.

19. Dan Miron, *The Prophetic Mode in Modern Hebrew Poetry* (Milford, CT: Toby, 2010), 373.

20. Ibid.

21. Avineri, *Making of Modern Zionism*, 218.

22. Yitzhak Laor, *Anu kotvim otach moledet* [Narratives without natives: Essays about Israeli culture] (Tel Aviv: Hakibbutz Hameuchad, 1995), 5.

23. In contrast to the political historians or the historians of literature, who are committed to an empathic view, for Hannah Naveh, Michael Gluzman, Yitzhak Laor, and other professors and critics of Hebrew literature, the exclusive language of the second and third aliyot, expressed the contours of national struggle and the creation of myths or teleological narratives that relied on the image of David and Goliath, the few against the many, the sons of light versus the sons of darkness, and so on. According to Hannah Naveh, the generation of 1948 "established itself in relation and via the occupied language." See Hannah Naveh, "Al ha'ovdan, al ha'shchol, ve'al ha'evel ba'havaya ha'Israelit" [On loss, death, and mourning in Israeli existence], *Alpaim* 16 (1998): 88–89.

24. As will be shown below, Deleuze and Guattari refer to the "minor" as the "language [that] is affected with a high coefficient of deterritorialization," meaning the opposite of the placed, centralized, powerful, or major. See Gilles Deleuze and Félix Guattari, *Kafka: Toward a Minor Literature*, trans. Dana Polan (Minneapolis: University of Minnesota Press, 1986), 16.

25. Diary, undated entry from October 1933, Zarchi Archive, pp. 33–34.

26. I use this term in a different way from Edward Jayne's explanation of *negative poetics* as a form of misrepresentation, which he defines as the *differentia specifica* of literature. See Edward Jayne, *Negative Poetics* (Iowa City: University of Iowa Press, 1992), 46. I think of negative poetics as a form of writing that encounters the norm or convention of its time and tries to subvert or undermine it. A critical thought of that kind does not answer to Jayne's dualistic model of truth and lie, reality and dream, and so on.

27. Na'ama Rokem, *Prosaic Conditions: Heinrich Heine and the Spaces of Zionist Literature* (Evanston, IL: Northwestern University Press, 2013), 119.

28. Haim Toren, "Divrei ha'kdama lidmuto shel Israel Zarchi" [Introductory words to the future of Israel Zarchi], in the posthumously published *Israel Zarchi: ha'hof hanichsaf: spiurim* [Israel Zarchi: The wishful shore: Stories] (Jerusalem: Eruven Mass, 1950), 9–10.

29. Ibid.

30. Diary, undated entry from May 1931, Zarchi Archive.

31. Israel Zarchi, *Yamim yechefim* [Naked days] (Tel Aviv: Mitzpe, 1935), 190.

32. Different histories of melancholy describe this development, among which are a few classics discussed in this book: Raymond Klibansky, Erwin Panofsky, and Fritz Saxl, *Saturn and Melancholy: Studies in the History of Natural Philosophy, Religion, and Art* (London: Nelson, 1964); Jean Starobinski, "L'encre de la melancolie," *La nouvelle revue française* 123 (January 3, 1963): 410–23; Wolf Lepenies, *Melancholie und Gesselschaft* (Frankfurt am Main: Suhrkamp, 1969); Robert Burton, *The Anatomy of Melancholy*, ed. T. Faulkner, N. Kiessling, and R. Blair (Oxford: Clarendon Press, 1989).

33. It is interesting to think about the role of melancholia when juxtaposed with another medical-philosophical concept that has clear political and personal implications: stasis. For an analysis of stasis, see my "Nihilism as Stasis," in *The Politics of Nihilism: From the Nineteenth Century to Contemporary Israel*, ed. Roy Ben-Shai and Nitzan Lebovic (London: Bloomsbury, 2014), 13–33.

34. Giorgio Agamben, *Stanzas: Word and Phantasm in Western Culture*, trans. Ronald L. Martinez (Minneapolis: University of Minnesota Press, 1993), 11 (my emphases).

35. Ibid.

36. See Aristotle's discussion of melancholy in his *Problems* 30.1, translation in *The Nature of Melancholy from Aristotle to Kristeva*, ed. J. Radden (Oxford: Oxford University Press, 2000), 57.

37. Agamben, *Stanzas*, 18.

38. Klibansky, Panofsky, and Saxl, *Saturn and Melancholy*, 219.

39. Chartier is quoted in Klibanksy et al., *Saturn and Melancholy*, 225.

40. For a comprehensive history of the Warburg school and Panfosky and Saxl's work on Dürer's *Melencolia I*, see Emily Levine, *Dreamland of Humanists: Warburg, Cassirer, Panofsky, and the Hamburg School* (Chicago: Chicago University Press, 2015), 10–11. For a short and succinct analysis of the specific context for Panofsky and Saxl's work on the topic, see Claudia Wedepohl, "Warburg, Saxl, Panofsky, and Dürer's *Melencolia I*," in *Schifanoia: A Cura dell'Instituto di Studi Rinascimentali di Ferrara* 48–49 (2015): 27–44.

41. Klibansky, Panofsky, and Saxl, *Saturn and Melancholy*, 217.

42. The study was rejected by Benjamin's committee at Frankfurt University, destroying any chance for Benjamin to have an academic career. See Walter Benjamin, *Ursprung des deutschen Trauerspiel*, in *Gesammelte Schriften* I (Frankfurt am Main: Suhrkamp Verlag, 1991).

43. Walter Benjamin, *The Origins of the German Tragic Drama*, trans. John Osborne (London: Verso Books, 2003), 142.

44. Ibid., 144.

45. Ibid., 139.

46. Agamben, *Stanzas*, 26.

47. Eric Santner, *On Creaturely Life: Rilke, Benjamin, Sebald* (Chicago: Chicago University Press, 2006), 89.

48. Benjamin, *Origins*, 149; Benjamin is quoting Karl Giehlow, "Dürers Stich Melencolia I und der maximilianische Humanistenkreis," *Mitteilungen der Gesellschaft für vervielfältigende Kunst* 26, no. 2 (1903): 29–41; see also 27, no. 3 (1904): 6–18; 27, no. 4 (1904): 57–78.

49. Benjamin, *Origins*, 149.

50. Ilit Ferber saw Benjamin's sadism as a close relative of Freud's lost object of the melancholic. See Ilit Ferber, *Philosophy and Melancholy: Benjamin's Early Reflections on Theater and Language* (Stanford, CA: Stanford University Press, 2013), 41.

51. Gershom Scholem to Walter Benjamin, 20 September 1934, *The Correspondence of Walter Benjamin and Gershom Scholem 1932–1940*, trans. Gary Smith and Andrew Lefevre (New York: Schocken, 1989), 142.

52. Benjamin, *Origins*, 152.

53. Roberto Esposito, *Terms of the Political: Community, Immunity, Biopolitics*, trans. Rhiannon Noel Welch (New York: Fordham University Press, 2013), 27 (my emphasis).

54. Ibid., 30.

55. Ibid., 32–35.

56. Ibid., 36.

57. Ibid.

58. Roberto Esposito, "Community and Nihilism," in *The Italian Difference*, ed. Lorenzo Chiesa and Alberto Toscano (Melbourne: re.press, 2009), 40–465.

59. For the political analyses of the melancholic topoi in modern Hebrew literature, see Yitzhak Laor, "Sipur al Ahava veChoschech: Taamula, Narkicism veHamaarav" [A story of love and darkness: Propaganda, narcissism and the West] in *Mitaam* 7 (September 2006): 67–90; Michal ben Naftali, *Al Ha'Prishut* [On asceticism] (Tel Aviv: Resling, 2009).

60. Nurit Zarchi, *Mischakei B'didut* [Games of loneliness] (Tel Aviv: Yediot Ahronot, 1999), 21.

61. Diary, undated entry from 1944, Zarchi Archive.

2

THE EARLY NOVELS

Z ARCHI'S FIRST TWO NOVELS, *YOUTH* (1933) AND *NAKED Days* (1935), take place in an open and unsettled space, bare and empty. Sand dunes, desert land, the drying stony fields do not offer much consolation to the farmers. In fact, openness itself becomes a threat.

Zarchi hardly mentions the Arabic population and portrays the Jewish settlers as struggling. The pioneers keep trying, and failing, to occupy the open space and fill it with signs of habituation and a sense of direction, but emptiness fights back. The barren land gains the characteristics of active agency and resists attempts to occupy it. Furthermore, open spaces seem to invade the houses and the cultivated land. A majority of Zarchi's early protagonists get lost in the vacant land, a place without signs, direction, or a guiding voice. They also seem to fail to communicate with their fellow pioneers, allowing an uneasy silence to fall between them. The stories move away from any sense of a telos or fulfillment. The melancholy that accompanies the effort to occupy the land is pathological because it repeats in different ways, in different registers of tone, and in different semantic levels, the resettlement effort. Melancholy becomes a state of existence in Palestine.

1. The Melancholic Pioneer: *Youth* (1932)

The historian of psychology Eran Rolnik wrote of the Jewish pioneer, the *halutz* (pioneer), that he was "unconsciously torn between his commitment to realizing Zionist ideals and his yearning for his parents," a crack in his idealistic world that made "the young pioneer . . . fight a 'terrible battle' with himself."[1] One of the first psychoanalysts of the yishuv, who declared that the pioneers stood in urgent need of mental care, wrote that the halutz struggled "with an easily comprehensible longing that has been sacrificed to his [Zionist] ideal."[2] In Zarchi's stories, the "terrible battle" has resulted in the pioneer's losing all sense of direction.

This loss makes Zarchi's writing relevant to our time. While he presents Zionist settlement activities as a series of struggles with a desert wilderness, his poetics emphasizes, within this conventional discourse, the presence of creaturely life and temporal boundaries. In the midst of youth—at the peak of bodily energy, erotic drive, and idealism—Zarchi gives us apathy and stagnancy, the frustration of all eros.

In *Youth*, the lack of motion implies loss and an open, confusing, unoccupied space. In the opening scene the utopian hopes of the protagonist, Uri, encounter the conditions of the setting: "Deep sand covered the road, the sand dripped between the wheels, and it was impossible to urge the animals on."[3] Having gone to Palestine to cultivate a land of milk and honey, by the end of the story Uri is driven to suicide; if the beginning promises a fulfillment of erotic passion, the end shows his wife aborting their child and leaving him. Never able to find a place of his own, he spends his time wandering. Other characters in the novel experience hunger, unemployment, boredom, and frustration, displaying a continual sense of drifting without a goal.

The Zionist clichés about the heroic old settlements, about fighting the heat and draining the swamps, about confronting *falakhs* (Arab farmers) and Bedouins, about the stout male body and the dancing collective body, turn to dust. When idealistic workers and farmers are not in conflict with the land, they go up against the alienated and resentful bureaucrats of the Rothschild estate and Zionist organizations.[4] A vast gap opens between Rothschild's bored, hedonistic clerks and the farmers on the brink of starvation. One of the wastrels visits a rural settlement: "The car pulled over at one of the stores, Binyamin Lubinsky got out, went into a store, and after several minutes returned holding a big paper bag. He said, 'This is how I do it. Without provisions I can't get going. I also have a newspaper and a book with me in the car at all times. That way I can spend hours in it without being bored'" (53).

In contrast to the failed farmer who narrates the novel, Lubinsky readily takes control of his space. Unlike those whose wagons sink in the sand, he drives his big car from one colony to another, representing the interests and power of the baron. The socioeconomic gap between the two men—the farmer Uri and his rival, the urban bureaucrat—shapes the core conflict of the novel, marking the distance between those who have power and those who do not. The conflict is not only ideological: The woman the protagonist loves is caught between Uri's passion and the comfort offered by the rich Lubinsky; but Uri never confronts Lubinsky himself or the sense of a widening gap between classes and between the Zionist ideal of equality and reality.

At the center of the novel, mirroring this helplessness, is the diatribe with which an anarchist exposes the discursive assumptions made by the idealistic settlers in their struggle with the affluent bureaucrat: "As I've said more than once, you laugh at every serious subject. You dismiss and ridicule everything. Rather than look for an escape, rather than even revealing the reality for all to see, you cover it up with trivia. . . . Thousands of fresh young lives are suffocating and withering because of hypocrisy" (77–78). The protagonist merely records these trenchant comments, which are instantly dismissed by the settlers.

But skepticism takes over the narrative: A story that opens with great hopes for individual and collective redemption ends with its obliteration. The tone is quite Nietzschean, as is the allusion to "the Europeans of the day after tomorrow":[5] "Maybe these children will be the people of tomorrow, the generation of redemption? . . . A thread of sadness flickered in his heart: we also once had a child. . . . We had and did not have" (173).[6] Idealism and a fervent wish for a community exist in this novel alongside the critique and transcendence of these very desires. The loss of direction and accompanying melancholy that Zarchi so often deployed are used to expose the inherent expectation expressed by idealistic and utopian language. Whereas the opening of the novel follows "a [new] road, meaning: a hop, a jump, a fast connection to the world, the discovery of new horizons and grand potential for action" (12), it concludes with Lubinsky taking over the road and Uri crying, in his desperation, "to the mountains, to the open space, to wander along unpaved roads, climb on the standing rocks" (178). By the end of the novel, the emptiness of the natural space replaces the promise of the utopian community.

The historian and literary critic Gershon Shaked (1929–2006) explained the serial disappointments of Zarchi's early characters by dwelling on their failed relations to society, which he identified with a native literary position: "Much like [Yosef Haim] Brenner's protagonists, [Zarchi's] protagonists fail in their attempts to create permanent relationships," yet "the author repeatedly affirms the conventional values of contemporaneous pioneer society."[7] Shaked focused on Zarchi's characters' pathological relation to reality. Indeed, the lack of meaningful connections and the failure of the men and women of *Youth* and other early novels to tie their dreams to reality are among Zarchi's most distinctive traits. Shaked might have missed that, but Zarchi's repetitive stress on the failed aspects of existence charged his figures with an unconventional beauty, offering an alternative to the triumphalist's discourse of collective utopia. Their failures bespeak a larger, collective failure.

2. Melancholic Lessons

Youth was published in 1933 thanks to the insistence of Haim Nahman Bialik (1873–1934) and Yaakov (Jacob) Fichman (1881–1958), an acclaimed author and an editor.[8] Bialik and Fichman helped Zarchi in spite of the stylistic gap between their own writing and that of the younger author. In contrast to the ironical works of Bialik, Fichman, Brenner, and Shai Agnon—all of whom utilized the poetic distance between the limited perspective of the protagonist and the much richer and more critical consciousness of an implied author—Zarchi's melancholy closely tracked his protagonist's perspective. Several publishers rejected *Youth* before Asher Barash (1889–1952), a central figure in the literary scene of the early yishuv and the founder of the Gnazim Institute (home now to Zarchi's manuscripts), accepted it in the summer of 1932.[9] Zarchi copied into his diaries a few sentences from the rejection letters he had received; one publisher wrote, "Many chapters would be suitable as novellas. They shouldn't be joined as a novel."[10] Zarchi wondered, "Are they really so afraid of reality? And here I have described it openly."[11] A few weeks later he wrote, "This is the first book, . . . and I felt that something had ended. I myself was like a wrung lemon. A dried-out fig. . . . And then the first pages of *Naked Days* started coming to me."[12]

When he began work on his second novel, Zarchi was also translating a play by the expressionist Ernst Toller (1883–1939). All trace of this never-published translation has vanished. Could it have been in the suitcase his daughter lost to the bulldozers? Without the manuscript, we can only surmise why Zarchi chose Toller. A Jewish-born anarchist and communist, an expressionist playwright who won the Kleist prize, and a leading intellectual, Toller served as the head of the revolutionary Bavarian Soviet Republic for exactly six days in 1919, for which he served five years in prison. After a brief return to writing plays, he was exiled in 1933, and six years later hanged himself in his hotel room in New York. Zarchi's interest in Toller—in his diaries he calls him a "hero"—belonged to his broader engagement with radical left-wing views.[13] It is not a mere coincidence that Zarchi's next translation project was an anarchist classic, Heinrich von Kleist's *Michael Kohlhaas* (discussed in chap. 4).

The books written during this period should be discussed in the context of another father of Hebrew literature, S. Ben-Zion (1870–1932). Nowadays forgotten, during the 1920s and 1930s Ben-Zion (the pseudonym of Simcha Alter Gutman, father of the painter Nahum Gutman) stood at the heart of the literary yishuv and was mentioned by Zarchi as an important inspiration, a recurrent topic of discussion.[14] He died as Zarchi was finishing *Youth*.

Ben-Zion received harsh judgment from the same critics who criticized Zarchi. For example, Jospeh Klausner—a professor of Hebrew literature and Zarchi's mentor at the Hebrew University—wrote that Ben-Zion "was unable to express significant events, significant national sorrow, and significant celebration" of the Jewish settlement in Palestine. Yet Klausner also pointed out that Ben-Zion did not blindly accede to Ben-Gurion's dictates "and was therefore hated by both the left and the right."[15] The majority of Ben-Zion's writing explored the period that preceded Zionism, looking at the difficulties of living in exile, confronting antisemitism, and daily life in the Jewish eastern European market town, the *shtetl*. A few stories dedicated to the *halutzim* featured tragic endings.[16] Some critics described Ben-Zion as a misanthrope, a disciple of Ahad Ha'am (Asher Ginsberg, 1856–1927), the critic of political Zionism. (Zarchi admired Ahad Ha'am, calling him in one diary entry "the great Hebrew.")[17] Ben-Zion's editorial impulses far exceeded the norm. According to Agnon, Brenner once paid a call on Ben-Zion, and when he idly opened a magazine lying in his host's study, he discovered red corrections littering one of the articles. Because he had written the piece himself, he had a few choice words for his would-be Max Perkins.[18] Agnon shared Brenner's disrespect of Ben-Zion, but for a slightly different reason: Zarchi reported in his diaries that Agnon had stopped talking to a friend who declared Ben-Zion—rather than Agnon—the most interesting writer of the period.[19]

But mostly Ben-Zion was seen as a depressive writer who "considered himself an outsider writer, an outcast, with no links to the [ruling] party."[20] Agnon, the sharp and cynical observer, described him as "a prophet of disasters and one who laments the silence of the divine spirit and every day and its creator."[21] Bialik, who was Ben-Zion's student for a while, described him as "detached from the local Israeli life, depressed and bitter."[22] And yet everyone agreed that with Ben-Zion's death a period in the history of Hebrew literature had ended.

What was it about this difficult, melancholic outsider that appealed to Zarchi? Maybe it was his refusal to engage with any camp, be it literary, political, or even social. Maybe the attraction was his linguistic innovations and his eagerness to criticize just about anything and anyone. In the collectivist atmosphere of the early yishuv, such an approach came as close as one can imagine to literary anarchism—and to Zarchi's admiration of anarchist literati such as Ernst Toller and, as will be discussed later, Heinrich von Kleist.

3. Diary Excerpts from the Early 1930s: Zarchi as Kästner's Fabian

After he finished *Youth*, Zarchi decided to enrich and widen his intellectual horizons. Perhaps the passing of the great outsider, Ben-Zion, convinced him he needed to explore unfamiliar areas. As his diaries show, it was clear to him that he would be an author. Such a calling required more than observational skills. To make a proper study of literature, history, and philosophy, he decided to attend Hebrew University, and he turned to Bialik for references and assistance. Soon he found a letter of acceptance in his mailbox. "Studying," Zarchi wrote in a letter thanking Bialik, "will certainly be an important component in my future literary work."[23]

The rather mature college student appears to have done very well in his literature and philosophy classes. In October 1933 he wrote in his diary, "I took the final exam in [Hugo] Bergman's course, writing about a long year's worth of material on logic and epistemology—and I succeeded. A year and a half ago, I was watering or hoeing. . . . Strange!"[24] Among the friends he made in Jerusalem was his new mentor's nephew, Yehuda Arie Klausner, the father of Amos Oz, and Haim Toren, a writer and critic who became his closest friend. He also met the young writers later labeled the "Jerusalem group": Ezra Hamenachem, Asher Barash, Yosef Aricha, Ari Even-Zahav, and Yaakov Orland. Even-Zahav went on to become the academic secretary of the university's humanities faculty, and Orland rose to fame as a poet. Such contacts proved helpful when, in October 1937, Zarchi was offered an administrative post at the university, a job he kept until 1944.[25]

His studies allowed him to start widening the context for his writing. During the 1930s he traveled for long periods, first to see the lands surrounding Palestine, then to London. These trips took place under the sway of a romantic influence, particularly that of Heinrich Heine, whose grave he visited in Paris's Montmartre Cemetery. During this period, an often lovesick Zarchi sounded like an enthusiastic poet who could not separate his imagination from reality. For example, here is Zarchi's entry from September 3, 1934: "Jerusalem. Only a brief trip to Haifa in the midst of preparing for an exam. Beside me sits a girl named Esther. Is it so again? The heart is not its old self. Is it so? That restlessness that I recognize oh so well." A week later he describes another meeting with the same woman. He calls her "Birdie" and other nicknames, mostly borrowed from romantic novels and poetry. Alongside these amorous references are poems by Rilke that Zarchi copied into his notebook and read aloud to Esther.[26] This short but intense affair was not an anomaly, as others followed. He met a mysterious, English-speaking woman who went by the name of Rosa Fränks during a vacation in Tiberias; yet when he tracked her to an apartment in Tel Aviv, he discovered she was a very married Mrs. Buchholtz. Meanwhile, his on-and-off affair with Esther was becoming more serious. Zarchi continued to copy poems from Rilke, Heine, and Goethe into his diary, filling pages with stormy thoughts about his affairs and sexual hopes. The fantasies took a gradual literary and psychoanalytical form. In one diary entry from the period he reflected: "Freud, my rabbi Freud, what would you say to this? What a strange feeling one gets when thinking about Oedipus and Greek mythology, or the love affair with a mother, a sister, a loved one."[27]

In late December 1934 and early 1935, he reported intensive work on his new novel, *And the Oil Flows to the Mediterranean*. He had discovered that Esther was having an affair. He contemplated breaking things off, but then realized that romantic fantasies were not his alone and asked himself, "Won't I forgive you?"[28]

At least one of Zarchi's friends saw him as a follower of the neoromantic movement that appeared in Germany in the 1920s and 1930s. In a diary entry dated April 22, 1935, Zarchi wrote about his friend's comparison of him with Erich Kästner's Fabian, from his eponymous novel: "How strange it was to hear from Jacques . . . that I am Kästner's Fabian, who cannot find a way to participate in the destruction of the past, the construction of the future. Fabian drowned because Kästner couldn't provide him with a way of life—and me? He is sure that it is only a temporary depression as a kind of wish to escape everything. I only want to be shut up with my book in my room, away from the whole world and so on. I was amazed that someone had seen through my soul in such a way."[29]

I choked when I read this diary entry. It proposed a certain key to Zarchi's use of melancholy. Erich Kästner (1899–1974) is known nowadays mostly for such children's books as *Emil and the Detectives* (1929) and *The 35th of May* (1931), in which he depicted both the great hopes inspired by the founding of the Weimar Republic and the hardships the republic went through. During the late 1920s, though, he was celebrated for his poetry, journalism, and criticism, and he identified with the Social-Democratic Party. His attacks on the Nazis made him a hero in the eyes of the moderate left wing; communists and anarchists ignored or mocked him. In a short fragment analyzed in chapter 4, Walter Benjamin treated Kästner as the representative of a moderate, bourgeois politics and the epitome of a "left-wing Melancholy."[30] I will return to Benjamin's "left-wing melancholy" in the beginning of chapter 4, but before I do, let me say a little more about Zarchi's relation to Fabian.

Fabian, the protagonist of Kästner's only work of fiction aimed at adult readers, is a man whose romantic failure mirrors the failure of the Weimar Republic to win the hearts of its citizens and defend them from the rise of fascism. The novel was published in 1931, two years before Hitler's rise to power. Much like Kästner's "hopeless man"[31] and his "sorrow of the heart" [*Herzleiden*], Zarchi found that his "temporary depression" proved to be a perpetual state; he connected it to German *Sturm und Drang* and the ancient philosopher Epicurus (341–270 BC), who explained, "It is ridiculous to hasten your own death because you're bored with life, when you're doing the same thing by the way you live."[32] In his diary Zarchi wrote: "Influenced by Goethe, by Epicurus. Exhausted from the sorrow. Would give up a lot so as not to suffer in the absence of a lot. . . . I'm exhausted."[33] Epicurus's name occurred often in Zarchi's diary during this period, especially in connection with reflections that resonate with the philosopher's thinking on atomism or finality. Linking him to Goethe was natural, as the latter had developed a theory of natural communication as a relation between atoms.

Reflecting about melancholy, from ancient Greece to modern Germany, connected Zarchi to his own present and sense of drama; Esther and Zarchi separated for a period, and in July 1935 he wrote about another love affair.

A painful scene he described sounds as if it could have been taken straight from one of his stories:

> The two of us in our room. Naked. A knock.
> "Who is it?"
> "Esther!"
> My heart almost stopped. I found some strength.
> "I can't come to the door right now, but I'd like to see you. Tell me when. Later. You'll be around, won't you?"
> "I'm leaving tomorrow." (I could sense that she was in agony.) "I don't know where I'll be."
> "All right."
> "Good-bye."
> "Good-bye."
> All was silent.
> I searched for her all night. The next day as well, but she was nowhere to be found.[34]

Zarchi published his second novel, *Naked Days*, in 1935. He opened the novel with an epigraph from *Faust*:

> Fate's gift to him's a spirit always driving
> On and on, allowed free rein,
> And in its headlong striving
> It overlaps the joys of earthly living.
> I'll drag him through a wild existence
> Through flat want of significance,
> I'll see him dangling in it, fixing, cleaving
> And meat and drink will hover over
> The lips of his never-to-be-sated craving.[35]

The romantic tradition often referred to these lines, in which Satan sets out his program for Tantalus. Schelling quoted them in *Philosophy of Art* (1802–1803), and Hegel did in *The Phenomenology of the Spirit* (1807). By joining in, Zarchi positioned himself as a Hebrew descendant of that tradition, embracing the darker face that suspected the scientists and, more generally, the belief in material progress. Yet his act was also part of the idealist tradition that adopted wholeheartedly the belief in utopias, the principle of absolute truth, and an obsessive melancholic search, Fabian-like, for a "way of life."

4. *And the Oil Flows to the Mediterranean* (1937)

In 1938 Zarchi finally married another Esther, Esther Hanani, who had immigrated from Vilna to Palestine in 1925 and worked as a teacher. The

couple had two daughters, Nurit and Michal. Nurit told me that his children's names represented to Zarchi the natural elements of fire and water.
He had already given her name to the heroine of *And the Oil Flows*.[36] A later
series of Zarchi's diary entries, written during a tour of the deserts of Iraq,
conveys a perspective one would identify nowadays as regional or postcolonial in its investment in local scenes, on the one hand, and disgust at the
colonial influence, on the other hand. For example, here are the entries for
May 20 and 21, 1934, in Baghdad ("Mesopotamia"):

5/20

Everyone shook their heads: Iraq? There? You lunatic! . . . Two days' worth of
desert . . . and when you see the desert the blaze of summer winds, the local
Bedouin, and suddenly at the end of the ride a sea of those European fascist
hats, you have contradictory feelings. . . . It reeks of cheap nationalism.

5/21

The museum. Mesopotamia 3,000–3,500 B.C. After that, Assyria, Babylon. . . .
The enormous statues evoke many thoughts. . . . Perhaps humanity isn't pro-
gressing at all?[37]

After his return, Zarchi started working on his third novel, which was
published three years later. Much like its predecessors, *And the Oil Flows to
the Mediterranean* tells the story of a man who wanders without a clear aim.
When we first meet Gideon Barkai he descends from the settlement, after
his attempt to grow crops on a rocky mountainside has just failed. And his
failure is not unique: It seems as though most of the inhabitants of Iliya ("up
high"), a small village in the Galilee, are on the brink of starvation. People
work hard to survive, but the younger generation is heading off to the city,
leaving both the land and the idealistic discourse behind. After Barkai also
fails to win the love of Nurit, he decamps for Haifa, replacing one hardship
with another and swapping one mountain (Galilee) for another (Carmel)
and the language of idealism for the language of materialism. Unable to
reconcile himself with either, he is left hanging between two worlds. First
Barkai follows his idealistic dreams: He dreams of working for the electric
company so as to bring light to people's homes, but he is turned away from
the utility company. He finds his way to Solel Boneh, the Zionist construction firm that had long cooperated with the British colonialists, but he ends
up losing that job as well. When his former love turns up in Haifa, he makes
a mess of things with her. Unemployed and on the brink of despair, Barkai

follows a vaguely worded suggestion and makes his way to the desert. There he traces the material route of light (electricity) back to its source—the oil gushing from the sandy wastes—only to return to Haifa empty-handed. Here again, Barkai never reaches the place he dreams of, the oil wells of Iraq. Rather, his is a pendular movement utterly lacking a telos. Large parts of the novel take place at night, accompanied by a sense of confusion, absence of purpose, blindness, and failure.

After losing all other jobs, and after days spent aimlessly in the desert, Barkai takes a temporary job at a British oil company. The colonialists are pumping the costly cargo and building pipes that will help them transport the oil to ships at Haifa harbor that will carry it to England. It is in this context, in the middle of the desert, that he befriends a Jewish communist and a Bedouin rebel, and witnesses the outbreak of the Bedouin revolt against the British, shortly before watching its violent suppression and returning to Haifa. Upon his return he tries his luck one last time with Nurit, and inevitably he fails.

Barkai is a melancholic protagonist but not a tragic one. There is no rise-and-fall movement in the novel, nor is there any catharsis. Barkai's wanderings enable us to watch—from a distance—the large historical events and political structures that accompany the clash between world empires and rebellious tribes as well as the conflict between idealism and materialism. All the while our wanderer never judges or reflects on what he sees; he simply experiences it through a growing melancholy.

The reader observes the gaps between the idealists' settlement and the hedonistic urban life through Barkai's eyes—or through the failing eyes of his senile grandmother: "One of her senses still remained alive and alert, and moreover it was increasingly intensifying: the desire for money. She could no longer keep track of all the changes in currency, some measure of how long she had lived. . . . Voraciously, the old lady charged at the treasure. She counted and counted, without even knowing any more which digit came first."[38] This moribund woman is not far from Barkai's friend Zvi Caspi, a far younger materialist. Caspi (the word means "silver") is a fellow refugee from Iliya and has shared Barkai's path, fleeing the idealist's utopia of the land to embrace modern urban life. In the novel Caspi shifts from cultivating the land, ironically, to selling land and real estate, betraying the ideals of his socialist village.

In contrast to Caspi, who cares only about getting rich, Barkai never quite deserts the idealistic terminology. A different desire had driven Barkai from his home: He had set out in search of love. Nurit, the love of his youth, had moved to Haifa and become involved with a rich man. When Barkai reveals his soul to his old friend, Caspi goes to speak to Nurit. Here we are offered a different point of view on Barkai's personality, implying his relation to the romantic tradition in general and to Nietzsche's critique of the romantic tragedy specifically. During his conversation with Nurit, Caspi, advocating for his friend, connects the dots:

> A romantic, you say? Ah, no. . . . Romanticism always morbidly admires the past, which is unhealthy. It adheres to past traditions with such devotion. We are all infected with this disease to some degree. I myself had this inclination, but studying natural science cured me. Our profession [i.e., selling real estate] demands a healthy approach. And for Gideon [Barkai] it is a different matter, I think. Gideon is a rationalist on the one hand and a dreamer on the other. But his dream is always directed toward the future. How shall I say this? If he is a romantic at all, then he is a romantic of tomorrow. (137)

In short, Caspi describes Barkai as the quintessential idealist. Much like Nietzsche's Zarathustra or his "European of tomorrow," Barkai declares the failure of worn-out ways—in his case, the socialist utopia and capitalism's hedonism. Zarchi's melancholy, however, is a far gentler sentiment than Nietzsche's drive toward nihilism and the will to power.

The symbolic use of the protagonist's name is another indication of that melancholic alternative. The name "Barkai" is taken from the Midrash, where it means "the morning star," Venus. It appears most famously in the wisdom literature of the Ben Sira parables. There, "Barkai" is equated with Hillel Ben Shahar (Hillel, son of Dawn, Lucifer for the Christians), the opposite of Saturn, the star of twilight.[39] Yet the name receives an ironic overtone in Zarchi, when considering that Barkai, as the "romantic of tomorrow," becomes the representative of twilight, Saturn, and failure rather than resurrection, dawn, and success.

For Barkai, new friends made in the oil fields—a Jewish Marxist named Shlomo Narkis and a young unnamed Bedouin rebel—reveal two quite different aspects of existence. The rebel inspires a romantic and distinctly Oriental dream:[40] "He was a sort of partner in meaning. . . . [He taught me] the great song of pining for a distant and desired loved one" (175). The Marxist reveals the mechanism of the Zionist political system: "Sometimes things were said which Gideon had long since felt but could only now articulate. . . . We do not feel the other's pain, we only surmise it, as we simply surmise the existence of a falling star. But somewhere out there, in the vast reaches of infinity, an entire world has shattered" (185). Barkai learns about the Nietzschean "rebellions of the weak" and learns to admire Nietzsche from Narkis, the charismatic and self-centered revolutionary. The two friends also discuss Rousseau and Voltaire, precipitating an intense series of exchanges on the power of the dispossessed, the passion "to approach the king, spit in his face, curse him, and say to him: And who are you really? A king? You are a wretched dog" (186).

Narkis explains to Barkai how workers and the middle class can put to use their ability to reconfigure the world: "If they stopped working for one day, the world would have no bread to eat, no water to drink, no clothes to wear, and no train to travel on. And then they could come to the rulers and say, 'Kind sirs, will you please step down? Otherwise you will die of hunger and thirst'" (197). Later he adds, "One has to know one's way in the world, and this incident here in the desert is but a small link in a long chain binding near and far, uniting many worlds. One must not live a tranquil life in a warm little corner one has found for oneself, even if it is a spiritual corner, as whole worlds shatter" (200). Narkis has no doubts undermining his sense of absolute truth and his own ability to teach it to the oppressed nomads of the desert.

Indeed, the workers at the oil company call for a general strike, but it fails. Narkis, Barkai, and the other organizers scatter. Barkai's revolutionary lesson is a melancholic, not a utopian one. As he heads back to Haifa, Barkai speaks briefly with a man on a train: "When he heard that Gideon was from the land of Israel, his eyebrows shot up almost until they reached the hair on his head. He said, 'From the land of Israel, huh? I hear the Jews are building a new state there, is that so?' Gideon smiled, was silent for a moment, then said musingly, 'State or no state, we're trying to catch our breath, like every oppressed people. That is all'" (291).

And the Oil Flows is a novel about melancholy, but it is equally dedicated to a new understanding of space, individual and collective, discursive and geographic. The plot introduces space from unconventional perspectives, as it is seen from the eyes of poor Jewish settlers, urban capitalists, British colonialists, and the native population. The politics of space is crucial to understanding the novel and its unique use of melancholy. The set of spatial oppositions that occupy its center depicts a clear conflict between complacent opportunism and idealistic failure on the one hand, and oppressive imperialism and hopeless rebellion on the other. The gallery of characters I discuss above presents the reader with that spectrum of possibilities; Barkai, at the center of the narrative, is the champion of failed opportunities, but his recurrent failures shed light on his materialist surrounding.

How does the novel reflect the concrete political situation unfolding at the time of Zarchi's writing? Zarchi wrote his novel in 1935 and 1936. An entry he made in his diary the day after completing the first draft reads, "Gideon Barkai (why does my heart quiver when I mention this name?) is a new Don Quixote, despised, but dear, dear to me that is."[41] Zarchai's thoughts came at an especially difficult time for the Jewish-Arab relationship in Palestine, and for the relationship of both communities with the British. The Arab rebellion arose as an expression of national consciousness that rejected both the British colonialist and the Jewish settler. As Eric Hobsbawm showed in *The Age of Extremes*, the 1930s were "a crucial decade for the Third World, not so much because the Slump led to political radicalization, but rather because it established contact between the politicized minorities and the common people of their countries."[42] Resistance to British rule spread across the Middle East and India; the "crisis of colonialism," which started with local movements, became an international movement that brought "the end of empires."[43]

Between 1932 and 1936, as D. K. Fieldhouse and other historians have shown, at least six new Arab political parties were established.[44] Arab nationalism grew from a locally organized initiative to a national phenomenon capable of establishing the basis for a "national-unity government of Palestinian Arabs."[45] Among the first to notice this change was the leader of political Zionism, David Ben-Gurion, who pointed out that the Arab population in Palestine changed from a "wild and fractured mob, aspiring to robbery and looting" to "an organized and disciplined community, demonstrating its national will with political maturity and a capacity for self-evaluation."[46]

Zarchi was among the first to realize the implications of this transformation. Zarchi's story could be read as a cultural transformation in a disputed space. In *The Arab Jews: A Postcolonial Reading of Nationalism, Religion, and Ethnicity*, Yehouda Shenhav analyzed the close connection between the Zionist movement of the 1930s and British colonialism in Iran and Iraq, using as a case study the very construction company for which the young Zarchi and his protagonist worked: "Solel Boneh's presence there beginning in the 1930s paved the way for key Zionist figures and networks of Zionist emissaries to visit various parts of the Middle East."[47] Shenhav presented the company as a stand-in for Zionism:

Reflecting the inherent duality, not only of the company, but also of the Zionist movement as a whole, Solel Boneh ventured into the Abadan region [on the Persian Gulf] holding two different passports, so to speak. One of these identified it as a Zionist operation, symbolic of the success of the Jewish national project in Palestine; the other, as a business enterprise in the service of British colonialism. Solel Boneh operated by balancing the legitimization it was given by these sovereign sources (Zionism and European colonialism), while speaking in several voices simultaneously. Striking the necessary balance to operate in the region was no simple matter, because relations between Zionism and British colonialism did not always run smoothly, and also because the Jewish workers at Abadan were not a monolithic group.[48]

As Shenhav points out, the impact of colonialism must be considered in terms of mechanisms, not ideology; economic forces such as Solel Boneh could have helped the colonialist regime and still have identified with a socialist agenda. Zarchi, who himself worked for Solel Boneh, paid close attention to those mechanisms of control and addressed the same cultural and spatial divisions between the European (and Jewish) pioneer and the native—Arab, Arab Jew, and even the pan-Arabic European. This language of separations could only project a polar opposition between the mechanism of colonialist control (mediated through work), on the one hand, and an atmosphere of imminent revolutionary change and a transformation of the political geography, on the other hand.

Barkai observes and learns the two but never gets involved. The novel ends by coming full circle. That is, its final image is of an urban melancholic ascending a mountain at sunset. No longer is there any thought of some idealized settlement; no longer is there any hope for a sacred collective. Instead, there is a vista, viewed by one man, alone: "He walked slowly, halting at times, and he saw the city at his feet, or the sea at the city's feet. His heart weighed heavy in him. What was his heart, in fact? A wick that cannot reach the burning oil? . . . When he opened his eyes, the sun was already setting far away at the sea's blue horizon, big and blazing, red with the blood of the sorrow of Being. Soon the sun had set and disappeared. Tomorrow it will rise again" (301).

Barkai's failure suggests a larger failure. He bows his head and accepts the bursting of his idealistic dreams. There is no big drama here, no tragedy. Instead we return to the beginning of the novel, and the descent from the failed settlement. The space around the protagonist has not changed. Just as in Cervantes's *Don Quixote,* life simply pushes on, leaving the confused and detached protagonist behind. The only hint of a grander narrative is the one supplied by nature itself: The sun, which sets like the personified "sorrow of being," will rise again, suggesting the modest scope of the grand human drama.

If time refuses the temptation of human life, space gives in to its political allure. The body of the pioneer, or its collective appearance in organizations such as Solel Boneh, represents the attempt to take over the aboriginal space, to signify it according to European codes, and to charge it with known terms, borrowed from the colonialist discourse. Then again, while Zarchi spoke the idealistic language of the pioneers, he never adopted their militant and chauvinistic discourse. In short, in spite of being an Ashkenazi Jew, Zarchi wrote from the perspective of "in-betweenness" and viewed the agents of Zionist power with a mixture of admiration and suspicion. This ambivalent voice is exactly where Zarchi's melancholy hovers and where a wide crack opens. Melancholy is the witness testifying about the presence of an ontological gap.

Little of Zarchi's perspective was decipherable for the critics of the time. One well-known critic of the period, Mordechai Robinson, accused Zarchi of "chronic psychological detachment, consisting of a certain degree of negation of [the right to] settle [in Palestine]."[49]

Robinson was correct in his observation concerning the "detached" effect but not the meaning behind it. Zarchi consciously tried to keep his distance from the collective and spatial convergence. Yet Zarchi's critique was not meant to end with "negation" as much as what Giorgio Agamben calls "pure difference": In *Stanzas* Agamben wrote about ambivalence or the "topology of the unreal" as the point of transformation from the romantic topoi to the modern celebration of melancholic fetish, pathologies, depression, and the abnormal.[50] The critical praxis, he observed, was born when the erasure of separations in space became too obvious to ignore: "We must still accustom ourselves to think of the 'place' not as something spatial, but as something more original than space. Perhaps we should think of it as a pure difference."[51] Such a pure difference is weighed not in terms of topographic space, national boundaries, ethnic distinctions, and the like, but rather in what Zarchi relied on, the distinctions between the aimless movement and its absolute absence. It is the seemingly minor difference between utopian (transcendental but frustrated) hope and (aimless) living movement, on the one hand, and deadly paralysis, on the other. Thinking about the closure of the novel in light of its beginning illuminates the difference between grand hopes and minor realizations or between aimless wondering and stagnation. Barkai, and not Caspi, the real estate agent, is the source of reflection and critique in this novel. So Barkai, like Zarathustra and Moses, is left to descend from the mountain, sobered by the extent of human greed. However, a marginal and melancholic prophet of the modern self, he is left to console himself with the repetitive movement of time, beyond spatial limits. If the question that opened the novel was how to overcome failure, the one that concludes it is how to integrate it.

5. Minor Literature as a Melancholic Type

In his short study of the Swiss author Robert Walser, written in 1929, Walter Benjamin discussed the contribution of the "minor genre": "The real challenge is to take advantage of the contemptible, unassuming potential of this form to create something which is alive and has a purifying effect."[52] Half a century later, Gilles Deleuze and Félix Guattari have developed this thinking about the reviving and corrective function of the "minor" into a complete theorization of "minor literature," in terms that could easily apply to Zarchi's novels. His protagonists are all "losers," defeated by their own ambitions, by their dreams, by their families, their communities, and the land. They have been beaten by the romantic and organic principles that they believe in. They are often impotent, both metaphorically and literally. Yet they lose and fail in order to expose a certain immanent boundary and, as a result, to overcome it.

In their study, ostensibly of Kafka but subtitled "Toward a Minor Literature," Deleuze and Guattari write about a literature of "nomads without law." Written in a "major language," typically that of an occupier or colonizer, this category, they assert, possesses "a high coefficient of deterritorialization."[53] In this sense, for them the epitome of minor literature, Kafka's literature and his German, "marks the impasse that bars access to writing for the Jews of Prague and turns their literature into something impossible—the impossibility of not writing, the impossibility of writing in German, the impossibility of writing otherwise."[54] Minor literature, a melancholic mode, marks the limit of the acceptable and possible. Its vital force ties the individual story to the collective: "The individual concern thus becomes all the more necessary, indispensable, magnified, because a whole other story is vibrating in it."[55] Minor works expose the limits of major language, pinpointing its blind spots. They celebrate "a revolutionary machine-to-come, not at all for ideological reasons but because the literary machine alone is determined to fill the conditions of a collective enunciation that is lacking elsewhere in this milieu: literature is the people's concern."[56] Minor literature has the possibility of revolutionizing language—and more than language—because of its ability to work under the radar of major literature and other forms of representation. As Paul Patton explained, this subversive ability had to do with periods of social change and key concepts for Deleuze and Guattari's philosophy, such as becoming, lines of flight, nomadism, and "metamorphosis machines," or the kind of thought that "consists in stretching out a place of immanence that absorbs the earth."[57]

Much of what Deleuze and Guattari said of Kafka may be said of Zarchi as well. Both men wrote "stories that stop because they cannot develop into novels, torn in two directions that block any way out."[58] They are, in other words, *incomplete* in essence. Kafka's novels falter in such ways, often literally so; they do not end or they end abruptly. Zarchi's narratives open an incomprehensible gap between the idealistic promise and the poor realization. Both Kafka and Zarchi's protagonists fail to take initiative and change a destiny set by "major language" and by the consensus around them. Their failure as characters reflects the failure of the narrative to represent reality in an authentic way and of the narrator to employ an active mode of storytelling.

The passive characters in Kafka's stories, and the dreamy figures in Zarchi's, shape a storyline whose obvious center is a mimetic failure and a cracked literary machine. The reality in both Kafka and Zarchi's stories refuses to be documented. Zarchi's stylistic and thematic choices also fit Deleuze and Guattari's model of "minor literature." For one, Deleueze and Guattari show how minor literature avoided a structural opposition of minor and major in favor of a subversive relation that challenges the major from within. Zarchi's novels and short stories, written during the 1930s and 1940s, seemed to fulfill the criteria established by the major literature or the consensual political discourse of the time, but they ignore the expected telos, the realization of the utopian ideal and the call for action. The serial failure of mindless protagonists to carry out any of Zionism's projects by becoming pioneers or establishing families marked the meeting of minor and major, as melancholy met the expectations of the time. In this way, Zarchi's stories propose a correction to modeling "minor literature" after Kafka. If Kafka's task is a major one, namely, the dismantling of major language and literary models, Zarchi's modest hope is to integrate an alternative, a truly "minor" key to the major melody of the sovereign language.[59]

As I showed in the first chapter, the protagonists of *Youth* (1932) and *Naked Days* (1935) answer these criteria, as does the hero of *And the Oil Flows*, Gideon Barkai. All men are passive figures who reflect much more than they act, dream more than they do, and answer a general idealist demand for change without ever taking an initiative of their own. The most distinctive action of those characters is leaving a place, with the hope that a change of scene would change their destiny, and instead they become "nomads without the law," as mentioned above.

Zarchi's most obvious example of minor literature was inspired by a visit to England. In 1937 he took a leave of absence from his job at the Hebrew University, following an invitation he received to spend an academic year in London, with the support of both the university and the Zionist Histadrut (union). During this year he audited classes, explored the rich cultural offering of the British capital, and met with intellectuals and political representatives. While in England, Zarchi reexamined the ties connecting his politics and his poetics, past, present, and future. He insisted that his role in England was one of a wondering intellectual, not of a Zionist representative. Still, he relished spending time with prominent cultural Zionists. For example, in one of the letters to Haim Toren from London, Zarchi wrote excitedly about a visit with Simon Rawidowicz, a pacifist who criticized the idea of a Zionist grab of Palestine. Like Ahad Ha'am, Rawidowicz believed that the Jews should establish a spiritual but not a political center in Palestine. The two men hit it off: "He didn't settle for one five- or six-hour meeting. . . . He appears to think that I have some merit and vigorously insisted that I arrange another meeting, and so I will."[60]

In addition to such meetings, Zarchi visited with his heroes of bygone days: He saw manuscript letters by Heine, Goethe, Byron, and Shelley. When he stood at Heine's grave in the Montmartre cemetery, he was "close to tears."[61] This attraction to the romantic authors is connected with what Heine biographer Jeffrey Sammons called the struggle "with a psychologically originary tendency to melancholy and pessimism,"[62] echoing Theodor Adorno's observation in his well-known "Heine the Wound" that "romantic expressivity is a myth atrophied by its growing 'self consciousness as a literary language.'"[63] Drawing on romantic imagery but resisting its absolutist internal inclination, both Kafka and Zarchi produced literature as an answer to burning political problems, for it turned self-consciousness into a deeper investigation into the incompleteness of language itself. In Zarchi's literature, the Zionist attempt to revive and reterritorialize the ancient

Hebrew instead helped to further deterritorialize it, revealing the gaps that were opening between the dream of realizing the ancient prophecy and the concrete results.

Zarchi conveyed to Toren his impressions of London in a long series of letters. Those letters formed the basis of the memoir *Traveling without Luggage* (1938), an account of his year abroad dedicated simply to "my friend."[64] A striking shift of mood stands out when we compare the inspired and happy reports he sent from London with this travel memoir Zarchi wrote soon after. While the letters are filled with individual optimism and romantic idealism, in the memoir Zarchi framed his own happy experiences in the context of the overwhelming shifts of history and his own pacifistic and pessimistic views: "The shadow of the bayoneted gun extends across all countries. And traces of shadows are visible everywhere, and there is no refuge whatsoever, . . . and they appeal to you from cinema newsreels, and from notices in the world's most democratic entities, such as the kingdom of Britain, whose advertisements pressure you: 'Join the modern army!'"[65] Scribbled in the margins of the manuscript is the following: "The prophecy in the book (by me) about war breaking out: written before war broke out."[66] From such notes it is clear that Zarchi viewed Britain, in 1938, in his usual dual manner. Alongside his admiration for Byron and Shelley and the liberal state lay his jaundiced thoughts on the country's colonialist history.

In a section of *Traveling without Luggage* devoted to Hyde Park he wrote:

> I had almost been seduced by the charms of the nocturnal garden, when my eye suddenly fell upon a speaker whom I could not look away from. He was tall and slender, wore no necktie, and possessed a dark fervor. . . . As the words that rushed so passionately from his lips became clear, I listened carefully: "During the war—I murdered men during the war! I did not kill, I murdered! With my own bare hands I spilled the blood of beautiful young healthy people— my hands spilled this blood! I murdered mothers' sons, and the tears of the mother of a foreigner are as bitter as the tears of our own mothers. Imprison me, sentence me to death, for I have murdered! But none of you will! After all, it was legally sanctioned murder, and I was even called a loyal and worthy son of my country!" (41)

Like his anonymous orator, Zarchi expresses highly critical, often maudlin views. The law for him was not only the basis of equality and democratic order but also the means by which mass murder was carried out, as his orator declares: "It was legally sanctioned murder, and I was even called a loyal and worthy son of my country!" (41) Tradition is not only a communal force, but it also operates as a tool of coercion. As he wrote in his earlier novel, *Naked Days*: "I am not a keen follower of tradition. I do not ascribe holiness to any porridge simply because it has been cooking in the same pot for many generations" (60). Indeed, whether in the novels or the memoir, Zarchi's protagonists are "nomads without the law," or at least nomads who are skeptical about the law.

After a friend took him to see Eton, that bastion of the British aristocracy and political elite, Zarchi reported a discovery that had shocked him, quoting the words of his guide: "The students here are not only pounded with lessons, but lashes too, plain and simple. A method? No, tradition. A disobedient student asks for a lashing himself, punishment which is executed on a wooden step designated for this purpose—the sages of Eton think it is easier to bear a lashing than the pangs of conscience. . . . Are you appalled? I am too. As I was wrestling with this outrageous news, my English neighbor whispered to me: 'Shelley and Gladstone were reared here'" (62).

In a letter he sent his friend Haim Toren on July 8, 1938, at the end of his year abroad, Zarchi reported that his route back from London had taken him through Antwerp and Paris. In Antwerp, he wrote, he was invited to speak to a Jewish audience. Because he was seen as a representative of Zionism, the group had invited him to speak about politics in Palestine. "You know me and know how far removed I am from this topic," he complained, "how I suffer because, at a time when our land and nation are so troubled, literary matters are far removed from the hearts of our readers. . . . I am obligated to pay this tax to the diaspora, and I will talk twice, most probably, about politics and literature."[67] An apolitical literature whose object is the political would stand, half a century later, at the heart of Deleuze and Guattari's discussion of "minor literature."

Zarchi returned from London with a stronger and more urgent commitment to the idea of Jewish return, but he connected that idea to the very opposite of the rhetoric of Zionism, to a traditional Jewish literature, and his politics also stood at odds with those of Zionism's secular and political writers. At the conclusion of his small memoir, he cited the medieval poet Yehuda Halevi: "I shall worry about neither property nor household / Nor wealth, nor any lost thing" (125).[68]

The epilogue to the short memoir was written after Zarchi returned to Palestine. His view was pessimistic and dark but not hopeless: "Much blood has been absorbed by the roads running through the land, and it is smeared on every rock and path. The blood of the past seeps into the blood of today, but a hope wide as the desert is forever extending from them" (126). One recalls the corrective aspect of the "minor genre," as Benjamin calls it, or "minor literature," as Deleuze and Guattari identify it.

Zarchi's travelogue received little attention from the critics. The author and editor Yaakov Fichman wrote a short review in *Moznaim*, the official organ of the Zionist association of authors (Agudat HaSofrim), sounding, like Gershon Shaked after him, the naïve-alarm: "These quick travel notes, observations, and fragments sometimes reveal more about their writer than anything else. . . . These little chapters, in which juvenile innocence has not expired, stand on their own right."[69]

Zarchi's travel writings are minor in the Deleuzian-Guattarian sense: They present an individual search for meaning in a language that questions its own norms and codes. Trying to shape such dualism as a coherent form of expression could lead to a paradox or a distanced allegory, as was the case with Kafka. But in Zarchi's case it exposed the rupture between the individual will and the collective formulation, or between the idealist promise and the failure of major literature. *Traveling without Luggage* possesses an episodic and deterritorialized structure, resisting the Zionist narrative of secular redemption or territorial realization. Zarchi's closure expresses a future hope that would distance itself from the bloody past and the present by not realizing them. In this sense, it diverges from the genre described by Deleuze and Guattari, with its opposition between center and margins. As Shai Ginsburg noted while writing about another melancholic writer of the early yishuv, Yosef Haim Brenner: "Whereas literature is commonly perceived at the center of the Hebrew discourse of the nation, one should conclude that, contrary to common critical practices, one cannot set the center of that discourse against its margins. . . . On the contrary, it appears that challenge and subversion permeate that national discourse through and through."[70] Indeed, like Brenner and Kafka, Zarchi utilizes subversion in order to permeate the national discourse. Unlike them, however, he never transgresses the melancholy and dreamy helplessness of his protagonists. His point of diversion is where his melancholy takes over the narrative, balancing the idealism and questioning the idea of Zionist return, but this is also where it stays. If there is any sense of redemption in Zarchi's work, it is offered by the act of writing itself. Only literature could imagine the hope of departure from a road soaked in blood without negating its existence. Nevertheless, if a critical mission, it is a limited one: Zarchi never takes the next step Brenner and Kafka took, turning the power of language against his own sense of self and the ability of his language to convey an authentic sense of reality.

If so far I argued in favor of reading Zarchi as a case of "minor literature," it is important to note where he diverges from Deleuze and Guattari's model. While books like *And the Oil Flows, Youth*, and *Traveling without Luggage* offer a model that answers the criteria that minor literature displays in more sophisticated works by Kafka, they also depart from it. The protagonists seek the lost past rather than the "echo of the future" Deleuze and Guattari found in *The Trial* and "The Metamorphosis." If Kafka's protagonists are simple people who are left suspended or isolated in space, without context, Zarchi's protagonists are men and women of action who keep failing. They are not necessarily passive, just wrong. Unlike Kafka's static characters, they slowly shift from greater activity to melancholy and passivity. If Deleuze and Guattari describe minor literature as a system of passion rather than the creation of new laws—Kafka's protagonists keep desiring objects and responses, especially those they cannot achieve—Zarchi's protagonists answer, by the end of the story, to the law of melancholy. If Deleuze and Guattari depict the transcendentalism of the law via its affinity to both passion and power, in Zarchi it is the unrealized passion that undermines power, law, and any form of transcendentalism. Contra Deleuze and Guattari, sometimes it is beneficial to look not only at minor literature written by major writers but minor literature written by minor writers. Melancholy, a marker of the minor, helps us expose the factors that undermine the norm, both literary and political, as well as those factors that strengthen norms and conventions. It does so by taking apart the constructive and materialist nature of urban space and replacing it with wild nature on the one hand, and with the ingrained redeeming potential of language on the other.

Notes

1. Eran Rolnik, *Freud in Zion: Psychoanalysis and the Making of Modern Jewish Identity*, trans. Haim Watzman (London: Karnak, 2012), 45.

2. Ibid. See also Rakefet Zalashik, "Psychiatry, Ethnicity, and Migration: The Case of Palestine, 1920–1948," *Dynamis* 25 (2005): 412.

3. Israel Zarchi, *Alumim* [Youth] (Tel Aviv: Mitzpe, 1933), 3. Page numbers for subsequent quotes for *Youth* follow this edition and will be given in line. All translations are mine.

4. The Baron Edmond Benjamin James de Rothschild (1845–1934) is one of the most influential figures of the early history of the yishuv. His investment in the early Zionist settlement was not limited to his capital but involved his closest and most efficient administrators, who helped in educating, training, and supervising the young pioneers. For that purpose, Rothschild purchased lands in the center and north of Palestine, established the Palestine Jewish Colonization Association (PICA). As Elizabeth Antebi argued, most of the historiography about Rothschild's activity has been biased one way or another. For a critical reading of his activity, see her "Baron Edmond de Rothschild (1845–1934): From HaNadiv (The Benefactor) to HaNassi (The Prince)," in *Jewish Studies at the Turn of the 20th Century*, vol. 2: *Judaism from the Renaissance to Modern Times*, eds. Judit Targarona Borras and Angel Saenz-Badillos (Leiden: Brill, 1999), 251–56.

5. In a famous passage from *Beyond Good and Evil* Nietzsche warns the "Europeans of the day after tomorrow" to consider pessimism their current political horizon; he concludes with a prophetic sentence: "Alas! If only you knew how soon, how very soon, things will be . . . different!" See *Beyond Good and Evil*, part 7, section 214. Friedrich Nietzsche, *Beyond Good and Evil*, trans. Judith Norman (Cambridge: Cambridge University Press, 2002), 109.

6. Ellipses are in the original.

7. Gershon Shaked, "Meotam Hasichim She'biladehem ein Etzim: Al Yetzirato shel Israel Zarchi" [From those saplings, without which one finds no trees: About Israel Zarchi's writing]," *Bitzron: Rivon Le'sifrut, Hagut U'mechkar* 4, no. 15 (1982): 13.

8. Zarchi thanked the two in different places. See, for example, Zarchi to Yaakov Fichman, 1 July 1933, Israel Zarchi Archive, file 8, no. 17609 (6-4805), Gnazim Institute, Tel Aviv. As the letter indicates, Fichman, who edited the organ of the Hebrew Writers Association, *Moznaim* [Scales], invited Zarchi to send him any new stories. Zarchi sent Fichman his first novella, *Samson of the Perfume Market*, in 1933.

9. Nurit Govrin, "Ha-Nistarot ba-niglot: 'Al ha-shirah veha-prosah shel Asher Barash" [About the poetry and prose of Asher Barash], in *Keri'at ha-dorot: Sifrut 'ivrit be-ma'aglehah* (Tel Aviv: Gvanim and Tel Aviv University Press, 2002), 1: 259–80. For the formal letter of acceptance of *Youth* by Barash, see Diary, 9 July, 1932, Zarchi Archive, file 171, K-3694.

10. Undated diary entries, 1932, Zarchi Archive, file 171, K-3699, p. 23.

11. Ibid.

12. Ibid., 26.

13. Undated diary entry, 1932, Zarchi Archive, file 171, K-3694, p. 36.

14. A diary entry recalls a conversation with Agnon about Ben-Zion. See Diary, 4 March 1942, Zarchi Archive.

15. Joseph Klausner, "S. Ben Zion Hamesaper" [S. Ben-Zion the narrator], *Ha'aretz*, 15 December 1920. See also Nurit Govrin, "Naftulei Yetzira: Hamishim Shana Le'Ptirat S. Ben Zion," *Siman Kria'a: Rivon Meorav LeSifrut* 16/17 (April 1983): 579.

16. Among the latter, see "Massaot" (1900) about travels in Palestine, including imaginary treks to snowy mountains with bears; "HaSa'ar Mitcholel" [A storm is coming] (ca. 1903) about the stormy life and bloodshed in Palestine; "HaSolelim" (1908) about the pavers of roads in Palestine; "Al HaMishmar" (1918–20) about the life of the guards in Palestine, which ends with death; "Yekutiel" (1924) about a pioneer who emigrates to Palestine but misses his home in Europe; and "Olam Katan" (posthumous) about missing life in Europe and the parents' home.

17. His comments were upon hearing about Ahad Ha'am's death. Diary, 3 January 1927, Zarchi Archive.

18. Haim Beer, *Gam Ahavatam, Gam Sin'atam* [Their love and their hate] (Tel Aviv: Am Oved, 2006), 111.

19. See also Diary, 25 October 1933, Zarchi Archive.

20. Govrin, "Ha-Nistarot ba-niglot," 579.

21. Ibid., 588.

22. Ibid., 578.

23. Zarchi to H. N. Bialik, 8 January 1933, the Bialik Archive, Correspondences, Tel Aviv. I would like to thank Shmuel Avneri, the director of the Bialik Archive, for his assistance in finding this letter.

24. Diary, 25 October 1933, Zarchi Archive.

25. In a diary entry dated 30 October 1937, he wrote: "A position in Even-Zahav's department. . . . I agreed but deep inside was hoping for a savior, so I don't need to take it. The savior didn't come and I had to agree, with a sense of relief." Diary, 30 October 1937, Zarchi Archive.

26. In September 1934 Zarchi copied Rilke's "Zum Einschlafen zu Sagen," a lullaby to a loved one, which links the lines "the clocks call striking to each other" and "a strange man passes yet / and rouses a strange dog." Rainer Maria Rilke, *Translations from the Poetry* (New York: Norton, 1993), 61. See also Diary, unspecified date in September 1934, Zarchi Archive.

27. Diary, 10 December 1935, Zarchi Archive.

28. Ibid.

29. Ibid.

30. Walter Benjamin, "Left-Wing Melancholy," in *Selected Writings*, ed. Michael W. Jennings, Howard Eiland, and Gary Smith (Cambridge, MA: Harvard University Press, 1999), 2: 424.

31. Diary, 10 December 1935, Zarchi Archive. See also the characterization of Fabian's world as "hopeless" in Fred Rodrian, "Notizen zu Erich Kästners Kinderbüchern," in *Neue deutsche Literatur* 8–9 (1960), 117–29.

32. Translated and analyzed by Peter Toohey in *Melancholy, Love, and Time: Boundaries of the Self in Ancient Literature* (Ann Arbor: University of Michigan Press, 2004), 123, 325n34. Toohey argues that the term *taedium* was first used in a letter Seneca sent to Epicurus.

33. Diary, 22 April 1935, Zarchi Archive.

34. Diary, 19 July 1935, Zarchi Archive.

35. Johann Wolfgang von Goethe, *Faust: The First Part of the Tragedy*, trans. David Constantine (London: Penguin, 2005), 62–63.

36. Interview with Nurit Zarchi, 23 December 2013.

37. Diary, 20–21 May 1934, Zarchi Archive.

38. Israel Zarchi, *Ha'Neft Zorem La'Yam Ha'Tikhon* [And the oil flows to the Mediterranean] (Jerusalem: Israeli Publishing, 1937), 37. Page numbers for subsequent quotes for *And the Oil Flows* follow this edition and will be given in line. All translations are mine.

39. This is not the place to ponder about the genealogy of the term Barkai, but it is interesting to note that one finds allusions to Ben Sira's use of the term in the medieval theology of Meister Eckart, the modernizer of the German language. See, for example, George J. Brooke, *Intertextual Studies in Ben Sira and Tobit, Essays in Honor of Alexander A. Di Lella* (Washington, DC: Catholic Biblical Association of America, 2005).

40. I mean "Oriental" in the sense Said described it: "Orientalism as a Western style for dominating, restructuring, and having authority over the Orient . . . Without examining Orientalism as a discourse one cannot possibly understand the enormously systematic

discipline by which European culture was able to manage—or even produce—the Orient politically, sociologically, militarily, ideologically, scientifically, and imaginatively during the post-Enlightenment period." Edward W. Said, *Orientalism* (London: Penguin Books, 1995), 3.

41. Diary, 2 March 1936, Zarchi Archive.

42. Eric Hobsbawm, *The Age of Extremes: The Short Twentieth Century, 1914–1991* (London: Little, Brown, 1996), 214.

43. Ibid., 215.

44. D. K. Fieldhouse, *Western Imperialism in the Middle East 1914–1958* (Oxford: Oxford University Press, 2006), 163.

45. Tom Segev, *One Palestine, Complete: Jews and Arabs under the British Mandate*, trans. Haim Watzman (New York: Henry Holt, 2000), 368.

46. Ben-Gurion quoted in Segev, *One Palestine*, 370.

47. Yehouda Shenhav, *The Arab Jews: A Postcolonial Reading of Nationalism, Religion, and Ethnicity* (Stanford, CA: Stanford University Press, 2006), 38.

48. Ibid., 23.

49. "Sh'lilat Yishuvit," literally the "negation of settlement." See Mordechai Robinson, "Motivim Yishuviim (Hatlishut shel Zarchi)" [Motifs of settlement: Zarchi's detachment], *Ha'aretz*, February 12, 1937. See also the discussion in Aviva Mahlo, *Ben Shnei Nofim* [Between two landscapes] (Jerusalem: Reuven Mas, 1991), 137.

50. Giorgio Agamben, *Stanzas: Word and Phantasm in Western Culture*, trans. Ronald L. Martinez (Minneapolis: University of Minnesota Press, 1993), xviii.

51. Ibid.

52. Walter Benjamin, "Robert Walser," in *Selected Writings*, 2: 257.

53. Gilles Deleuze and Félix Guattari, *Kafka: Toward a Minor Literature*, trans. Dana Polan (Minneapolis: University of Minnesota Press, 1986), 16.

54. Ibid.

55. Ibid., 17.

56. Ibid., 18.

57. Paul Patton, *Deleuze and the Political* (London: Routledge, 2000), 136. For the sake of clarity, I ignore here the subtle work of differentiating between the four different types of deterritorialization and reterritorialization, as well as the differentiation between relative and absolute deterritorialization. However, more could (and should) be done with those theoretical observations in the context of melancholy.

58. Deleuze and Guattari, *Kafka*, 41.

59. Kafka keeps reflecting about his natural inclination to destroy expectations, for instance, the "talkativeness" or "talking shop" of a certain "Dr. K.," who "becomes conscious of his proficiency, there are associations with every story. . . . Some I also destroy by asking questions." Diary entry from October 13, 1911, in *The Diaries of Franz Kafka 1910–1913*, ed. Max Brod, trans. Joseph Kresh (New York: Schocken Books, 1976), 75.

60. Diary, 8 July 1938, Zarchi Archive, file 171: Correspondence Zarchi-Toren, cases 69577–586. David N. Myers describes Rawidowicz as a thinker who "tacks away from the political margins toward the center." As Myers shows, Rawidowicz adopted a critical position inspired by Ahad Ha'am's cultural Zionism. Zarchi's melancholy implied the reverse course, from the center to the margins, even if inspired by similar sources. See David N. Myers, *Between Jew and Arab: The Lost Voice of Simon Rawidowicz* (Hanover, NH: Brandeis University Press, 2008), 99, 104.

61. Ibid.

62. Jeffrey L. Sammons, *Heinrich Heine: Alternative Perspectives, 1985–2005* (Würzburg: Königshausen and Neumann, 2006), 83.

63. Theodor Adorno, "Heine the Wound," in *Notes to Literature*, ed. Peter Uwe Hohendahl and Sander Gilman (Lincoln: University of Nebraska Press, 1991), 84.

64. Undoubtedly meaning Haim Toren, the recipient of Zarchi's letters from London and Paris.

65. Zarchi, *Massa Le'Lo Tz'ror* [Traveling without luggage] (Jerusalem: Hotza'at Ha'Sfarim Ha'Eretz-Israelit, 1939), 29. Page numbers for subsequent quotes for *Traveling without Luggage* follow this edition and will be given in line. All translations are mine.

66. Zarchi Archive, file 171, "Notes."

67. Zarchi Archive, file 171, correspondence: Zarchi-Toren, case 69577–586.

68. For the full poem in an English translation, see Joseph Yahalo, *Yehuda Halevi: Poetry and Pilgrimage* (Jerusalem: Hebrew University Press, 2009), 108.

69. Yaakov Fichman, "Masa Belo Z'ror," *Meoznaim* 9, no. 2 (Summer 1939): 267.

70. Shai Ginsburg, *Rhetoric and Nation: The Formation of Hebrew National Culture, 1880–1990* (Syracuse, NY: Syracuse University Press, 2014), 148.

3

JERUSALEM, MESSIANISM, EMPTINESS

1. Repetition and Obsession

The movement of Zarchi's protagonists, who set out into sandy wastes or walk back and forth between their failed utopian dreams and the sad reality of everyday life, is the same back-and-forth movement as the one described in chapters 1 and 2. Like a manic depressive, Zarchi's stories shift between ecstatic hope and deep disappointment. Although much of my discussion of Zarchi's melancholy thus far has emphasized his protagonists—their rhetoric and individual preferences—his key ideas are more readily found in the landscape, where he conceptualized his notion of melancholy in spatial terms. Nothing demonstrates the spatial arrangement of melancholy better than Jerusalem, the city of syndromes, ecstasy, and false hopes. Jerusalem, we shall see, served as an ideal space for Zarchi's poetics, especially because it was a perfect case of deterritorialized and reterritorialized space, or as Deleuze and Guattari explain, it is "a map and not a tracing," that is, a two-dimensional image representing an idea rather than a three-dimensional experience of an actual space.[1] Following this sharp observation, one could identify Zarchi's Jerusalem as a rhizomatic map of melancholic repetition and obsession, lost traces and retroactive reflection. In the following section I examine an impossible urban terrain that projects an embedded sense of loss of direction as well as the lack of goal or organization. The effect, and affect, I argue, is one of a melancholic repetitive mode that breaks away from "tracing" and, furthermore, from any stable subject, a linear movement, or a well-framed sense of territory. Zarchi's pre-1948 understanding of melancholy as a deterritorialized space contrasts with the post-1967 configuration of the united city under Jewish sovereignty as the mark of the (unwilling) victor, the suffering soul of the (necessary) killer.

2. Jerusalem: Deterritorialization

During the 1940s, Zarchi wrote about Jerusalem. He had been living there since the early 1930s, but it took him almost a decade to take it up as his subject. Once he started, his stories concentrated on the landscapes and symbolism of the ancient city. His metaphorical language changed and, with it, the literary field he occupied and its associated political implications.

His first Jerusalem book was a short novel—which he would later regret[2]—dedicated to and named for Mount Scopus, site of the new Hebrew University campus. In describing a young student walking in the streets of east Jerusalem, without a sense of direction or of time, Zarchi projects a deep alienation that he must have felt himself during his days as a student a decade earlier: "Weeks passed. . . . He did not know how many, for something strange persisted during those weeks. He only knew that he found himself between day and night and was hung there above an abyss with no bridge to support him."[3] Part of the confusion is the result of the protagonist's philosophical questioning (he is a philosophy major) that echoes Zarchi's own skepticism: "It is not clear whether history is the study of the past as it actually occurred, because history is not the study of this past, but rather of what has been preserved in our knowledge of it" (217).

After this work came a series of novellas and more novels that explored Jerusalem and its symbolism. The historical setting slowly moved backward, from the present to the late nineteenth century, and from the secular and free-floating life of students to the mythic language of the Yemenite settlement in Jerusalem or the mystical and messianic Ashkenazi orthodox community.

Zarchi's Jerusalem differs from the conventional image of the city as a sacred place, the ritualistic center for the three monotheistic religions and a key symbol for the eschatological and revivalist image. Zarchi presented the city—like other authors of this time—as a disappointment, but added to it a detailed description of an isolated, melancholic space without a center, a great burial ground, gray, desperate, and hopeless—both politically and emotionally.[4] Only rarely—and briefly—did the city in Zarchi's work experience moments of personal, literary, or religious transcendence, what the philosopher Rebecca Comay calls "the sublime abstraction which finds power in disempowerment."[5] In his Jerusalem stories Zarchi projected his sense of disempowerment on the city and the aesthetics of its geography. Similarly to Deleuze and Guattari's argument concerning Kafka's tactics of deterritorialization, disempowerment in Zarchi's novels serves to charge the familiar landscape and consciousness with a different understanding of an a priori space and time, or a counterhistory. But let's slow down, for a short while, the advance of the philosophical train and observe its movement again—as we did in chapter 1—in biographical and literary terms, as the author Amos Oz described Zarchi, and Jerusalem, in his own memoir.

3. Amos Oz's Zarchi

The letter and diary entries Zarchi wrote during this period say little about his personal life. Yet a recent autobiographical novel by Amos Oz provides a poignant and intimate glimpse of Zarchi. Based on Oz's childhood recollections, the excerpts below, from his *Tale of Love and Darkness*, describe Zarchi the man and offer a look at his friendship with Oz's parents:

> Today the name of Israel Zarchi is almost forgotten, but in those days he was a prolific young writer whose books sold many copies. He was about my father's age, but by 1937, when he was twenty-eight or so, he had already published no fewer than three books. . . . He too studied Hebrew literature with Professor Klausner at Mt. Scopus, though he arrived in the land a few years before my father did and had worked for two or three years as an agriculture laborer in the colonies of the Sharon. Zarchi made his livelihood doing clerical work at the university. He was a dainty man, absent-minded, shy, rather somber, with a soft voice and a soft step, his body meager and delicate—I could never manage to picture him holding a hoe or a pickaxe. . . . His thin face was very pale and dreamy. As he walked it seemed that he did not trust the ground he stepped on, or conversely, worried that his steps were hurting the ground. He never looked at me when we spoke—his brown contemplative gaze was almost always fixed on the floor. I revered him because I was told that he was not like other writers: the whole of Jerusalem wrote scholarly books, put together from notes, from other books . . . but Mr. Zarchi wrote books "out of his own head." . . . On winter evenings a few members of my parents' circle used to get together sometimes at our place or at the Zarchis' in the building across the road: Haim and Hannah Toren, Shmuel Werses, the Breimans. . . . The Zarchis were not only Father's former landlords but also dear friends, despite regular arguments between my revisionist father and Zarchi the "Red": my father loved talking and explaining and Zarchi liked to listen. . . . Esther Zarchi, for her part, tended to ask questions, and my father enjoyed giving her extensively detailed replies. Israel Zarchi would turn to my mother sometimes, with downcast eyes, and ask her opinion as though begging her in coded language to take his side in the argument.
>
> In 1947 [the publisher] brought out my father's first book, *The Novella in Hebrew Literature, from Its Origins to the End of the Haskalah.* This book was based on my father's master's thesis, which he wrote for his teacher-uncle,

Professor Klausner.[6] [After the first copies arrived] Father's happiness lasted for three or four days, and then his face fell. Just as he had rushed to the post office every day before the package arrived, so he now rushed every day to Achiasaf's Bookshop in King George V Avenue, where three copies of *The Novella* were displayed for sale. Day after day the same three copies were there, not one of them purchased. And it was the same the next day, and the day after that. "You," Father said with a sad smile to his friend Israel Zarchi, "write a new novel every six months, and instantly all the pretty girls snatch you off the shelves and take you straight to bed with them, while we scholars, we wear ourselves out for years on end checking every detail, verifying every quotation, spending a week on a single footnote, and who bothers to read us?" . . . And then suddenly, a couple of days later, on a Friday evening, he came home beaming happily and all a-tremble like a boy who has just been kissed in front of everyone by the prettiest girl in the class. "They're sold! They've all been sold! All in one day!" . . . [To celebrate, Mother] suggested the two of them go to the Edison Cinema. . . . I was dropped off with the novelist Zarchi and his wife, to have my supper there and behave myself until my parents got back, at nine or half past. "Behave yourself, you hear? . . . If Mr. Zarchi is working, just find yourself a toy or a book and sit as quietly as a mouse! . . . And so off they went . . . and Mr. Zarchi suggested I go into his study, which, as with our flat, was also the bedroom and the sitting room and everything. That was the room that had been my father's when he was a student. . . . Mr. Zarchi sat me down on the sofa and talked to me for a bit—I don't remember what he said, but I shall never forget how I suddenly noticed on the little coffee table by the sofa no fewer than four identical copies of *The Novella in Hebrew Literature*, one on top of the other, like in a shop. Among them was, I knew, one that Father had given to Mr. Zarchi with an inscription. I just couldn't understand why he would have the three others, and it was on the tip of my tongue to ask, but at the last moment I remembered the three copies that had just been bought that very day, at long last, from Achiasaf's Bookshop. I felt a rush of gratitude well up that almost brought tears to my eyes. Mr. Zarchi saw that I had noticed them. He did not smile but shot me a sidelong glance through half-closed eyes, as though he were silently accepting me into his band of conspirators, and without saying a word he leaned over, picked up three of the four copies on the coffee table, and secreted them in a drawer of his desk. I too held my peace, and said nothing to him or my parents. I did not tell a soul until after Zarchi and my father had died—the former while he was still in his prime. I told no one except, many years later, his daughter Nurit Zarchi, who did not seem overly impressed.[7]

4. The Jerusalem Novellas, Early 1940s

In December 1939, shortly after his return from England and the completion of *Traveling without Luggage*, Zarchi wrote a short story set in the stony passages of the old city of Jerusalem. In "Samson from the Perfume Market," first published in *Moznaim*, the organ of the Hebrew Writers Association

(Agudat HaSofrim), Zarchi fused a romantic tragedy with an ironic presentation of the Samson story.[8] Here a love affair doomed by class conflict reads like an updating of *Romeo and Juliet*, in which the Samson of the story comes to a sorry end at the hands of the family of the girl he loves.[9] Having forced their sister to separate from her lover, whom they consider inexcusably ignorant and poor, her brothers threaten to kill him if he sees her again. He gives in to their demands and quits his job, taking instead the job formerly held by a blind mule; it is Samson's brute strength that turns the millstones that grind wheat into flour. He moves to a cave, becoming one of the living dead: "The initial smell of the hollow is musty, chill—the breath of old stones" (37). This olfactory description echoed in many of Zarchi's stories set in the caves and graves and catacombs of Jerusalem.

Sidestepping high drama, the story stays in the realm of "minor literature" (as described in chap. 2) and refuses the temptation of catharsis or downfall. And unlike the biblical Samson, Zarchi's protagonist did not bring the house down on the heads of his enemies; instead he buried himself alive. The story presents a model closer to the baroque *Trauerspiel* than to the structures of Jewish, Greek, or Elizabethan drama. But why? What does Zarchi earn from such an aesthetic choice?

The motion of Samson is that of the millstones he turns, round and round. The repetitive movement of his body also marks the circularity of the melancholic mind, unable to break away from its own dead end. It is the movement of a hopeless animal that grinds time itself into minute particles, dragging life out into innumerable identical moments. The story is framed as a pastiche—adapting and shrinking the scope of both *Romeo and Juliet* and the story of Samson and Delilah—yet melancholy resides in the background as an unrealized potential. Any convergence between the personal and the collective, the mythic and the individual, will and impotence, implies melancholy: "The young men saw that he wasn't moving, and said to him, 'But you are Samson! Show us some of your heroic feats.' His answer emerged as a sad murmur: 'I . . . I am Samson, but my seven locks have been shaved off'" (43). Here, the betrayal is carried out not by Delilah, a pagan woman, but by the brothers of the Jewish girl: "And you, who are you, you ignoramus, to covet a girl from a good family?" (40). Class, not ethnic identity, is what separates the two.

Only one person stands up to the brothers: "Their mother grew angry and said, 'And what about us? Why were we born rich? And now we bow before the gods of money?'" (42). In a place where the rich and poor live side by side, Zarchi demands, why make enemies or bring in foreign gods? It is enough that a man brings disaster down on himself: "And so this wheel has become the center of his bleak life, a peg to hang from in an endless night" (47). In the epilogue to the short story, the narrator speaks of Samson as one too weak to chance death in a final confrontation with his enemies. A sense of uneasy and unsolvable melancholy replaces the catastrophic tone of the biblical story.

Shortly after he published "Samson from the Perfume Market," Zarchi wrote another story that updated a Torah story while extending the motif of the millstones and their repetitive movement: "Millstones of the Wind."[10] (The Hebrew title is "Reichaim shel Ruach"; *ruach* means both *wind* and *spirit* and the alliteration stresses the hyperbolic contrast between the heaviness of the stones and the lightness of air or noncorporeality.) This story follows Hannah, the adopted daughter of Rabbi Yaakov, a miller. To parallel the latter part of Hannah's long and sad life, Zarchi recounts the decline and fall of Jerusalem, from the city of myths and dreams to the place of madness and death.

The story opens with the symbolic decision to situate a mill outside the walls of the old city, representative of the efforts secular Zionists made to leave the boundaries of Jewish orthodoxy. Jewish extramural settlement was supported by the philanthropy of Sir Moses Haim Montefiore (1784–1885), a rich banker of Jewish-Italian origins and president of the Board of Deputies of British Jews. Montefiore had a windmill built and around it the settlement known as Mishkenot Sha'ananim. Zarchi invented a fictional figure, Rabbi Yaakov, who agrees to run the windmill. Rather than heed the family members and old friends who urge him to return to the old city, Rabbi Yaakov pursues his perverse course. He marries Hannah against her will to a rebellious cynic, and the couple joins him at the new windmill. In taking the job at the mill, Yaakov indicates that money is a secondary consideration: "He saw the act of construction as the beginning of redemption, and the minister he saw as one of the wealthy people of yore, coming to revive a ruined land. His mission was, in its entirety, a good deed. . . . But some were not pleased that Rabbi Yaakov now devoted less time to study, that he no longer visited the temple in both the morning and in the evening, that he did not join the conversation after prayers had concluded" (54).

As happens so often in Zarchi's fictions, those who break with the status quo are punished. Life outside the walls is harsh, and the mill fails. The men are the first to escape the hardship and disappear. After the death of

Rabbi Yaakov, Hannah's husband leaves her with the children, their sons scatter, and Hannah is left all alone. Deserted, poor, and lonely, she goes mad, raving about messianic time. "And as Hannah had forgotten Jerusalem, so Jerusalem too had forgotten her. . . . Her shadow trudged across Jerusalem, the shadow of days gone by, a forgotten immemorial memory" (69–70). Once again, as with the Samson story, the conclusion is infused with an uneasy melancholy rather than an apocalypse, and with forgetting as the counterhistory of remembrance, success, and catastrophe.

Here, as in a number of his other stories, Zarchi demonstrated a fine sensitivity to womanhood. The story that started with the well-known tale of a "major" historical narrative and the place of a dynamic male protagonist shifts to a story of "minor" figures and history, represented through a female perspective and a counterhistorical narrative. As the narrator explains, Hannah saw all of the mistakes her husband made, but she could do nothing to resist or amend them. She comes to signify the failed hope of early Zionism, a system hobbled by a lack of sensitivity to social issues and inflicted with male chauvinism and egocentrism. Jerusalem, in that context, wears a melancholic attire of a two-dimensional, circular and decentralized city.

Notes

1. Gilles Delezue and Félix Guattari, *A Thousand Plateaus: Capitalism and Schizophrenia*, trans. Brian Massumi (Minneapolis: University of Minnesota Press, 1987), 12.

2. See note from 20 December 1944, in "Lists, Conversations, Meetings" file, sig. K-3700, Zarchi Archive, Gnazim Institute, Tel Aviv.

3. Israel Zarchi, *Har HaTzofim* [Mount Scopus] (Jerusalem: Ahiasaf, 1940), 29. Page numbers for subsequent quotes for *Mount Scopus* follow this edition and will be given in line. All translations are mine.

4. Avner Holtzmann followed the literary depiction of Jerusalem during the British Mandate, in that way, as "a deep foreign notion in relation to Jerusalem. While identifying themselves as the heart of the Zionist revolution, these authors and their friends shared the notion that Jerusalem, the actual and symbolic heart of the pre-Zionist Yishuv, was not relevant to the changes that characterized the time, but set aside, captivated by its own past, alienated and far." See Avner Holtzman, "Yerushalaim HaMandatorit baSifrut HaIvrit" [The mandatory Jerusalem in Hebrew literature], in *Yerushalaim biTkufat HaMandat: Ha'Asiyah ve'Hamoreshet*, ed. Yehoshua ben Arie (Jerusalem: Yad Itzhak Ben Tzvi, 2003), 370–92. Here, p. 376.

5. Rebecca Comay, "The Sickness of Tradition: Between Melancholia and Fetishism," in *Walter Benjamin and History*, ed. Andrew Benjamin (London: Continuum, 2005), 90.

6. Yehuda Arie Klausner (1910–1970), Amos Oz's father, was born in Odessa and emigrated to Palestine in 1933. He was a literary scholar who—under the influence of his uncle, the scholar Joseph Klausner—wrote a series of researches dedicated to Jewish and Hebrew literary texts. Yehuda Arie Klausner worked for many years at the National Library in Jerusalem and engaged especially with the Hebrew bibliographical database that includes, as of 2011, 90 percent of all Hebrew bibliography in the world since the fifteenth century. The chairman of the initiative was Gershom Scholem, and Hugo Bergman sat on the supervising committee.

7. Amos Oz, *A Tale of Love and Darkness*, trans. Nicholas de Lange (New York: Harvest, 2005), 125–26, 134–35. An important portion of the text quoted above does not appear in the English translation and so has been inserted and translated by Yael Kenan and myself for this book. I would like to thank Amos Oz for consenting to allow me to translate and publish this portion from his book.

8. Israel Zarchi, "Shimshon Mi'Shuk Habsamim" [Samson from the perfume market] in *Israel Zarchi: Yalkut Sipurim* [Israel Zarchi: A collection of stories] (Tel Aviv: Yachdav, 1983), 37–47. Zarchi submitted the individual story to Yaakov Fichman, the chief editor of *Moznaim* on July 1, 1933. See Zarchi Archive, file 8, sig. 17609 (6-4805). Page numbers for subsequent quotes for "Samson from the Perfume Market" follow this edition and will be given in line. All translations are mine.

9. No other names are mentioned in the story.

10. Israel Zarchi, "Reichaim shel Ruach" [Millstones of the wind] in *Israel Zarchi: Yalkut Sipurim*, 48–71.

4

POLITICAL THEOLOGY AND
LEFT-WING MELANCHOLY

1. Rebecca Comay and Wendy Brown:
Benjamin's Left-Wing Melancholy

If the hidden matrix of Zionism is a political-theological view, a melancholic Zionist finds it embedded in a particular dualistic view. If Zionism, as Hillel Cohen argued, developed a "dual consciousness," a "Jewish spark" next to crude nationalism, then it was constructed on the basis of both victimhood and decisionism.[1] In a recent book about the origins of Hebrew poetry, the literary and political analyst Hannan Hever argued that early Zionist Hebrew literature tried to "shape an authentic sense of reality that is nonliterary, in the service of the collective norms of the *halutz*, the new Jew, who tried to control his space using un-mediate measures of control of the landscape and the nature of the land."[2] But the history of Palestine was bound to induce a theological dimension in the land, positioning the halutz as a "subject and a sacrificial victim who would redeem the people."[3] Hever placed at the heart of his analysis three concepts: Carl Schmitt's analysis of political-theological decisionism, Walter Benjamin's understanding of the relationship between law and violence, and Giorgio Agamben's recent analysis of the state of emergency.

In a brilliant short essay, Rebecca Comay cited Freud, Panofsky and Saxl, Benjamin, Julia Kristeva, Agamben, and others in presenting melancholy as a dualistic language, paralyzing and ecstatic at the same time. She showed that the melancholic state of mind generally implied a lost object and an inability to overcome that loss. But for her, the story did not end with a Freudian decline to pathology: "The sublime abstraction which finds power in this disempowerment threatens to evaporate the object into an

aesthetic phantasmagoria which would adapt the subject to the require-
ments of the present. . . . The structure of melancholia in this way begins
to bleed into that of fetishism. . . . The fetishistic split which maintains the
contradiction between knowledge and belief—traumatic loss on the one
hand, redemptive totality on the other—provides no protective contain-
ment of its antitheses, but rather implicates both within a contaminating
porosity and oscillation of one term into the other."[4]

How does this junction between the political-theological and melancholy help us to understand Zarchi? How does it help us understand
early Zionism? During the 1940s Zarchi learned, gradually, how to com-
bine his ideas about melancholy with the views of the ancients. For him
it was a countermechanism, that is, a system that enabled him to subvert or even dismantle the consensual views of his generation. The power
of melancholy lies in its liminality; like Deleuze and Guattari's "minor
literature," it allows the writer to work inside and outside conventional
language and norms. Zarchi turned to it while bringing ancient mythical
texts and figures—Samson and Hannah, for example—into the modern
age. After all, the convergence of the ancient and the modern was already
in the air, as it was the lifeblood of Zionism. As I show in this chapter,
Zarchi's analysis of messianic temporality was central to his thinking.
His particular contribution, in that respect, was the creation of a melancholic temporality that was grounded itself in what Comay calls "a
split fetishism"; looking at the present always with the filter of victimhood and decisionist logic meant a recurrent need to translate the double
loss—the loss of one's own past plus the loss of the ability to mourn it—to
a melancholic apparatus, or a fetish. If we recall Anita Shapira's observation, quoted earlier, that Zionist leaders constructed their utopian ideology on the basis of an "acceleration of history," then Zarchi's melancholy
slows it down by forming a counterhistory. Figures such as Hannah,
Samson, and Gideon Barkai are all messianically utopian radical idealists and unpredictable romantics in the grip of irrational passions, but
their failure ensures the collapse of messianism as a possible horizon,
individual and political. Their melancholy is always bleeding into a fetish
that unites the traumatic loss and the redemptive totality with a messianic understanding of Zion.

These melancholy protagonists express themselves in the idealistic
discourse while carving out a counteridealist niche within it. They do not
answer the expectations of progress, and they fail in political and personal

terms; theirs is a quasi-religious vocabulary used to express a secularized messianic vision, but they fail in achieving even that.

Comay's theory relies heavily on Walter Benjamin's analysis of melancholy. Benjamin was the first to connect melancholy with idealism, on the one hand, and a secularized form of political messianism (what Comay calls a "fetish") on the other hand. During the 1920s and 1930s Walter Benjamin examined both melancholy and messianism, analyzing their roles in the secularization and politicization of theological concepts. I will show how these concepts shed light on the political acceleration of history, the result of Comay's above-mentioned "split." Max Pensky observed in that context: "Benjamin sees the convoluted paradox of melancholy writing in its particularly political dimension. Melancholy infects any political cause that it seeks to support, for the melancholic's support (of anything) is always tinged with the atmosphere of meaninglessness. Politically, meaninglessness translates into resignation, the precise negation of decisiveness. A melancholy politics thus glides into a secret, half-willing collaboration with the forces it seeks to oppose. . . . Benjamin thus argues that *contemporary* melancholy writing must necessarily lose the appearance of political detachment."[5] In other words, while observing the relevance of melancholy to the culture and politics of his time, Benjamin criticized it as a form of cooptation. Even as early as his first scholarly work, *The Origin of German Tragic Drama* (1928), he observed: "Melancholy betrays the world for the sake of knowledge. But in its tenacious self-absorption it embraces dead objects in its contemplation, in order to redeem them."[6] Like Freud, Benjamin contrasted melancholy with mourning, but for the opposite purpose. As Ilit Ferber put it in a recent book about Benjamin's use of melancholy, "the melancholic devours his lost love-object in order to retain it; in demonstrating his endless loyalty, he destroys it."[7] This description, I argue, is an accurate depiction of Zarchi's melancholic relation to Zionism.

Benjamin criticized the melancholic "betrayal of the world," or his object of love, but also pointed at its potential. Devouring and destruction have the potential to release the subject from the melancholic obsession. Lacking a purpose other than devouring and destroying, the melancholic thinker can recover what has been forgotten and create a narrative that runs contrary to the history written by the winners. Such was the achievement of Benjamin's poets, who saw the power of melancholy as something lyrical, allegorical, and philosophical: Johann Peter Hebel, Hugo von Hofmannsthal, and Stefan George.

As mentioned in the introduction to this book, in "Left-Wing Melancholy" (1931) Benjamin attacked Erich Kästner as one of the key literary representatives of the German Social Democrats, saying that his (and their) "political meaning exhausts itself in the reversal of all revolutionary reflexes, insofar as they ever could have touched the bourgeoisie, into objects of distraction, of amusement, made available for consumption."[8] In other words, the romantic melancholy of bourgeois writers, Benjamin perceived, is nothing other than the sterilization of revolutionary tendencies. How to avoid this fallacy? Benjamin positioned the aesthetic mechanism—Foucault would call it a *dispositif* or *apparatus*—before any ethical value or any political norm. The bottom line is pretty simple: No critique that serves the power structure can be truly critical. Melancholy exposes the false pretentions of the critical voice, which unpacks the liberal left's instrumentalization, even fetishization, of melancholy. As Benjamin had written in his study of German drama, "All essential decisions in relation to men can offend against loyalty; they are subject to higher laws. Loyalty is completely appropriate only to the relationship of man to the world of things."[9] It is this loyalty that melancholy exposes and betrays, and it is melancholy that is betrayed by those aspiring only to the material world.

In the introduction I mention also the short essay by Wendy Brown, which argued that "left[-wing] melancholy is Benjamin's unambivalent epithet for the revolutionary hack who is, finally, attached more to a particular political analysis or idea—even to the failure of that idea—than to seizing possibilities for radical change in the present."[10] For that reason, "left melancholy represents not only a refusal to come to terms with the particular character of the present, that is, a failure to understand history in terms other than 'empty time' or 'progress.' It signifies, as well, a certain narcissism with regard to one's past political attachments and identity that exceeds any contemporary investment in political mobilization, alliance, or transformation."[11] This failure to grasp the world outside idealistic terms, even when they've failed to signal chance, creates a fallacy; these terms simply miss the dispositive that is defining the power. "It is a Left that has become more attached to its impossibility than to its potential fruitfulness. . . . [It is] caught in a structure of melancholic attachment to a certain strain of its own dead past."[12] Rather than devouring and destroying the rotten set of norms, a left-wing melancholic would reminisce about his glory days and portray the present and the future as a history in decline.

How relevant is all this to the revival of Hebrew during the first half of the twentieth century and to Zarchi's own use of melancholy? Zarchi's rhetoric is a perfect case for Brown's theorization of left-wing melancholy because he situates himself and his protagonists on the left and their success or failure within the scope of the idealistic discourse. Yet Zarchi presents a diversion or an alternative to this theorization as well. The failure repeats itself too often, too many times, in too many novels. It takes its own life and transcends, if that is indeed the term, the idealistic discourse that generated it. The glow of olden days and their sacred values yield to a recurrent crisis of realization.

In order to characterize the failure—and its accompanying melancholic effect—better, we have to focus on the crack that exposes the weakness and the repeated failures of the idealistic system. The crack appears when we shed a political-theological light on the idealizing "dual consciousness" and its ingrained secularist worldview.

2. On Secular Redemption and Theopolitics: Joseph Klausner and Uri Zvi Greenberg

Joseph Klausner was Zarchi's mentor at the Hebrew University and maintained that authoritative position until his protégé's death, despite routine political disagreements between the two men and their very different takes on literature. Klausner is known not only as one of the fathers of Israel's first university but also as the foremost authority on Hebrew literature. Born in Lithuania to traditional Jewish parents, he shed his religious beliefs during his education in Odessa and Heidelberg. In 1919 he immigrated to Palestine and six years later, having published a number of important studies of Jewish and Christian messianism, he was appointed the head of the young university's new department of Hebrew literature. Among his major works are *The Messianic Idea in Israel* (1908), *Jesus of Nazareth* (1922), *From Jesus to Paul* (1931), *The Land of Israel during the Time of the Second Temple* (1927), and the six-volume *History of New Hebrew Literature* (1936–1950).[13]

Klausner assumed the leadership of the Hebrew revival, presiding over the Committee for the Hebrew Language, which helped in regulating the reform of the revived language and established the autonomous body known as the Academy of the Hebrew Language. Along with Eliezer Ben Yehuda he proposed new terms and linguistic practices, linking them to the language in the Bible. Less apparent, Klausner was one of the initiators of what I call "political-theological Hebrew." He envisioned a close relationship between theological concepts and modern political forms; in this work he was joined by a number of his political and philosophical rivals—Martin Buber, Y. L. Magnes, Hugo Bergman, and Gershom Scholem, all foes of European nationalism associated with the binational—that is, the Jewish-Arab confederative ideal of *Brith Shalom* (Covenant of Peace) and Ahad Ha'am's cultural Zionism.[14] Zarchi's affiliation with Klausner's rivals did not contribute much to his teacher's appreciation of his books, but it never hurt the personal relationship between the two, most probably because the younger man never challenged the older directly.

Having initiated a long engagement with messianism in his dissertation (submitted in Heidelberg in 1902), Klausner brought his thoughts on the topic to a magisterial conclusion in a new edition of his 1908 *The Messianic Idea in Israel* (ha-Ra'yon ha-meshihi be-Yisra'el), republished in 1950. The new edition is dedicated—not without a wink—to the memory of his bitter rival, the first president of the Hebrew University, Yehuda Leib Magnes. Klausner placed messianism at the heart of political Judaism, from ancient times to his present, and identified the core of Zionist ideology with the notion of an end-of-time return to Palestine. An introductory passage reads, "I have endeavored to bring into relief the *universalistic* (which is still very far from cosmopolitan) and the spiritual part of the Messianic idea; but along with this I have found it right, for the sake of scientific objectivity, to emphasize also the national and political part."[15] The contrast between the positive universalistic and the negative cosmopolitan ideology, as Klausner saw it, accorded his understanding of nationalism in messianic terms; he assumed, as Carl Schmitt wrote in *Political Theology* (1922), that modern sovereignty demanded the secularization of theological concepts. He believed that the secular aspects of messianism naturally promoted a national ideal, and he ignored any evidence to the contrary: "How is it possible to explain this wonderful phenomenon: the marvelous development of the Messianic idea in the midst of a unique people, Israel, to such a degree that there is nothing like it in any other nation? The answer to this question is to be sought in the ancient history of the Israelite people. The Messianic expectation is the *Golden Age in the future.*"[16]

Along with his friend and political ally, the poet Uri Zvi Greenberg, Klausner shaped what Hever recently called "a messianic political-theology," the view that the return to Zion realized the ancient promise for the redemption of the people.[17] Uri Zvi Greenberg (1896–1981) is considered one of the most important Hebrew poets of the twentieth century. His messianic approach and open identification with the Revisionist and anti-Arab positions of Zeev Jabotinsky's party made him the darling of the messianic right wing in the Jewish yishuv and the state of Israel. Greenberg's messianism expressed itself in ideological, geopolitical, and intellectual terms, identifying a purist and an anti-European position, grounded in the ancient territory of Zion. As Eran Kaplan put it: "Greenberg denounced the eagerness of Jews to accept pacifism, which he argued had nothing to do with teachings of the Hebrew prophets but with the decadent influence of German liberalism on Jewish intellectuals. He also condemned the tendency of those who were the victims of European violence to admire the culture of their oppressors."[18] According to Hever, since the partisans of the messianic view could not identify their own position with the European fascist movements, they described the socialists as belonging to "the tradition of fascist thinking."[19] Greenberg, as Dan Miron showed, "declared himself to be the true heir and corrector to M. Brenner's wrong—European and socialist—interpretation. Referring to the Brenner precedent and positioning himself as Brenner's heir, [Greenberg] then responded . . . by declaring: 'I shall make this non-poetic word—politics—sing.'"[20] During the 1920s Greenberg declared that Klausner and his circle—one that Greenberg explicitly identified with—offered, in Hever's words, "a messianic-mystical solution. . . . The aspiration to establish a Jewish state became for them an irrational hope to revive the kingdom of Israel in the present," the legacy of which is visible in the post-1967 settlers' movement.[21] This form of decisionist messianism is the exact opposite of Benjamin's view of melancholy as a form of anti-decisionist meaninglessness.

Klausner expressed similar opinions in a study of early Christianity, concluding with the following prophecy: "The politico-spiritual Messianic ideal of Israel will be realized in all its fullness, and the Jewish people will dwell in their land historically, and will speak their language historically, and Judaism in the form of ethico-prophetic monotheism will spread over all the world."[22]

Here is an eschatological image that fuses past, present, and future. Prophecy, embedded in the history of the genre, supports an affirmative relation to Jewish identity. But whom does it exclude? Who is kept outside this image? Klausner's image excludes quite a few of his "enemies," from the pragmatic centrists to the peaceniks, his colleagues. The rift seems inevitable, yet Klausner continued to cooperate with his rivals.

In *The Question of Zion*, Jacqueline Rose carried out a psychoanalytical investigation into the heart of Zionist aspirations and the political-theological discourse, which she contrasted with the radical left-wing position of Buber, Magnes, Bergman, and Scholem. She contended that melancholy enabled them to reconsider Klausner's political-theological messianism: "Imagine how hard it must have been to pull against the drift, to have been anything other than euphoric in 1948. Today [that position] is the still-resonant, melancholic counternarrative to the birth of a nation-state."[23] Rose put her finger on a pertinent issue, namely, the disappearance of such proposals from the public sphere and the rise of a melancholic worldview by the small remnant of peace activists and supporters.[24] In her analysis, however, Rose missed an ongoing cooperation of those historical binationalists with the messianic and euphoric discourse, not on ideological grounds—the subject of her study—but on the basis of a shared linguistic mechanism. While Klausner, Buber, Greenberg, and Zarchi had many political and ideological differences, they shared the same discursive platform: the revival of Hebrew. A more precise and less naïve reading of the period has to examine the revivalist apparatus that conditioned the potential and the limits of political thinking, much beyond any ideological setting. Other positions that diverged from that platform—the alliance of communist Arabs and Jews, the critics of colonialism, the anarchists who opposed a Jewish state—were excluded from the official discourse, even when it presumed a critical stand.[25] The very core of modern Hebrew assumed a pure point of difference, namely, a sovereign separation between the Jew and the Arab, or what Gil Anidjar called "a permanent attribute" of both one's sense of sovereignty and his enemy.[26]

Zarchi's writing belonged neither in the critical camp nor among the loyal Zionists. A melancholic, he subverted the discourses of both groups, which shared an essentially utopian character. In response to pressure to ally himself with one position or the other, he shifted to an allegorical mode. In the following section I show that this did not save him from criticisms from Greenberg or his centrist friends. Zarchi's melancholy did not adhere to the principle of revival, that is, the exclusion of the Arab or the Jewish-Arab, as shown below.

3. Orland: Zarchi versus Greenberg

During the 1940s Zarchi often visited Klausner at his house, where he met a few literary dignitaries, among them Uri Zvi Greenberg. Zarchi often brought with him his friend Yaakov Orland (1914–2002), who kept notes on the group's interactions and later published them. A Zarchi-Greenberg exchange recorded by Orland reveals that the two writers hewed closely to the conventional political-theological jargon of the day.

Here are some of the exchanges important for our discussion[27]:

"But Klausner and Kabak and Shalom Ash say—" / bursts out Israel Zarchi / our novelist friend, gloomy-eyed and generous of pen, / who arrived, small and slender, / unnoticed at the top of the stairs, / and stood there throughout, quietly listening from afar. / "They do, huh?" Uri Zvi leans and tilts his head and looks down / ready to take on the new arrival. / "Huh! Well, ain't this guy cute!" / He speaks with disdain, / half Hebraized Yiddish and half Yiddishized Hebrew. / "And so what if they do? You can speak too! / When you do, tell them that I know better!" / After a tense silence and the blink of a pair of blazing eyes / his wrath rears up / and he carries on, sounding a bit hurt, / "As you well know, / I grappled with the crucifix in Poland / before I disembarked in Jaffa. / I mean then, in the early 1920s. / Believe me, I know the face of Christianity. / Really. / All of us from this generation know its longstanding devotees and supporters / and nobody approves. / One can't talk to even one of them. / It is a desperate and conflicting and cruel bloody history, / as among bitter enemies. And it won't work out. / Not with the Westerners, and not with the Arabs. / Because both of them, the crusader's sword / and the Islamic sword, / are pointing toward Jerusalem, / and the consecration of death in the ancient East nourishes them. / The Arabs inherited Egypt's *Book of the Dead*, / and the Christians, the Roman myth of crucifixion."

"But Freud claims that Moses was an Egyptian. . . ." / This from a groveling Zarchi, standing right in front of him. / "He can claim all he wants! Some professors claim that Jesus was Aryan. So what? / It is a fact—there is no consecration of death in the Torah that was received at Sinai. / On the contrary, it is the tree of life, as everyone knows." / As Uri Zvi speaks, his Adam's apple lurches. / "And the afterlife? The resurrection? Our righteous Messiah?" / insisted Zarchi, / unaware of how he had come so close to the mouth of the volcano.

Suddenly Uri Zvi paled. / I had seen his face many times before. / Never as white as this. / He hunched his head between his shoulders / and jutted out his chin, / leaning against the fingers holding his cane. / His voice dropped an entire octave / and he sounded as if he were whispering. / "None of this belongs to Moses's Torah. We got this from the gentiles. / You surprise me. / Even Gersonides and Rabad and Hillel the Elder had trouble with this, / but you have understood it all?" / "But . . ." Zarchi would not relent. / Fire erupted from the mouth of the volcano, / and the entire floor shook, / and [Greenberg's] voice echoed like flints crashing down, / blazing like chunks of lava. "Mr. Egghead, I'd tell you something, / but I don't want to be suspected of idolatry. / But as you are a Hebrew writer, you ought to know. / Let me quote Tractate Hullin: / 'Whoever teaches an unworthy disciple is as one who throws a stone at Mercury.' / You should bring all your 'buts' to your book club in Tel Aviv. / They will print it in one of their journals—a thrill for you, I'm sure. /

"And now listen, fellow, and listen very carefully: / there is and there will be no peace between the gentiles and ourselves. / That is it. / As long as Judaism has that special quality / that provokes jealousy in those who lack it, / it will not do any good. / Do you hear me? Not a thing! / Two thousand bloody years between us and them! / It's like two thousand years in a laboratory / at your famous *Universität* on Mount Scopus. / No study has lasted longer, and no proof could be more scientific. / And this our people do not want to understand. Not before the war, / and not after the terrible catastrophe, / and not even now, with barbed wire running through the streets. They trust European decency, and the symbolic knowledge / of Western philosophy. / Our people do not understand that Egyptians, Canaanites, Babylonians, / Persians, Spaniards, Poles, Ukrainians, / Germans, and Britons / all represent the hatred of Jews, / religions of corpse offerings and persecution, / kings' skulls preserved in pyramids, / monks' skulls in the desert of Judea, / crossbones on the hats of SS officers, / the *Totenkopfverbände*, / on the arms of the *Einsatzgruppen*. / They all come from a single source, / the death symbols of the idolaters, / even the place where That Man was crucified, / called Calvary. / And that is the foundation of the survival / of the Jewish unity with the Creator, / which is the only bedrock of the Imago Dei. / That is why they cannot forgive us. They do not want us. / So what do I want with Ash and Kabak? / And by the way, Klausner does not say what you say." / "Did I say anything about what Klausner says?" / Zarchi replies with a mumble, / half-elated and half-embarrassed.

If for Greenberg the world is divided by political-theological codes between us and them, for Zarchi it must be investigated in terms of shared existence: Moses the Egyptian, metaphysical temporality for all, messianism that crosses all spatial and temporal boundaries. While Greenberg hands out commandments and preaches like a prophet to the not-yet-atoned, Zarchi hands out questions. For Greenberg the key is the political-theological separation; for Zarchi, it is a political-theological cooperation.

Yet Zarchi's literature exposes the gap between the hope for realization and actuality. Zarchi's utopianism is one of doubt and estrangement, not of armament and annexation. The opening to this chapter, discussing Comay, Brown, and Benjamin, dwelt on melancholy in a way that seemed to oppose a progressive and a redemptive time line, and a look at Zarchi's politics pushes in the same direction. An Egyptian Moses, as Freud described him, reopened the issue of the Holy Land to the equal claim of the "Egyptians." If life in Palestine were examined on the basis of an idealist, universal ethics, then melancholy undermined this—and any other—presupposed teleological narrative. Instead, it exposes the gap that occupies the heart of the dualist matrix.

4. Jerusalem and the Space of Descent

The role of Jerusalem in Hebrew literature has been well researched, and one might call it the quintessential "Zionist place," which Karen Grumberg defined in contrast to "the perceived wildness and chaos of the 'uncivilized' space beyond."[28] Writers made Jerusalem a mystical point connecting the idealistic and the real, the sacred and the secular, the biblical dream-city and the home of modern secular Zionists.[29]

Although Zarchi had lived in Jerusalem since the early 1930s, it wasn't until 1936, after he completed *And the Oil Flows*, that the city took its place at the center of his writing. In his diaries he offered a series of thoughts on its symbolic resonance as well as its political and geographic qualities. The British had tried to create a legislative body in which all the inhabitants of Palestine could participate, yet in 1936 the Arab minority revolted against the British colonialists and an increasingly militarized Jewish population. The insurrection continued for three years and cost the lives of about four hundred Jews and two hundred British soldiers; thousands of Arab Palestinians died.

In his diary, Zarchi reported "sounds of shots and news about destruction all over. I am studying for my final exam in philosophy."[30] When he returned after the year in London, he sighed heavily: "Jerusalem. That good homeland, flooded with blood."[31] Yet when he wanted a place to write, he chose the old city: "The entrance to the room is off a narrow alley—a hole in the wall, really—one has to bend down to enter. Why come here? Because I had to give my soul a shake, I had to search for the distant echoes that are still reverberating here."[32]

In "Samson from the Perfume Market" (1939), "Millstones of the Wind" (1940), and his other stories set in the city, Zarchi presented a very different Jerusalem. Zarchi's fictional Jerusalem possesses qualities both transcendent and sublime, yet it often seems to be deserted. The combination frustrates the reader: This place, this dream cannot be realized. The transcendental is left, in this case, an unrealized potentiality. To the secular idealist dream and religious wealth of Jerusalem, Zarchi added another level of symbolic failure. His reviewers and critics acknowledged this frustration but did not identify its sources; they usually focused on his idealistic tone and ignored or rejected the critical aspects of his writing. Because he rejected the collective transcendence or left it hanging in the air, a form of transcendence they saw as the only possible outcome, they felt short-changed. Before delving into Zarchi's particular interpretation of Jerusalem as a place of collective failure, I first offer some context for that failure.

Dan Miron wrote of the third aliyah's efforts to find in Jerusalem "a different poetics"; the group of authors who emigrated during that period granted the city a conceptual and a metaphorical power, which Miron contrasted with the power of mimetic description. Ezra Susman, a close colleague of Zarchi's who was among those recasting Jerusalem, recalled looking down at the city from the summit of Mount Scopus, peering "through the twin screens of heat wave [*hamsin*] mist and the mist of tears."[33] The metaphor of the mist serves to connect the personal with the environmental, translating it into an individual landscape of sensation and ecstasy. Zarchi, in contrast, dedicated long passages to depictions of the filth, heat, ruins, and neglect of the actual city. He did not try to mimic the physical conditions of the city, but no "mist of tears" clouded his view, either.

Among the better-known analyses of Jerusalem as a literary symbol, Nurit Govrin's work focused in particular on duality in symbolic language. According to Govrin, "In Jerusalem, more than anywhere else, especially once actual contact with it began, the duality between the heavenly Jerusalem and earthly Jerusalem is intensified."[34] Govrin paid special tribute to the literature of the old yishuv, singling out S. Ben-Zion, who believed that Jerusalem ought forever to be "a house of prayer of all religions."[35]

Like the better authors of the day who went beyond conventions—Ben-Zion, Yosef Haim Brenner, and Shai Agnon—Zarchi viewed the city dualistically and critically. His detailed descriptions, delivered by his dreamy protagonists, convey estrangement and lack of continuity. The idealistic mania of his protagonists accompanies the pilgrimage to Jerusalem and usually moves in two steps: It starts with a high idealist language and ends with a pile of ruins, a city of anger, fights, and grime. In spatial terms Zarchi's Jerusalem is a city without a center, whose walls are crumbling, positioned in a no-man's-land between the existent and nonexistent. In *Jerusalem's Ornaments* (*Iturei Yerushalaim*, 1942), a series of fragments and the most "Jerusalemite" of his writings, he wrote: "Shrouded in dreams stands the wall-encircled city. And the dreams are numerous and varied, some grand and elevated and some very sad. A cloud of glory hovers in the highest heaven and sorrow and agony are laid beneath a hidden step."[36] This idealistic depiction of the city, occurring early in the narrative, contrasts with later descriptions: "Abandoned houses of prayer, whose walls are bleak and whose closets are sealed and whose cracks are clasped by hyssop—there is no sadder sight: for it is not only a matter of faith, but a scene of failed purpose, . . . a temple, as it were, divorced from any divine spirit" (13). And further:

> Of the ten sorts of problems that descended on the world, nine assailed Jerusalem. And the problems the ancient city encountered were not temporary ones, here today, gone tomorrow. No, these are real problems, problems that never expire, and they are fruitful and multiply, it seems. One begets another and so forth. Some are physical problems: one is lame and another is handicapped, . . . and some are mental defectives, for the one thing Jerusalem does not lack is lunatics. This one shouts out over and over again: "I am Solomon!" And proclaims himself to be an incarnation of the Messiah. And that one sees the entire world as senseless. . . . When morning comes, and the sun gilds the edges of dreary walls and awakes the stones with a bright light, they come out of their lairs and nooks and their damp basements, spitting and coughing and dragging a wrecked body, some with a wooden leg and others with the remainder of their body, whatever they have left—a shadow of a man and a broken doubtful human. . . . And when the sun sets, as the shadows collect on the walls, they congregate in the small yard. . . . The mentally damaged know no peace. . . . They carry on their bony and feeble shoulders all the woes of the nation. They determine the course of the elements; they blow the wind and make rain pour. Sometimes they surpass human suffering and sometimes they sink below it, and splendor and degradation mingle in them. (18–19)

In other words, Jerusalem—the sacred symbol of the Jewish people—functions in Zarchi's story much like a demonic utopia, whose dark light shines with illness and decay. Rather than a division between the heavenly and the earthly city, here is a division between an earthly city and an infernal underworld that meets the two with a demonstrable effect. For Zarchi, Jerusalem possessed a persona like that of Benjamin's melancholic prince or demonic creature—or like the human protagonists in his stories. As with the opposition between the ideal and the real, so we find in the melancholic city an existential opposition between survival and madness, life and death, the surface and the underworld, the simple routine and the hellishly chaotic. Here again Zarchi shapes a set of oppositions he then leaves hanging and suspended. His protagonists almost never make the choice, or a decision of their own. Much like Agnon, a source of inspiration during this period, Zarchi populates the Jerusalem stories with mad dogs and melancholics.[37] Jerusalem gives them a context, surrounds them with walls, or opens its gates for them. It serves not as a metaphor as much as a mechanism that enables the creation of metaphors of suspense.

Jerusalem also functions here as hyperbole. Marking the realization of a historical dream and the promise of transcendence, it also incorporates an essential threat of collapse and destruction, but that as well is never materialized. Zarchi's poetics is original in its ability to position the two dimensions simultaneously and to construct an ongoing and radicalizing antinomy that collapses into itself.

In his chapter on melancholy and community, Roberto Esposito described melancholy and community in much the same way as Zarchi's description in *Jerusalem's Ornaments* as "the originary melancholic, lacerated, and fractured character of community."[38] The Zionist place could be considered in such terms, or as Zarchi wrote, "a fault and a wound that a community experiences not as a temporary or partial condition but as the community's only way of being" (28). At the very center of both history and myth, Zarchi unearthed what Esposito characterized as the ultimate individual-collective convergence of melancholy, "like an unbreakable wall [*limite*] that a community hurls itself against and bounces back from, unable to cross. Or Melancholy is like the Thing, *la chose* or *das Ding*, that is impossible to realize."[39]

5. Curriculum Vitae

Before elaborating on Zarchi's next text—the darkest and most radical engagement with melancholy he ever wrote—I want to supply a few personal coordinates for him. Those will become crucial for the later part of his life, thinking, and career.

The Hebrew University's archive includes Israel Zarchi's curriculum vitae, a manuscript compilation of his work life that he had submitted in October 1937, before taking a secretarial post in the university's Office of Pedagogy.[40] He claimed "over a year and a half of secretarial work in a family business (factories, etc.), extensive agricultural training outside Warsaw before coming to the Land of Israel in 1929."[41] A short biographical narrative indicated that after his work as a farmer and construction worker, he had taken some courses as a student-at-large before enrolling as a full-time student. He mentioned 1939 as the beginning of his postgraduate studies and his aspiration to earn a doctoral degree. "In addition to Hebrew," he wrote, "I speak, read, and write German, English, Polish, and Yiddish. Approximately three years ago I brought my parents to the Land of Israel, and they are financially dependent on me."[42]

Shortly after he was hired, Zarchi requested and received special assistance from the university in order to support his parents. In August 1942 he announced that, thanks to the support he was receiving from David Senator and A. M. M. Shneorson, two of the directors of the university, he had decided to reduce his work hours by one-half so that he could dedicate more time to his literary work. In 1943 the costs associated with raising a child—Nurit Zarchi had been born in October 1941—obliged him to apply again for special assistance, and again he mentioned that he was the only source of support for his parents.

A severe bout of depression drove him to another appeal in August 1944, and the university granted him a year's paid vacation, yet it was of dubious therapeutic value, as it ended with his hospitalization.[43] In the fall of 1945 he was hospitalized again, and the university agreed to pay for his travel to a sanatorium. Shortly thereafter Zarchi applied for early retirement; he planned to dedicate himself to literary writing. In spite of these frequent leaves of absence, he maintained a warm relationship with both faculty and administrators, many of whom sent congratulatory letters when he won the Jerusalem Prize in 1947.

6. *The Guesthouse* (1942)

During the early 1940s Zarchi's rhetoric changed. The change occurred gradually, and it appears to have been linked to a growing awareness of the destruction of European Jewry on the one hand and disappointment with his chosen homeland on the other. Melancholy, which he had long used to depict Zionist pioneers, became a general mode. As apocalyptic imagery became a more common element of his writing, melancholic rhetoric framed both a revisionist interpretation of the past and dark forebodings of the future.

He was not alone in this regard. Beginning around 1940, many leaders of the Jewish yishuv in Palestine held similar views. For example, Martin Buber was writing about political theology and political messianism during the 1930s and about destruction and apocalypse during the 1940s.[44] Rommel's invasion of Egypt in the summer of 1942 inspired politicians of the Zionist yishuv to speak seriously of collective suicide, another Masada.[45] Although such a grim course was forgotten once the military threat vanished, a general sense remained that a reckoning was not far off.[46] The fear of imminent destruction appears in one of Shai Agnon's finest novels, *Only*

Yesterday (1945), and his unfinished novel, *Shira* (mostly written between 1948 and 1950). In *Shira* destruction is connected to the protagonist, a German-Jewish scholar named Manfred Herbst (literally "autumn"), whose lover, Shira (literally "poetry"), embodies the eros and the redemptive force he sees in the Hebrew language. In line with the era, the wise philologist fails to create a useful intellectual product (the thousands of file cards he collects fail to add up to a coherent system), and his love for Shira, a rather assertive nurse, flounders. Agnon's views on apocalypse vary over this period, but melancholic and apocalyptic motifs continue to reverberate as an open, unrealized threat in his writing.

In contrast, Zarchi's *Guesthouse* (*Malon Orchim*), a unique piece in his own oeuvre, realizes the apocalyptic promise. It was published in 1942 in *The Destroyed House of Our Grandmother* (*Bet Savta She'Charav*), a collection of three of Zarchi's novellas concerned with the destruction of European Jewry.[47] The few critics who had read Zarchi's previous books liked it, but the collection, like everything else he wrote, was mostly ignored. Among the three novellas, *The Guesthouse* is the most complete and the most innovative. The different layers of the narrative not only expose the melancholy of the German Jews who cannot work the idea of the Middle East into their conception of highly acculturated European lives, but its explicit and hidden references to both the Jewish and the Christian apocalypse form an intertextual world that swallows up the narrative in its final pages.

On the surface, the plot of *The Guesthouse* is very close to the plot of *Shira*: In both cases the decline of European Jewry is presented alongside the alleged indecipherability of an erratic Levant. Yet Zarchi's depiction of German-Jewish immigrants in crisis is both less ironic and more pessimistic than Agnon's, producing a catastrophe without catharsis.

The title of the novella—like Zarchi's later novel, *Unsown Land*—comes from the prophecy of Jeremiah: "Oh that I had in the wilderness a lodging place of wayfaring men; that I might leave my people, and go from them! For they be all adulterers, an assembly of treacherous men."[48] Zarchi's novella concentrates on a single place, the hostel or guesthouse, in which a small group of German-Jewish refugees are lodged after escaping the Nazis. As in Jeremiah, the lodging place becomes not only a temporary hostel but also a place of reflection and reconsideration.

In addition to the fascination with apocalypse, other elements of *The Guesthouse* set it firmly in its time. The characters' biographical details link

Fig. 4.1 Israel Zarchi ca. 1942. © Israel Zarchi Archive, Gnazim Institute, Tel Aviv; used with permission.

them to the yishuv, and the more we know about the German-Jewish intellectuals of the 1940s, the more acute appears Zarchi's (and later Agnon's)
critical depiction of the redemptive attraction of European emancipation
and Jewish nationalism. Jewish memories of nineteenth-century emancipation and of secularization sharpened the notion of an abyss opening under
them once the racist segregation of the twentieth century set in. Zarchi's
novella offers a critical view of this history by concentrating on the figure
of a German-Jewish judge who represents the high ideals of German legal
culture grounded in Enlightenment universalist values, a well-known type
in the *yishuv* of the period.[49]

Gershom Scholem, Buber's close colleague at the Hebrew University
and Walter Benjamin's close friend, offered a different, but equally worri-
some, critique of Enlightenment and emancipation. For him, the difference
between right-wing reactionaries and left-wing liberals was marginal, for
liberals ended up reaffirming the power structure, albeit in a "gradual" way:
"Among gentiles the most vigorous advocates on behalf of Jews were actually those who predicted explicitly and consciously the impending disappearance of Jews as Jews. . . . Liberals had hoped the Jews would gradually
vanish."[50]

Klausner, Scholem, and Agnon had little in common politically, but
all were critics of liberalism and Jewish assimilation, and all, in contrast to
Kafka or Benjamin, saw Jewish immigration to Palestine and the revival
of Hebrew as a solution to the plight of European Jewry. In that sense they
did not differ much from representatives of political Zionism. As the historian Roni Stauber described it, David Ben-Gurion, the head of the Jewish
Agency, the executive political body of the *yishuv*, and later the first prime
minister of Israel, "claimed that the very fact of establishing the state built
the bridge between it and the time before the destruction of the Temple, and
instilled in the hearts of those living there that they were the heirs to Israel's
ancient kingdom."[51] Interestingly, the revivalist view [*tehia*] relied on a clear
catastrophic understanding of the reality, for, according to Ben-Gurion,
"the recent past no longer exists. . . . It was destroyed in the Holocaust."[52]

Zarchi's story positions the revival of Hebrew—and the distance of
his liberal German-Jewish protagonists from it—in the context of a biblical catastrophe and a failed messianic return. Interestingly, the catastrophe
shapes an impending future, not a past event: The title of *The Guesthouse*
refers to Jeremiah's desperate realization that he would not be supported
by his people, a community he deemed immoral and, like the city where

he dwelt, doomed to destruction: "For the mountains will I take up a weeping and wailing, and for the habitations of the wilderness a lamentation, because they are burned up, so that none can pass through them; neither can men hear the voice of the cattle; both the fowl of the heavens and the beast are fled; they are gone. And I will make Jerusalem heaps, and a den of dragons; and I will make the cities of Judah desolate, without an inhabitant" (Jeremiah 9:10–11). In a comment on this passage, the medieval Jewish philosopher Maimonides wrote:

> A person who lives in a place where the norms of behavior are evil and the inhabitants do not follow the straight path should move to a place where the people are righteous and follow the ways of the good.
>
> If all the places with which he is familiar and of which he hears reports follow improper paths, as in our times, or if he is unable to move to a place where the patterns of behavior are proper, because of [the presence of] bands of raiding troops, or for health reasons, he should remain alone in seclusion as [Eichah 3:28] states: "Let him sit alone and be silent."[53]
>
> If they are wicked and sinful and do not allow him to reside there unless he mingle with them and follow their evil behavior, he should go out to caves, thickets, and deserts [rather than] follow the paths of sinners as [Jeremiah 9:2] states: "Who will give me a lodging place for wayfarers, in the desert[?]"[54]

Maimonides read Jeremiah in the context of Eichah's lament and in relation to the prophecy of destruction of the late prophets and asceticism. In other words, the prophet who chose a nomadic life as a minor rebellion against the corruption embedded in major norms or social consensus won the sympathy of Maimonides much as he did Zarchi's—that is the tension explored in *The Guesthouse*.

A deeper discussion of his text can explain how Zarchi adapted melancholy to the new political reality, to a modern hermeneutics of the prophecy of destruction, and to literary conventions of his time. I begin with the surface of the story, the appearance, behavior, and typical expressions of its protagonists.

The main protagonist of the story is Judge Simon, who displays qualities—such as punctuality and formality—characteristically affiliated with the *yekkes*, the German-Jewish immigrants to Palestine. Like other German Jews in *The Guesthouse*, he lives like a nomad—settling neither here nor there, no longer in Europe yet not truly belonging to the Middle East, living in his own bubble. Julia Kristeva's theory of melancholy explains such spatial disengagement as a metaphor for the loss of object relations, "an abyssal suffering that does not succeed in signifying itself and, having lost meaning, loses life."[55] This is exactly the process that unfolds in the story. Rhythm marks the duality of order and absence of meaning from the first page. As Zarchi writes:

> And against the wall between the two couches stands the tall long-case clock, whose pendulum produces a sound faint yet festive, and every half-hour it tolls once and at the hour it marks the time with a metallic sound as deep as a heavy-clappered bell. . . . And the echo of distant fine days rises from every piece of furniture, and sweet longing lodges in the lavish carved wood, reviving with the muffled sound of the clock, rejoicing with the beats of its deep heart. And here, in the corners of this room, the Nathans find a haven in the lonely hours of foreignness. . . . [There] one can search for the echo of a distant, vanished sound. (137)

The ticking of the living room clock signifies both the regulations of the house and the transformation of the chaos of the outside world into order. In due course the ticking reverses the work of time, counting back to the end of both meaning and life.

As a gap opens between order and meaning, the judge obeys the beat of measured time. "He removes a heavy watch from the pocket of his vest, measures it with a placid gaze, lifts his eyes, and focuses on the long-case clock as it temperately ticks, meticulously comparing the hands of the small clock with the hands of the big clock, and states, 'Yes, we still have plenty of time, my dear Mrs. Nathan: there are exactly two and one-half minutes until the designated time. Yes, now, if we repeat the sentence, there will be exactly . . . two and one-half minutes remaining" (137–38). By the story's end this fetishistic obsession with accuracy and strictness will have been exhausted. For example, the longing to exclude and block the entrance of alien elements into the house will have been frustrated: "Mrs. Nathan would choose her tenants very carefully. Now, when the land was overflowing with ragamuffins from all corners of the globe, especially from Germany, who could guarantee that those coming to reside in her house were decent, respectable people? . . . As the authorities did not address this, she had to investigate those who came to dwell under her roof" (139).

As the historian of culture Rakefet Sela-Sheffy showed, German Jews "were viewed with ambivalence; they were viewed as quite different from the dominant cultural norms of the time."[56] This suspicion arose from their reluctance to abandon their European ways: "They disapproved of the ugliness of contemporary politics and maintained an apolitical stance, an intermediate position common among the right-wing nationalists of the

Weimar Republic."[57] A study has found that during the first few decades of the Israeli legal system, 36 percent of the supreme court judges were German Jews, as were the first long-term minister of justice and a majority of the legal administrators and legislators.[58] Sela-Sheffy believed they gave the legal system a clear "formalist orientation" based on "the rule of law" and "a strict sense of order."[59]

The Guesthouse describes a group that clearly feels alienated from its Levantine surroundings, and experiences the same melancholic alienation established in *And the Oil Flows* and *Youth.* A growing gap between order and meaning, individual and surrounding, past and present is showing in psychological and discursive terms. The lodgers point to a rhyzomatic or a deterritorialized relation to reality. The judge explains this logic to his fellow lodgers: "A young seedling can still be uprooted and planted in new soil, but I am an oak that has been cut in two—when someone tried to uproot me my roots snapped and remained buried in the earth" (161). The metaphor of snapped roots takes us back to the grasping roots of *Youth,* Zarchi's first novel, and anticipate a later story, "Sambatyon," where he wrote of the plant "whose root does not reach the soil."[60]

Another individual who enters the guesthouse and resists transplanting the untransplantable is the Polish Jew. An uncouth fellow whose German is heavily accented, he cannot grasp the landlady's strict regulations nor the judge's dependence on them for his internal sense of order and mental stability. The fastidious judge becomes greatly frustrated when this outsider proves incapable of properly managing his silverware. The narrator's voice, empathic and ironic at the same time, allows the reader to identify with the suffering of the melancholic judge while acknowledging the futility of his scrupulousness.

The judge possesses a unique voice for the time; he not only acknowledges his difficult situation and his delusional bubble but, in a rare moment, he also sets his sober acknowledgment of failure within a much bigger delusion. Speaking of Zionism, he says, "This entire attempt to build a state—it will all be blown away by the wind, it will all blow over like the foam of the sea. . . . A state may be established here in accordance with local natural law, but that is not what you were hoping for" (161). His loss of hope in the future enables him to see just how destructive the Zionist enterprise could be for any sense of continuation and life: "The judge sank into a strange immobility. After the war's early days he had become perfectly still and was not interested in anything" (196).

The Guesthouse extends Zarchi's intensive exploration of melancholy and collapsing political norms. It is the melancholic judge, of all people, who sees the reality of the time, and in spite of his own fetishistic relation to the past he courageously faces the present and the future. The other lodgers, who turn a blind eye to the hopelessness of their situation, cannot grasp the situation: "Late that night Mrs. Nathan left the room. . . . The night was dark, and the windows facing the garden were open as if facing a vast abyss. She was gripped by fear and went to sleep with a heavy heart" (172). The plot leads slowly, as with the ticking of the clock, to its catastrophic end. But under the sign of an approaching disaster an examination is taking place, an evaluation of the distance between German-Jewish norms and Zionist expectations, between the discourse of order and the Zionist emphasis on the New Jew. Mr. Nathan, the owner of the house, explains to his tenants: "Imagine that! My son Michael, who received such a proper and meticulous education, brings me a glass of water without a coaster! And when I spoke to him about it he laughed! . . . You see, it is not that we are running short of something, but that neglect has become an ideal!" (177).

When the outside world, mediated in either Hebrew or heavily accented German, bursts the bubble of the German-Jewish microworld, everything falls apart. But here again Zarchi does something out of the ordinary. Rather than turning the story into a personal and symbolic tragedy, he fashions a universal apocalypse, signifying that a bridge between Jews and Christians (in this case) is still possible. The closure of the novella reminds the reader of Heinrich von Kleist's *Michael Kohlhaas*, which Zarchi translated from German to Hebrew while writing *The Guesthouse*. There is good reason to think that Zarchi drew inspiration from Kleist's suicide, killing his partner before shooting himself, for his own narrative. But the relation and impact go under the plotline or story of life. Evoking the Christian cataclysm, Zarchi uses the voice of a man who challenges both the order and the law of the land as he narrates the suicides of the judge and his wife, reported here indirectly: "One night the sound of Mrs. Simon's cry rang out of the judge's room, frightening all who heard it. . . . It was the cry of one lost in the dead of night. The whimper carried through the halls of the house for a long while, and no one dared look into its cause" (197). The narrator portrays for us, in fact, not only the sorrow that accompanied the Simons' decision, but also the utter helplessness that the other lodgers felt and their inability to prevent such a deadly end, in spite of the preceding and present warning signs.

In the concluding lines of the novella, Mr. Nathan explains the situation, partially to himself, partially to his cat, Mimi: "An upside-down world has lost its values; all walls have been breached, and all bridges have been severed, and not even an alley remains." But the more he tried to explain to Mimi the chaotic horrors which have taken hold of the world, the more he realized that he could not grasp the confusion. . . . And the daily events, the blaze of deeds gallop in gale and in storm much like those tremendous stallions with their heads flung forward whose nostrils are a flare of fire and whose breath is a flame and whose manes flutter in the wind like torches" (207). With these lines *The Guesthouse* comes to its shocking end. It is shocking not only because the plot leads a sad situation to a double suicide, but because Zarchi contextualizes this conclusion in a world of rich and surprising apocalyptic literary allusions. For one, the opening phrase refers to a well-known poem, "Verkehrte Welt," by Zarchi's literary hero, Heinrich Heine (as discussed in chap. 2), and the last to the Book of Revelations and the Four Horsemen of the Apocalypse.[61] Although the poem describes the potential overturning of the world in favor of an intellectual estrangement, in Zarchi the change Nathan describes is absolute; the final passage changes the tone of the whole story, anticipating the author's turn to a mythic-legendary discourse as an alternative to the false pretense of order and regulation or the useless insistence on meaning, where meaning is no longer. In literary terms the story shifts from Heine's ironic critique to Kleist's desperate anarchism, from a topsy-turvy surface to a much deeper sense of havoc and mayhem where not only gestures but the structures of language itself fail.

In fact, the story's similarities to Kleist's *Michael Kohlhaas*, including the subterranean apocalyptic motive, indicate a much stronger influence and connection. As noted above, Zarchi translated Kleist's novella around the same time he wrote his own, and in both stories one notes a link connecting the failure of the judicial perspective to a crisis of sovereignty, ending with a mixture of major apocalyptic allusions and a "minor" critique of norms, the four horses of the apocalypse and the cat, Mimi. This Kleistian influence is worth exploring further.

In his interpretation of *Michael Kohlhaas*, Andreas Gailus explains that the horses Kleist's fierce protagonist refuses to hand over to the authorities are a metaphor for Germany's legal system. Kleist had written: "In the manifesto which he scattered abroad on this occasion, he called himself 'a viceroy of the Archangel Michael, come to punish with fire and sword, for the wickedness into which the whole world was sunk.'"[62] This self-professed viceroy, Gailus showed, positions himself as a counterforce to the legal system, a prophet who stands outside the corrupt laws of the state to project justice: "Inscribing Kohlhaas's action into a drama of religious dimensions, the hyperbolic phrase 'angel of justice' radically changes the parameters. . . . Kohlhaas's attack on the [sovereign aristocrat] turns into a cosmic drama, a struggle for the very possibility of truth and meaning."[63] Against the background of the French Revolution, Kleist sounded a call for the end of political authority and of any sovereignty not based on justice alone.

Kleist's novella presents the confrontation of anarchic will and fate, which resonated not only with Zarchi—recall his interest in Ernst Toller—but with other writers of his generation. Kafka loved the story, and his literary executor, Max Brod, wrote the introduction to Zarchi's translation, explaining that the affinity between Kleist "and the absolute is an affinity with a capital *A*. 'It is possible that evil spirits drive the world,'" Brod quotes from Kleist, "'but we cannot fathom it.'"[64] The notion that evil might be a driving force appealed to pessimists of all kinds. Kleist, Toller, and Zarchi all combined a penchant for melancholy and a commitment to anarchism. Brod, who did not know about Zarchi's *The Guesthouse* and its double suicide, believed that the sort of agony that drove Kleist to kill his beloved and himself also drove Kafka to write.[65]

Both Kafka and Zarchi, two "minor" authors in Walter Benjamin's sense of the word, were fascinated by the tragic pain and suffering Kleist described and its absolute claim to truth. *Michael Kohlhaas* goes beyond the metaphysical theme of a conflict between an individual and the system to explain the protagonist's obsession and willingness to sacrifice himself and his surroundings—a melancholic-masochistic choice. Kafka and Zarchi followed suit, attaching the fight for justice—as the figure of the judge, in Zarchi's story, presents it—to an individual effect, an obsession with personal realization and the collective settlement of the land. The ticking of the clock represents the growing gap between hope and reality that forced the writers of the 1920s to make quick adjustments and connect radical new forms of "minor literature" to an anarchic political-theology. The consistent presence of apocalyptic motives in Kafka and Zarchi is a good indication of that radical form of questioning.

The Guesthouse links a personal and a collective catastrophe through a linguistic and a normative failure. In personal terms, the melancholic—

Zarchi or his protagonist—sees only dead ends in the world. In his theory of melancholy Jean Starobinski explained: "The walls seem to press on, and the doors—we are waiting for them to open—are locking forever. Internal exile and external exile unite, and strangeness becomes the essential component of the self, in both personal and communal terms—strangeness that becomes so hard that it leads the will to escalate things, even if that leads to destruction."[66]

Zarchi was writing during what he considered a time of chaos and perceived destruction, but the perspective he gave to his story's narrator was removed from the specific historical situation. Still, the unspoken context seeped into his stories: "A tiny letter arrived [and explained] that a Jew cannot show up at the court anymore, and that he should hand over his cases to his next in line. The letter cut the judge's life in two: In it he saw the whole power and pain of the world, and its cruelty" (141). In a diary entry from December 1944 Zarchi wrote about the debate in the yishuv concerning the national and therapeutic role of literature during "the most horrible year in the history of Israel for generations."[67] His reaction proved characteristically skeptical: "Can the writers of the land of Israel describe at this time the horrors of Treblinka, while residing in Jerusalem?" Then he asked another question: "And yet, why did I write *The Destroyed House of Our Grandmother* or *Jerusalem Ornaments* or *Unsown Land*? Would I have written those in peaceful days?"[68] In other words, while the Holocaust provided the motivation and background to the story, the specific constellation of the story reflected a local relation and a limited point of view. Zarchi succeeded in writing, from Jerusalem, about the world Treblinka erased by attaching the affect of Jerusalem, melancholy, to the effect of Treblinka, apocalypse.

One finds in Zarchi's words and passages a modesty vis-à-vis history, a reluctance to take on the humanist presumption and telos of brit shalom, the peace movement, or the right-wing messianism of his teacher. The *imperfectum*, the flaws, the destructive power of reality itself—all were essential to his writing.

Indeed, throughout the 1940s Zarchi's diary and correspondence attest to increased depression, long before he received a diagnosis of terminal cancer. In a letter written to Haim Toren in 1946, a year before his death, he apologized: "Please excuse the brevity, but my mental state right now is disturbed and distracted."[69] His own clock was ticking fast, faster than his sentences.

7. Psychoanalysis: Freud, Butler, Kristeva

In 1935 Zarchi was writing about his personal life while referring to "my rabbi Freud," as mentioned earlier. When he contested Uri Zvi Greenberg's messianic theopolitics, he cited *Moses and Monotheism* (1939) as an authority. Many other indications cited above prove Zarchi's intense interest in psychoanalysis in both individual and collective terms. Even though he never quoted explicitly from Freud's theory of melancholy, his intense interest in melancholy as a psychological and a cultural-political phenomenon would not have let him ignore it altogether. Zarchi's poetics reflect something inherent about Zionist melancholy. In order to grasp the full extent of Zarchi's poetics, we must manage better our understanding of melancholy, so far discussed only in a sketchy way.

A good starting point is the specific history of Freud's essay "Mourning and Melancholy" ("Trauer und Melancholie," 1917). Freud realized at an early stage of his career that the roots of the melancholic image were grounded in the mythic representation of self-destruction, often discussed via the image of the black bile or the black dog. This connection provided the background for the modern perception of melancholy. Freud's interpretation followed earlier understandings that emphasized the primordial power that melancholy bore into the modern worldview. Consider the gift Friedrich Nietzsche presented to his friends Cosima and Richard Wagner in 1870. After an enjoyable evening during which he lectured on Greek drama, Nietzsche gave the Wagners a reproduction of Dürer's *Melencolia I*. On the back of the print, the philosopher inscribed his own "song of melancholy," which reappeared, a year later, in *Thus Spoke Zarathustra* (1871).[70]

In his poem, Nietzsche-Zarathustra compares melancholy to a snake and a vulture, to the fading light of the sunset and the devilish yearning for the abyss.[71] As Ulrich Finke showed, Nietzsche's understanding of melancholy as a critical voice reverberating at the very core of modern optimism and progress continued to trouble the next generation of artists and thinkers. Three decades after the poem was written, Thomas Mann would echo its understanding of modernity as an inherently ambivalent force in *Reflections of an Apolitical Man* (*Betrachtungen eines Unpolitischen*, 1918), by, as Finke wrote, "understand[ing] the spirit of Dürer in a similar way to Nietzsche as revealed by the engravings *Knight, Death, and Devil* and *Melencolia I*."[72]

I have mentioned earlier that Zarchi sounded rather Nietzschean in his early novel, *Youth*. And the Marxist Shlomo Narkis detects Nietzsche's nihilistic critique in *And the Oil Flows*. In the last novel Zarchi published during his lifetime, *Unsown Land* (1947), he gave another figure—a pioneer afflicted with malaria—the voice of a Nietzchean critic, alluding directly to *Thus Spoke Zarathustra* in order to undermine the Zionist collectivist rhetoric. In his later texts Zarchi attached a radical critique of Zionist realization to melancholy, desperation, and transience. Throughout his career, he engaged with Nietzsche, leavening the philosopher's understanding of modernity with a Freudian take that construed melancholy as a mode that killed the body while opening a new avenue to critique.

Freud wrote the first draft of "Mourning and Melancholy" in 1915, with the Great War in mind. Accordingly, he constructed an essential opposition between melancholy and mourning. As he explained it, the temporal order of melancholy was not one of late or missed opportunity, but one of pathological repetition leading to a sick and incomplete narrative, contrasted with the positive force of mourning, which led to an overcoming. In the published text, Freud further sharpened the opposition: "The melancholic displays something . . . which is lacking in mourning—an extraordinary diminution in his self-regard, an impoverishment of his ego on a grand scale. In mourning it is the world which has become poor and empty; in melancholia it is the ego itself."[73]

As different as the conditions were, the relation between them—the ill and repetitive versus the healthy and linear—Freud saw as tight: "The correlation of melancholia and mourning seems justified by the general picture of the two conditions. Moreover, the exciting causes due to the environmental influences are, so far as we can discern them at all, the same for both conditions."[74] In other words, Freud set melancholy at the threshold, between the biological and the symbolic, as an expression of masochism and hatred of "the other" within.

Judith Butler pointed out that for Freud melancholy was the result of the failure of the ego to find a substitute for the lost object it mourned. This failure resulted in a turn toward narcissism, which "exposes the fault lines in its own tenuous foundations."[75] She noted the difference between melancholy as a discourse and as a psychological effect, hanging the hermeneutic itself on a Nietzschean-Freudian "fabrication of conscience" that enabled Freud to suggest "a view of conscience as an agency and 'institution' produced and maintained by melancholy."[76] Ultimately Freud's study offered "a portrait of melancholia that continually blurs into his view of mourning," a "psychic articulation of ambivalence as 'a conflict between one part of the ego and the critical agency' [in] the formation of the super-ego."[77] Such internal conflicts, Butler showed, led Walter Benjamin to argue, following Freud, that "melancholia spatializes, and that its effort to reverse or suspend time produces 'landscapes' as its signature effect."[78] I have already suggested that Zarchi used his literary imagination to concretize such an understanding of an internal melancholic ambivalence in the empty space of Jerusalem. But in contrast to Benjamin and Butler's argument, Zarchi's melancholia temporalizes the empty space, and not the opposite. The "landscape" is always a representation of the protagonist's internal and temporal mechanism, used to suspend norms.

In her discussion of Freud's "Mourning and Melancholia" Julia Kristeva presented the double negation to which Freud pointed—the denial of the loss—as an "exile," the speaking of a dead language.[79] Melancholy belonged to a world devoid of signifiers; its self-referentiality brought it dangerously close to both narcissism and fetishism. As Kristeva reminded us, *The Iliad* gave us, in Bellerophon, the melancholic's tendency to self-pity: "Forsaken by the gods, exiled by divine decree, this desperate man was condemned not to mania but to banishment, absence, void."[80]

In contrast to Butler, Kristeva's view of melancholy is ahistorical and potentially redemptive; the emptiness of melancholy suggests a possible rise from the fall. Kristeva offers the chance of a retrieval of meaning from meaninglessness, an end to "melancholic cannibalism."[81] Yet, like Butler, Kristeva cites with approval Nietzsche's and Benjamin's interpretation of melancholy as a language of exposure and paradoxes, a language endowed with the potential to transcend itself. But while Nietzsche and Benjamin adopted a political position to criticize melancholy, in Kristeva melancholy is celebrated as a necessary stage in the ascent to a metaphysical position.[82]

If we try to pinpoint Zarchi's position along the axes sketched out by these critics, we find that Kristeva's position answers his idealistic expectations while Benjamin's position lies much closer to his critical view of Zionism. Although Kristeva relied on Benjamin's critique of idealism, she saw melancholy as a theological opening to forgiveness, whereas Benjamin understood it as a way to criticize both the metaphysics of idealism and the theopolitical structure of the divine miracle. For Kristeva, the threshold between secular idealism and theological miracles lay exactly where an opening was revealed in the everydayness; that opening was the love offered to the other. There a reevaluation of past, present, and future took place, and there the unconscious sense of guilt was first examined.

Kristeva's analysis bespeaks her Christian and European background. In Zarchi's Middle East, revelation and redemption do not add up to mutual understanding as much as a recognition that the self is somehow lacking. His idealists have carried with them the conditions—linguistic, cultural, social, and political—ensuring their failure. Rather than a spatial opening, his metaphors suggest a temporal one—the acceleration of time, the accumulation in a repetitive mode. As I show in the next chapter, this specific mode and those specific tropes are grounded in the concrete conditions of Zionist melancholy. This observation closes the circle and brings us back to Agamben's understanding of melancholy as a threshold or "a 'place' not as something spatial, but as something more original than space. Perhaps we should think of it as a pure difference."[83] This point of pure difference at the heart of the Zionist discourse will engage us in what follows.

Notes

1. Hillel Cohen, *Year Zero of the Arab-Israeli Conflict, 1929* (Waltham, MA: Brandeis University Press, 2015), 86.

2. Hannan Hever, *Lareshet et Haaretz, Lichbosh et haMerchav* [To inherit the land, to conquer the space] (Jerusalem: Mossad Bialik, 2015), 61.

3. Ibid.

4. Rebecca Comay, "The Sickness of Tradition: Between Melancholia and Fetishism," in *Walter Benjamin and History*, ed. Andrew Benjamin (London: Continuum, 2005), 90.

5. Max Pensky, *Melancholy Dialectics: Walter Benjamin and the Play of Mourning* (Amherst: University of Massachusetts Press, 1993), 11 (emphasis in the original).

6. Walter Benjamin, *The Origin of German Tragic Drama*, trans. John Osborne (London: Verso Books, 2003), 157.

7. Ilit Ferber, *Philosophy and Melancholy: Benjamin's Early Reflections on Theater and Language* (Stanford, CA: Stanford University Press, 2013), 59.

8. Walter Benjamin, "Left-Wing Melancholy," in *Selected Writings*, ed. Michael W. Jennings, Howard Eiland, and Gary Smith (Cambridge, MA: Harvard University Press, 1999), 2: 424.

9. Benjamin, *Origin*, 156.

10. Wendy Brown, "Resisting Left Melancholy," *Boundary* 26, no. 3 (1999): 19.

11. Ibid., 20.

12. Ibid., 26.

13. *Bi-yeme Bayit sheni: mehkarim be-historyah shel ha-Bayit ha-sheni* (Jerusalem: Mada, 1954); *Mi-Yeshu 'ad Paulus* (Jerusalem: Mada, 1954); *Yeshu ha-Notsri: zemano, hayav v'e-torato* (Jerusalem: Shtibl, 1922); *ha-Ra'yon ha-meshihi be-Yiśra'el* (Jerusalem: Masadah, 1950); *Historyah shel ha-sifrut ha-Ivrit ha-hadashah* (Jerusalem: Hotsa'at Sefarim Ahi'asaf, 1952).

14. I wrote about Martin Buber's theopolitics in "The Jerusalem School: The Theopolitical Hour," *New German Critique* 35, no. 3 (2008): 97–120.

15. Joseph Klausner, *The Messianic Idea in Israel*, trans. W. F. Stinespring (New York: Macmillan, 1955), 4 (emphasis in the original).

16. Ibid., 11 (emphasis in the original).

17. Hannan Hever, *Moledet Ha'mavet Yafah* [Beautiful motherland of death] (Tel Aviv: Am Oved, 2004), 18.

18. Eran Kaplan, *The Jewish Radical Right: Revisionist Zionism and Its Ideological Legacy* (Madison: University of Wisconsin Press, 2005), 120.

19. Hannan Hever, *Payetanim u'Viryonim: Tsemihat haShir haPoliti haIvri beErets Israel* [Poets and zealots: The rise of political Hebrew poetry in Eretz-Israel] (Jerusalem: Mossad Bialik, 1994), 145.

20. It is worth noting that Greenberg attacked here a socialist position that was identified, at the time, with centrist Zionism of the Ben-Gurion faction. Quoted in Dan Miron, *From Continuity to Contiguity: Toward a New Jewish Literary Thinking* (Stanford, CA: Stanford University Press, 2010), 162.

21. Hever, *Moledet Ha'mavet Yafah*, 148.

22. Joseph Klausner, *MiYeshu Ad Paulus* [From Jesus unto Paul] (Tel Aviv: Mada, 1940), 2: 291.

23. Jacqueline Rose, *The Question of Zion* (Princeton, NJ: Princeton University Press, 2005), 70.

24. Which includes, interestingly, a small Facebook group that named itself after Brith Shalom.

25. The history of anarchism in the yishuv and Israel still awaits its research. Recent publications that touched on such issues are, for example, Nurit Gertz, *Al Daat Atzmo: Arba'a Pirkei Haim Shel Amos Kenan* [In his own mind: Four chapters about Amos Kenan] (Tel Aviv: Am Oved, 2010); Meron Benvenisti, *Halom haTzabar haLavan: Autobiographia shel Hitpakchut* [The dream of the white sabre: An autobiography of awakening] (Jerusalem: Keter, 2010).

26. Anidjar grounds this separation in the Schmittian theory of sovereignty and Deleuze and Guattari's analysis of "the war machine." See Gil Anidjar, *The Jew, the Arab: A History of the Enemy* (Stanford, CA: Stanford University Press, 2003), 75–76.

27. Yaakov Orland, *Mivhar Ketavim* [Writings] (Jerusalem: Mossad Bialik, 1997), 3: 183–87. Orland reported the exchange using short lines for a prose poem.

28. Karen Grumberg, *Place and Ideology in Contemporary Hebrew Literature* (Syracuse, NY: Syracuse University Press, 2011), 6.

29. Efraim Aurbach noted the trope of convergence of worlds in the way the sages wrote about Jerusalem. See Efraim E. Aurbach, "Yerushalaim shel Mata vi'Yerushalaim shel Ma'la" [Jerusalem on earth, and Jerusalem of heaven] in *Yerhushalaim Le'Doroteeiah* [Jerusalem in the generations], ed. Efraim Aurbach (Jerusalem: Magnes, 1968), 156–71.

30. Diary, 12 June 1936, Zarchi Archive.

31. Diary, 16 October 1938, Zarchi Archive.

32. Diary, 20 August 1941, Zarchi Archive.

33. Dan Miron, *The Prophetic Mode in Modern Hebrew Poetry* (Milford, CT: Toby, 2010), 373.

34. Nurit Govrin, "Ledaber al ha'Kotel" [Talking about the Wailing Wall], in *Gag: KeTav Et LeSifrut* 5 (Winter 2001): 105.

35. Ibid., 116. Govrin is referring here to a popular trope in Ben-Zion's texts.

36. Israel Zarchi, *Iturei Yerushalaim, shvilim ba'Ir Ha'atika* [Jerusalem's ornaments: Trails in the Old City, 1942] (Jerusalem: Weinfeld, 1942), 6. Page numbers for subsequent quotes for *Jerusalem's Ornaments* follow this edition and will be given in line. All translations are mine.

37. The motif of the "mad dog" was discussed widely in the context of S. Y. (Shai) Agnon's novel *Temol shilshom* [Only yesterday]. Recently, Todd Hasak-Lowy analyzed this motif as the major door to open Agnon's melancholic topoi. See Todd Hasak-Lowy, "A Mad Dog's Attack on Secularized Hebrew: Rethinking Agnon's *Temol shilshom*," *Prooftexts* 24, no. 2 (2004): 167–98.

38. Roberto Esposito, *Community, Immunity, Biopolitics*, trans. Rhiannon Noel Welch (New York: Fordham University Press, 2013), 28.

39. Ibid., 28–29.

40. Israel Zarchi File, Hebrew University Archive, Hebrew University, Jerusalem.

41. Ibid.

42. Ibid.

43. His depression lasted for months. In a diary entry from December 1944, Zarchi wrote about "a strange day. And since it is not unique this year, it is better to remove it from the calendar. My inability to act, the fall of all dreams. All colors are waned. I cannot do anything, not even write a note in a commemoration notebook. . . . Everything looks pale and useless, a man who destroys himself over a needless thing, who exhausts his powers—spiritual and physical—over what cannot amuse but only bring sorrow [to the reader]." Entry from 20 December 1944, "Sketches, Meetings, Conversations," B-3700, 24, Zarchi Archive.

44. Martin Buber, *Torat ha'Neviim* [The prophetic faith] (Jerusalem: Mossad Bialik, 1975).

45. Sasson Soffer, *Zionism and the Foundations of Israeli Diplomacy* (Cambridge: Cambridge University Press, 1998), 34.

46. Ibid., 258.

47. Israel Zarchi, *Bet Savta She'Charav: Sipurim* [The destroyed house of our grandmother] (Tel Aviv: Misrad Habitachon, 1988). The entire book may be read at http://www.echon-mamre.org (last accessed January 7, 2015). *The Guesthouse* was republished in another collection, *The Secret Flame* (*Shalhevet G'nuza*) in 1943 and again in 1947. Page numbers for subsequent quotes for *The Guesthouse* follow the Misrad Habitachon edition and will be given in line. All translations are mine.

48. Jeremiah 9:2. See the King James Bible: https://www.kingjamesbibleonline.org/Jeremiah-9-2 (last accessed June 7, 2016).

49. As one of the leading supreme court judges of that period, Moshe Silberg (1900–1975)—born to an Orthodox family and educated in Frankfurt and Marburg—explained the tenuous role of the Jewish intellectual: "This was the position of the Jew in European society, as the emancipation started and as it reached its peak. Parlors were opened to him, while hearts were sealed. He quickly climbed the social rungs, but the ladder itself was pulled from beneath him and he remained hanging there, up in the air, detached from the ground, with no roots and no hold on society's foundations."

50. Gershom Scholem, *Dvarim Be'go* [In support of] (Tel Aviv: Am Oved, 1976) 1: 100. Scholem had criticized the German-Jewish support of assimilation and emancipation since his youth and explained, in several essays, how this movement had led him to view Ahad Ha'am's cultural Zionism as the only solution for the Jewish problem in Europe. For a recent study about the phenomenon and its presentation in Kafka, Scholem, Benjamin, and others, see Vivian Liska, *When Kafka Says We* (Bloomington: Indiana University Press, 2009), 108–10.

Political Theology and Left-Wing Melancholy | 85

51. Roni Stauber, *The Holocaust in Israeli Public Debates in the 1950s* (Edgware, Middlesex: Vallentine Mitchell, 2007), 55.

52. David Ben-Gurion to Nathan Rottenstreich, 9 January 1957, translated and quoted in Stauber, *The Holocaust in Israeli Public Debates*. See also Idith Zertal, *Israel's Holocaust and the Politics of Nationhood* (Cambridge: Cambridge University Press, 2005), 59.

53. Eichah is the name of the prophet identified with the Book of Lamentations, which follows Jeremiah in the Bible and laments the destruction of Jerusalem. It is the center of the ninth of Av liturgical ritual.

54. Maimonides, *Mishneh Torah*, trans. Eliyahu Touger. Available online at http://www.chabad.org/library/article_cdo/aid/910346/jewish/Deot-Chapter-Six.htm (last accessed March 13, 2015).

55. Julia Kristeva, *Black Sun: Depression and Melancholia*, trans. Leon S. Roudiez (New York: Columbia University Press, 1992), 189.

56. Rakefet Sela-Sheffy, "HaYekim BiSde HaMishpat veDfusim shel Tarbut Burganit BiTkufat HaMandat" [German Jews in the judicial field and forms of bourgeois culture during the Mandate period], *Iyunim BiTkumat Israel* 13 (2003): 297.

57. Ibid.

58. Eli M. Salzberger and Fania Oz-Salzberger, "The Secret German Sources of the Israeli Supreme Court," *Israel Studies* 3, no. 2 (Fall 1998): 164.

59. Sela-Sheffy, "HaYekim BiSde HaMishpat," 297.

60. Israel Zarchi, "Sambatyon," in *Yalkut sipurim* [A collection of stories] (Tel Aviv: Yachdav, 1983), 99.

61. "Verkehrte Welt" is poem no. 21 in Heine's cycle titled *Zeitgedichte* (Poems of Time, 1844). The poem begins with a line that later appears in Paul Celan: "This is a topsy-turvy world; we are walking on our heads." Celan refers both to the image of a world gone "topsy-turvy" and the image of an uprooted plant in the air. For a translation of Heine's poem, see Heinrich Heine, "A Topsy-Turvy World," in *Poems of Heinrich Heine*, trans. Louis Untermeyer (New York: Henry Holt, 1917), 260.

62. Heinrich von Kleist, *Michael Kohlhaas*, trans. Martin Greenberg (New York: Melville House, 1960), and at http://pdfs.mhpbooks.com/Kohlhaas.pdf (last accessed December 22, 2016).

63. Andreas Gailus, *Passions of the Sign: Revolution and Language in Kant, Goethe, and Kleist* (Baltimore, MD: Johns Hopkins University Press, 2006), 124.

64. Max Brod, "Heinrich von Kleist, Chayav veYetizrato" [Heinrich von Kleist: His life and writing], introduction to Heinrich von Kleist, *Shalosh Novellot* [Three novellas], trans. Israel Zarchi and Mordechai Temkin (Tel Aviv: Am Oved, 1982), 12.

65. Ibid., 25.

66. Jean Starobinski, "Die Tinte der Melancholie," in *Melancholie: Genie und Wahnsinn in der Kunst*, ed. Jean Clair (Berlin: Staatliche Museen, 2006), 63 (my translation).

67. Diary, 29 September 1944, Zarchi Archive, "collection of handwritten texts." Sections from the diary were edited and published by Haim Toren after Zarchi's death in Israel Zarchi, *Iturim*, 24.

68. Ibid.

69. Zarchi to Haim Toren, 7 April 1946, file 171, Sig. 69586, Zarchi Archive.

70. For a report about Nietzsche's gift to the Wagners, see Cosima Wagner's diaries, entry 6 November 1870 (letter no. 231): http://www.thenietzschechannel.com/bio/cosima.htm (last accessed June 17, 2016). Ernst Bertram argued that the engraving was not *Melencolia I* but

Ritter, Tod, und Teufel [Knight, Death, and Devil] from 1513, even though he admitted as well that Wagner himself researched melancholy as a theme. See Ernst Bertram, *Nietzsche: Attempt at a Mythology*, trans. Robert E. Norton (Champaign: University of Illinois Press, 2009), 38.

71. Friedrich Nietzsche, *Thus Spoke Zarathustra: A Book for Everyone and Nobody*, trans. Graham Parkes (Oxford: Oxford University Press, 2005), 259–63.

72. Ulrich Finke, "Dürer and Thomas Mann," in *Essays on Dürer*, ed. C. R. Dodwell (Manchester, England: Manchester University Press, 1973), 129.

73. Sigmund Freud, "Mourning and Melancholia," *The Standard Edition of the Complete Psychological Works of Sigmund Freud*, trans. James Strachey (London: Hogarth Press, 1917), 14: 246.

74. Ibid., 243.

75. Judith Butler, *The Psychic Life of Power: Theories in Subjection* (Stanford, CA: Stanford University Press, 1997), 172.

76. Ibid.

77. Ibid., 172, 174; Butler is referring to Freud in this quote.

78. Ibid., 174; Butler is quoting Walter Benjamin here.

79. Julia Kristeva, *Black Sun*, 53.

80. Ibid., 7.

81. Ibid.

82. Pensky contrasts Benjamin and Kristeva in similar terms. See his *Melancholy Dialectics*, 19.

83. Giorgio Agamben, *Stanzas: Word and Phantasm in Western Culture*, trans. Ronald L. Martinez (Minneapolis: University of Minnesota Press, 1993), xviii. See the discussion above in chapter 2, section 4.

5

IN AN UNSOWN LAND

1. Vis-à-vis Brenner and Agnon

During the 1940s Zarchi became more and more conscious of the impact of Yosef Haim Brenner and Shmuel Yosef (Shai) Agnon on Hebrew literature in general and on his own writing in particular. In a diary entry from 1944 he described a conversation he had with Agnon concerning Brenner. The entry starts with Zarchi's report about Agnon's claims and continues with his own evaluation of both Brenner and Agnon.

> **Agnon:** My dear fellow, I have grown tired of good words, as one begins to despise good food after eating too much of it. . . . Everyone writes with such fine words now, the like of which our predecessors could not imagine, but I find it worrisome that an entire generation prophesies in one and the same style. And I, I have contributed more to this sinful conduct than others. I have grown tired of all this, tired. . . . I have just finished reading Brenner's *Breakdown and Bereavement* [*Shkhol ve'khishalon*, 1920]. Brenner was not a stylish writer, and his Hebrew was not very good, but what he wrote is much better than our generation's stylish stuff. It is regrettable that I cannot say this to him, to Brenner. I am much too late. For all those years I was held back by something, and I did not even pick up the book I now hold in my hand. And I ought to have told Brenner what I thought. You see, when one has something to say, things from the heart and not from a book or hearsay, the appropriate words manifest themselves without any trouble or toil. . . . But we are all sick, and we lack a truthful idiom, and I have had enough of this proper style, and it sickens me.

> [**Zarchi's diary comment**]: I disagreed with him: I thought the heart of the matter lay elsewhere. I even suspected that the source for his—Agnon's—grievance lay in the many imitators he sees, imitators of his idiom and style, which he resents. I wanted to tell him that searching for words and idioms is not a matter of trends, but rather a struggle to find an original and vivid style. The Hebrew language is not yet second nature to us, and

we do not yet know how to modify our language so it resembles the way people on the street talk. So we have a need for the books from which we wish to fashion ourselves a language, and while it may not be Agnon we are imitating, we all turn back and draw inspiration from the same sources from which Agnon himself drew—some successfully and others less so. And the day will come when we [fashion] ourselves a new, good, and beautiful language, not a language of translation, and then there will also be a difference between styles and not everyone will prophesy with the same voice. But who am I to explain this to a man like Agnon, who spoke with all his heart. He is our beacon and our example.[1]

As Zarchi explains immediately after this entry, it was obvious to him that the "good words" and style Agnon had in mind were not Zarchi's but his own. The younger writer admired the elder, and he admitted openly that some passages of his short stories certainly sound much like Agnon. As Agnon scholars demonstrated in different places, Agnon became such a model for a whole generation of *yishuv* writers.[2]

Brenner and Agnon were the two key experimental modernists of Hebrew literature. Gershom Scholem identified Agnon as the "heir to the totality of Jewish tradition" and as the one who appealed to a "transformed" sense of "continuity of tradition."[3] A strong stress on tradition enabled Agnon to be more playful and experimental where language was concerned, but his narratives seem less politically relevant than Brenner's. In the Hebrew canon Brenner and Agnon are the equivalent to the great authors of American modernism: T. S. Eliot, Ernest Hemingway, and Gertrude Stein. In *Mourning Modernity*, Seth Moglen distinguished two forms of writing in American literature—the "political" writing of Eliot, Hemingway, F. Scott Fitzgerald, William Faulkner, Willa Cather, and Jean Toomer; and the "experimental" and "excluded" modernism of Zora Neale Hurston, H.D., Tillie Olsen, Langston Hughes, and William Carlos Williams, dedicated to "the work of social resistance."[4] Members of the latter group—to which Zarchi would have added Upton Sinclair—"shared the presumption that capitalist modernization was a contingent historical process that might be resisted, controlled, redirected."[5]

The logic of Hebrew, especially after its "revival" by Zionist authors, introduces a different logic. As I explained in chapter 1, Zionist writers paired a modernist style—European, mostly—with a revivalist approach to history—grounded in biblical terms. Those who wrote in Hebrew during the early twentieth century, such as Brenner, H. N. Bialik, or Zarchi's other favorite writer, S. Ben-Zion, were committed to a utopian revivalist, socialist, and collectivist narrative. Even Agnon, who stood out due to his explicit dependence on later Mishnaic sources, reformed the Zionist canon and Israeli Hebrew from within, by "playfully juxtapos[ing] the new Zionist allegories invented via biblical flora with traditional allegories of the Song's roses, mocking normative distinctions between the secular and the sacred."[6] Comparing this form of modernism to the English and American modernism that Moglen discusses highlights why it is harder to separate modern Hebrew literature's internal and external forms of critique. Does this matter for our understanding of Zionist melancholy? In contrast to the triadic model Moglen built for the American modernist generation, the interwar generation of Zionist writers, Zarchi among them, experienced the collapse of a social order and loss of old values as a positive effect. Their melancholy, in other words, followed from a radically different set of circumstances.

2. In the Wilderness, in *Unsown Land* (1946)

To find the traces of Brenner's and Agnon's influence on Zarchi, one should begin with his characters. Like those of his idols, Zarchi's protagonists—almost always male—are effeminate, spiritual, melancholic, erotically frustrated, and ideologically challenged. Much like Brenner, Zarchi was fascinated by antiheroes, the opposite of the classic Zionist pioneers. And like Brenner's protagonist Yehezkel Hefetz, Zarchi's male protagonists fail to answer the criteria Max Nordau posed for the muscular Jew.[7] In Brenner's *Breakdown and Bereavement* Yehezkel Hefetz arrives in Palestine as a young idealist who hopes to find his individual and ideological destiny and sense of fulfillment in the holy land, but he is physically weak, homesick, and desperate, and slides quickly into melancholy and then actual depression; he gets hospitalized after a nervous breakdown and then moves in with his family in Jerusalem. After a cousin falls in love with him, Hefetz's mental state continues to deteriorate, now stricken not only by the inadequate relation to the place and the ideology he failed to realize, but also with romantic guilt.

Much like Hefetz, Zarchi's protagonists fall into a melancholic mood after their failure as pioneers, as workingmen, or simply as men. Zarchi's protagonists differ from Hefetz, however, because they do not adopt the language of personal pathos, which Anita Shapira describes in her biography of Brenner as "melancholy, deformity, and tragedy. . . . [Hefetz's] melancholy is a mental illness; his deformity, the hernia; and the tragedy, his loss of sexual ability."[8] Brenner's narrative evolved from "a story of the downtrodden whose world has crumbled" to the revelation at its end, yet Zarchi's stories move in a more circular and limited mental space in which the close of the narrative mirrors its beginning.[9] While the two writers produced unmistakably modern stories with alienation at their cores, and flirted with the great telos of the creation of a Jewish state and with socialist values, Zarchi's stories did not end with catharsis. Like Brenner, Zarchi was conscious of his environment and the double alienation his protagonists experienced, first as Levantine Jews in Europe and again as European intellectuals in Palestine, but unlike Brenner, the gap in Zarchi's stories did not close. This double and unsolved identity is the paradox that forms the core of *The Guesthouse*, and the same one that informs *Unsown Land*, Zarchi's 1946 novel that won the prestigious Jerusalem Prize in 1947.[10]

Like *The Guesthouse*, *Unsown Land* is a title borrowed from the Book of Jeremiah. In a chapter of prophetic admonishment—meant to remind the people of Israel that God had fulfilled his part of the covenant but the people had not—Jeremiah recalled that he had been urged by God: "Go and cry in the ears of Jerusalem, saying, Thus saith the Lord; I remember thee, the kindness of thy youth, the love of thine espousals, when thou wentest after me in the wilderness, in a land that was not sown" (Jer. 2:2). God's dispute with the people leads to a long and bitter break. It will destroy not only the generation that refused to listen, but the following generation, too.

> Be astonished, O ye heavens, at this, and be horribly afraid, be ye very desolate, saith the Lord.
> For my people have committed two evils; they have forsaken me the fountain of living waters, and hewed them out cisterns, broken cisterns, that can hold no water. (Jer. 2:12–13)

Zarchi set his tale against the backdrop of the Biluyim period, which he had identified with the primordial moment of Zionism since writing *Youth* in 1932.[11] In *Unsown Land* Zarchi closed a circle, one that views origins from the possibility of annihilation. After the Holocaust, he came to identify the internal power of that crisis along the fault lines of its ideological structure. The circular movement is meant to unite the sense of cosmological, communal, and individual-psychological desolation.

Zarchi's novel is the fictionalized story of Yosef Magidov, a pioneer who emigrated from Russia to Palestine and settled in the town of Rishon

Le'Zion. He was committed to Russian anarchism and socialism in his youth and, after the 1882 pogrom, decided to leave his homeland to put his utopian ideals to the test. From the very first pages of the novel the key tension is between a secularist vision and a messianic, political-theological one. The internal conflict centers on the historical figure of Rabbi Shmuel Mohilever (1824–1892), one of the founders of the Hibbat Zion, the first community of socialist pioneers who believed in working and settling the land. Zarchi portrayed Mohilever as bearing a secularized, messianic fire: "His heart burns with love for the holy land. Thankfully we have arrived at this moment; these are signs of the coming of the Messiah."[12] But in the novel's first scene Magidov's trust in the coming of a messiah or a messianic time is shaken: "The air was humid and salty and relentless. The exalted vision, which had delighted his spirit all through the night, vanished suddenly, and its glory sank like a play of illusions. Suddenly his life purpose dwindled, and weak and feeble he lay on the deck, as if all of life's vital essence had abandoned him" (24).

For the ancient Greeks and Maimonides, such an experience would have been associated with a melancholic soul. But it is also the experience of the Israelite prophet Jeremiah, who unites the crisis of belief in Israel with a general sense of desperation and his own, individual despair when the Israelites ignore and even censure him. Magidov's name alludes to this tradition. In Hebrew, *Magid* means the one who speaks with a divine voice or prophesies; *Ov* (as in the book of Samuel, "Ma'ale baOv," the evoker [of spirits]) is part of another prophetic idiom implying the raising of a divine voice out of nowhere or the one who communicates with the dead. Zarchi's novel maintains its realistic tone throughout and gently guides the reader toward a semantics of desperation and desolation, alienation and death. Magidov meets with quite a few of the historical-mythological figures of the early *yishuv*, such as Yehiel Pines, Karl Netter, Yosef Feinberg, and Samuel Hirsch, who pass through the story like familiar ghosts. The settlement itself is described in a charged messianic tone, but it eventually fails, shattering all hopes. Even moments of ecstatic experience—for example, when the protagonist views the old city of Jerusalem from the burial site on the Mount of Olives, the mythical spot for exilic Jews, who wished to be buried there for the day of resurrection—imply potential collapse.

From the moment of Magidov's arrival at the settlement, obstacles gather like storm clouds. First, the Ottoman authorities demand his cooperation as a subject, and he witnesses conflicts between Arabs and Jews and between Orthodox Jews and the secular settlers. A friend introduces Magidov to the group of pioneers who settle in Mikveh Israel and work under Samuel Hirsch, then explains that everything he sees is part of bigger power relations, that Hirsch will stop at nothing to consolidate power over the property: "It is after all the farm of a nobleman . . . and he sees in us refugees who have escaped grave danger, here today and elsewhere by tomorrow" (47).

A deeper understanding of the power relations exposes the force mediating among the various agents. One young pioneer offers an undiluted critique:

> Covered in a black blanket lay a fellow with a large forelock. . . . No one introduced him to Magidov, as if he were of no account. When Magidov saw that the fellow did not address him, did not seem to notice him, he approached his bench and extended his hand in greeting. The fellow took his hand indifferently, embarrassing Magidov thoroughly, then turned his back to him to face the wall. An unpleasant silence enveloped the room. . . . Someone said to Magidov, offhandedly: "He is sick, possibly with malaria." . . . At that moment the fellow faced about and shouted furiously: "It's all lies! Do not listen to them! I am not sick! I am not sick! Not physically at any rate. But when I look around, I lose my wits. Why do we torture ourselves here? If we were wrong and came here too soon, without knowing where we were going, we ought to admit our mistake and go back home and wait for better days." (51)

This man's Nietzschean melancholic outburst undermines the group's celebration of unity and realization: "Suddenly the affectionate spirit that had hovered over Magidov's arrival evaporated, words that had been spoken quietly and humorously felt like empty platitudes, and the air of tranquility that had covered the house disappeared" (52). The words of the sick man remain in Magidov's mind long after he leaves the gathering. He befriends a similarly unhappy man, his only friend in the novel: "It was in Luria's nature to quickly switch from hope to despair, and he wondered what would become of them in this wasteland" (87).

Both Magidov and Luria fall in love with another ideal, this one in human form. Nadia—the name salutes the heroines Zarchi admired in Tolstoy and Dostoyevsky—is a beautiful young woman, newly arrived, who offers a romantic alternative to the hardships of the land: "Her long dress lingers between her legs and disrupts her. . . . Her braids are piled high, covered by a gray, wide-brimmed hat adorned with two white ostrich feathers" (91). For Magidov, Nadia represents not only the European ideal he left behind and yearns for constantly but also the very idea of critical melancholy, which is the same as the dream of "the ideal colony, [that] is written in our code of principles." Magidov "would see her occasionally at the colony and was surprised to see her so settled and morose, as if a cloud of sadness dwelt in her blue eyes and sullied her spirit. . . . 'Forgive me if I ask you something that is not clear to me at all: what is that ideal colony that you constantly talk about?' Magidov smiled in the dark: 'Ah, it is one of those beautiful dreams that cannot be realized'" (94–95). Later in the novel Magidov observes: "Her words were full of sorrow. Sadness afflicted her often lately, and now, too, standing so at the edges of night, there was a vast and gloomy loneliness" (141).

In Nadia, Magidov finds a countervoice, a countertemporality, and an alternative to his everyday life. Magidov encounters another countervoice, an old man walking along one of the roads leading to Jerusalem who responds to Magidov's secularized fetish of the land with a cynical and exhausted tone: "'We have heard such talk from Pines and Ben-Yehuda, and we have grown tired of it. . . . One lost what remained of the holy city, yet you have not built anything of the same value!' He bent down and picked up a small stone, shoved it toward Magidov's mouth, as if to show him that he was worthless, and then scornfully cast it aside" (110).

When Magidov tries to persist, repeating his belief in the secular ideals of Zionism, his interlocutor warns him away from a grave religious sin—the acceleration of (messianic) time. As I have shown above, historians of Zionism have described the core temporality of Zionist ideology as "catastrophic Zionism" or "political messianism," both with the "acceleration of history."[13] Magidov says, "But do we not seek your favor? We are trying to redeem the people of Israel, so that we can be a nation among nations!" To this the old man replied, "It is folly to rush the work of our righteous Messiah!" (110).

After a series of conflicts with the settlers and Rothschild's bureaucrats, a friend of Magidov's summarizes the lesson of *Unsown Land*:

> Only now do I understand the profound reason why Jews have longed so fiercely for the land of Israel over two thousand years, how it is [that] so many of them could have come and seen the land but then failed to respond to it. . . . For if they came and saw the land in ruins, its air of poverty and savage people, their hearts' desire would vanish, and they would no longer achingly yearn for it. . . . You see, let me be absolutely clear: there is no divine spirit in this place. . . . It is as if we were trying to bring back a faraway time and reinhabit it, but we fail to do so. (169)

Zarchi's exploration of melancholy exposed not only the internal conflicts of the different Jewish groups but also their conflicts with the local Arab "savage people." These conflicts often resulted from the willingness of the Arab locals, who were generally better farmers, to work for lower pay. At different points in the plot, the Arabs appear as the all-knowing fellahin, the peasants or agricultural laborers with large and happy families and an intimate understanding of the land. Unlike many Zionists—especially those of the late 1940s—Zarchi's characters treat these people warmly: "They disembarked from the carriage and invited the Arabs into it with great honor, until it resembled a hilltop filled with people" (199). Zarchi acknowledged that this naïve and hopeful view was hardly mainstream: "It became known within the Jewish community that some were leaving to live in remote areas among Arabs. . . . They told them to forget this folly and stop this nonsense" (203).

In a very different scene, just after the confrontation between Magidov and a Bedouin who had tried to rob him, the effect is similar:

> A strange feeling entered his heart, and he wondered how he had summoned the strength to beat a man senseless. He, who had never even hurt an animal, and was a pacifist. He stood there, in front of the man, ashamed, wondering what had happened to him. He started to feel sorry for this big man, sitting before him bawling like a baby. Sticking his hand in his pocket, he dug out a few coins and presented them to the Bedouin. When he looked back, he could still see the Bedouin sitting on the sand dune, following him with a gaze full of wonder and devotion. (231)

Such descriptions belong to an Orientalist discourse, which—as Edward Said showed—helped portray the local fellahin as the typical Semite, the one "by nature lacking the desirable qualities of Occidentals," or "at least four centuries behind the times, . . . dishonest, uneducated, greedy, and as unpatriotic as he is inefficient."[14] Zarchi's narrator indeed examines the Bedouin with an air of patronizing empathy but also a matter-of-fact approach to the situation. An examination of Zarchi's position vis-à-vis power demonstrates that his own view, inherently oppositional, was the result of feeling entrapped. The harsh critique expressed in this and other novels of his is usually turned against the institutions of Zionist ideology that are supposed to represent him. Magidov describes Rothschild's representatives and Rothschild himself as "lawless men, revolutionaries and insurgents, . . . nihilists who do not have God in [their] hearts" (295). The regime he imagines for this early Zionist body makes it sound like a totalitarian sovereign: "No one may have a guest to visit without asking permission from the clerks. Nor may he do anything at all, be it good or bad, in garden or field without proper orders. To make sure that all edicts hold firm, no farmer knows the boundaries of his fields, and anyone who refuses to sign an agreement effectively removes himself from society" (295).

Magidov's clash with the Zionist bureaucrats of his day echoes Jeremiah's conflict with the bureaucracy of the king Zedekiah. Jeremiah's conflict does not end with the disagreement between him and the court; instead it escalates to open hostility between him and the people of Jerusalem.[15] According to Jeremiah, an ethical "return" is the key to unite the people and their God, or the earthly and heavenly. But the people, and their secular sovereign, the king, refuse.

A similar conflict occurs in Zarchi's novel. The ironic result for the idealistic pioneers—the agents of the realization of the ancient prophecy of return—is that their hard work and high ideals become the bitter fruits of a failed return to Zion, and the promise of a new future reverses its direction and ends up as Jeremiah's unsown land. The political disappointment leaves just one consolation, namely, the revival of Hebrew. In opposition to the bureaucrats and Zionist politicians, Zarchi presents Eliezer Ben-Yehuda, the acclaimed reviver of the Hebrew language, by introducing an idealistic teacher who represents—as a follower of Ben-Yehuda—the messianic view of the language: "'Give us children, and we will speak Hebrew to them on the Sabbath and on the weekdays, and they will not know any foreign tongue.' . . . Magidov likes listening to the teacher . . . who never tires of praising and glorifying Ben-Yehuda in Jerusalem, making him out to be a kind of general coming to conquer the nation-citadel" (305–6). Language replaces politics and agriculture as the heart of a new messianic force. As "the teacher"—for this is how he is called in the novel, with no indication of either a first or a family name—explains to Magidov: "You work with a plow and shovel to resurrect the body of Israel, and we toil with our language to resurrect the spirit of Israel. Other nations have cannons and horses and vehicles of war, and they conquer all they can grab. But we have nothing but this hoe in our hand and Hebrew on our tongue, and these things alone can restore our land to us. . . . Up until this day you have known only the torments of redemption; now you will see that the pangs of language are even more painful than pre-Messianic pangs" (307–8).

In contrast to the language of the Zionists, Zarchi's Hebrew does not normalize its messianic content. Instead, thanks to the dualism of our author's idealistic excitement and his melancholic critique, it exposes the ruptured bipolarity at the core of Hebrew. Zionists spoke of a "sword of realization" that hung above ancient Hebrew, namely, the requirement to renew it as a retroactive proof for the ancient prophecy of return. They supported every effort to carry linguistic revival to its fullest realization.[16] Zarchi's Hebrew expresses a slightly different sense of realization. Rather than carrying the ancient language into its immediate realization in the present, his plot and vocabulary express a melancholic suspense. Rather than constructing the language of the present as an immediate activation of a past potential, Zarchi's novels open a critical dialogue with both past and present use of Hebrew. Let me explain this argument by returning once again to the hidden prophetic layer—expressed mostly via his allusions to the dark predictions of Jeremiah.

Unsown Land opens with the prophecy of Jeremiah and ends with a reference to the books of Ezra and Nehemiah: "Suddenly [Magidov] remembered a vow he had made while in the mountains of Jerusalem: he had sworn that if his mission was successful he would return home and read from Ezra and Nehemiah" (316). But instead of following Ezra's example, resettling the land and rebuilding the temple, Magidov's story ends with a sense of melancholic monotony. He moves in with a woman he does not love and has a child with her. Life, it seems, is very different from both the big promises of the prophets and the tragedies of the storytellers. Nature alone connects with Magidov's sad sense of duration and incompletion, as he looks out from his wagon on a land that seems forsaken and full of ghostly voices: "It seemed as if the wind that had blown in their wheels had died down; they remained in their place, lonely and helpless. The voices and lightning, the storm that had guided them, now settled into silence; the small group stood motionless. A pronounced loneliness clenched the handful of houses and closed in on them where they stood in the fields" (321). The same feeling appears in a later passage: "And the few, the tiny few who remained, fought for their lives in a small, remote village. Laboring in fields that cannot support their owners—was this the demise of the dream?" (336).

Not quite. The novel avoids the calamitous conclusion of *The Guesthouse*, but at the end of *Unsown Land* a weary protagonist once again explains the paradoxical contours of his world to his horse, this time with a touch of tender consolation: "Samson, my dear Samson, my good horse, my son is born," to which the narrator adds: "The entire village was enveloped in darkness and only the illuminating windows of his little house remain dangling in the blackness. The night receded. The azure of the sky grew deeper. The stars began to pale" (338). As in *And the Oil Flows*, the last image fuses hope and sadness, continuity and rupture, a simple everyday sunrise and the dissolution of messianic hope. The soft melancholic tone, suspenseful and realistic, enables the reader to transpose the prophetic "messianic pangs" of the opening of the novel to the painful language of everydayness in its end.

Zarchi published *Unsown Land* after much calamity and frustration. Several publishers rejected the manuscript. Shortly after Berl Katznelson (1887–1944), a leading Labor Zionist who ran both the daily *Davar* and the publishing house Am Oved, accepted it, he died, and publication was delayed again.[17] After another long period of tense expectation, Zarchi finally received an offer from Dov Sadan, the other important publisher of the *yishuv*, who was ambivalent about the book but still agreed to publish it. In fact, Sadan continued to criticize the book even after it had been shortlisted for the prestigious Osishkin prize. The prize committee, in considering the novel for its award, connected *Unsown Land* to the legacy of its namesake, Menachem Osishkin, a founding father of the Zionist movement who had died in 1945, the year before the award was made. Zarchi lost the prize to Agnon's novel, *Only Yesterday*, which had led the pack that year in both prestige and dimensions of the project. In his opening celebratory speech, Klausner, as head of the committee, completely ignored *Unsown Land*, in spite of his close relationship with Zarchi and its place on the shortlist.[18]

The only established prize Zarchi won was the prestigious Jerusalem Prize, but at that point he was already very ill and some feared that *Unsown Land* would be the last novel he would write.

Notes

1. Diary, 7 April 1944, Israel Zarchi Archive, file 171, "Different Manuscripts," Gnazim Institute, Tel Aviv. I quote here a large section of the entry because of its value for historians of modern Hebrew literature and because of its shrewdness.

2. For a general discussion of the first generation of writers in Hebrew and the relevant historiography of Hebrew literature, see Arnold Band, *Studies in Modern Jewish Literature* (Philadelphia: Jewish Publication Society, 2003), 179.

3. Gerschom Scholem, "Reflections on S. Y. Agnon," in *Commentary*, December 1, 1967, https://www.commentarymagazine.com/articles/reflections-on-s-y-agnon/ (last accessed August 1, 2018). For an excellent discussion of Agnon and the continuity of tradition, see Ilana Pardes, *Agnon's Moonstruck Lovers: The Song of Songs in Israeli Culture* (Seattle: University of Washington Press, 2013).

4. Seth Moglen, *Mourning Modernity: Literary Modernism and the Injuries of American Capitalism* (Stanford, CA: Stanford University Press, 2007), 9.

5. Ibid.

6. Ilana Pardes explains, in a beautifully written book, about the subversive hermeneutics Agnon used to alter modern Hebrew from within. See Ilana Pardes, *Agnon's Moonstruck Lovers: The Song of Songs in Israeli Culture* (Seattle: University of Washington Press, 2014), 69.

7. Max Nordau, "Jewry of Muscle," published originally as "Muskeljudentum" in *Jüdische Turnzeitung* in June 1903. An English translation can be found in *The Jew in the Modern World: A Documentary History*, ed. Paul Mendes-Flohr and Jehuda Reinhartz (Oxford: Oxford University Press, 1995), 547–48.

8. Anita Shapira, *Yosef Haim Brenner: A Life*, trans. Anthony Berris (Stanford, CA: Stanford University Press, 2015), 343.

9. Ibid., 345.

10. Israel Zarchi, *Eretz lo Zru'a* [Unsown land]. Zarchi worked on *Unsown Land* for a long time, starting in 1939 with research on the early days of the Zionist settlement, and completing a first draft in January 1944. The novel was published in May 1946.

11. Bil'u is the acronym for Isaiah 2:5, "*Beit Ya'akov Lekhu Ve-nelkha*" [Let the house of Jacob go!]. The movement was based on the refugees of the 1882 pogroms in East Europe who immigrated to Palestine and were identified with a socialist ideology and an emphasis on cooperative agricultural settlement and the revival of biblical Hebrew. By 1884 there were forty-eight members leaving Mikveh Israel and who were divided between two core groups: one that established Rishon Le'Zion, the other leaving the school to establish G'dera. Even though the two settlements survived, thanks to the continuous investment by the Baron Edmund de Rothschild who opposed the Marxist agenda of the group, the Biluyim left for the cities or went back to Europe. For a short definition, see the Jewish Virtual Library: http://www.jewishvirtuallibrary.org (last accessed June 17, 2016).

12. Israel Zarchi, *Eretz lo Zru'a* [Unsown land] (Tel Aviv: Am Oved, 1947), 18. Page numbers for subsequent quotes for *Unsown Land* follow this edition and will be given in line. All translations are mine.

13. Anita Shapira identifies these two descriptions with the core of Zionist ideology. See Anita Shapira, "Zionism and Political Messianism, Comments on Israel Kolatt's Paper," in *Totalitarian Democracy and After*, ed. Yehoshua Arieli and Nathan Rottenstreich (New York: Routledge, 2002), 355. For the acceleration of history, see Shapira, *Land and Power: The Zionist Resort to Force, 1881–1948* (Stanford, CA: Stanford University Press, 1992), 151.

14. Said is quoting here from a letter the Zionist leader Chaim Weitzman sent to Arthur Balfour on 30 May 1918. See Edward W. Said, *Orientalism* (New York: Vintage, 1994), 306.

15. Walter Bruggemann's classic interpretation has focused on this power struggle. See Walter Bruggemann, *A Commentary on Jeremiah: Exile and Homecoming* (Grand Rapids, SD: William B. Eerdman, 1998), 362.

16. For this and other concepts of "realization" (Hagshama), see Shapira, *Land and Power*.

17. "Upon the sudden death of B. Katznelson, which rattled the whole land, all my plans for my book seem to have been breached as well. I waited for a few days in my tense anticipation and low spirit. . . . But all I got was an evasive reply: while my book had been on B.K.'s desk on the day of his death, no written response was found and we must wait until matters are sorted out." Diary excerpts, 4 September 1944, Zarchi Archive, "miscellaneous" file.

18. The committee included Klausner, the agronomist Itzhak Volkani, and Max Solovietchick (later Menachem Solieli), the director of the education section at the Zionist National Committee. Historian of literature Dan Laor described the scene in his classic biography of Agnon: "Prof. Volkani congratulated Agnon on behalf of the Second *Aliyah*, then Prof. Klausner took the stage to read the explanation for the judges' decision, which he himself had written. . . . Klausner refrained from mentioning the titles of the other contenders, including two works by Israel Zarchi." Dan Laor, *Haye Agnon: Biyograpfyah* [Agnon's life: A biography] (Tel Aviv: Shocken, 1998), 366.

6

THE HISTORY AND THEORY OF
THE MELANCHOLIC DISCOURSE

1. The Cultural History of Melancholy

Melancholy and utopia, depression and mania, boredom and love, lack of judgment and the extreme state of clarity: Melancholy is always a double-edged sword. The history of melancholy, as described in Peter Toohey's comprehensive *Melancholy, Love, and Time* (2004) goes back to ancient Greek philosophy and to the roots of Western thought. Euripides described the melancholic state in his play, *Orestes,* as that which "oscillates between the poles of mad insanity and clearheadedness."[1] Even then it was seen as the simultaneous state of cool contemplation and the greatest torture. Since the end of the fourth century BCE it was identified with an expression of anger and frustration but also with Seneca's "depressive melancholy," with Hippocratic physiology of black bile and with Aristotle's perception of human excellence.[2] How deep did those polarities go? It was in its earliest framing in Greece, Toohey shows, that melancholy was analyzed in terms of "the surface of things, on the manifest, and on how the individual relates to the community."[3] The duality of *acedia* (depressive boredom) and madness, physiological symptoms and a state of mental apathy, individual ennui and political restoration varies from region to region and period to period, but it was shared and recognized by all post-Hellenistic cultures in the West, often in terms of an "epidemic."[4] Most interesting for the history and the sociology of melancholy is its intuitive relation to time, the apathetic linearity of its flow and the senseless repetition of its circularity. For Toohey, melancholic time was inherently connected to the culture of the West, or "part of a dialogue that engrosses boredom, melancholia, and lovesickness."[5]

As I mentioned previously, recent analysis has revealed that depression was common among Zionist pioneers, with a suicide rate well above normal during the early years of the *yishuv.*[6] Much of the research focused on male pioneers who left their European homes and Jewish families to work as laborers in Palestine, yet the psychological effect extended to women as well. For example, Deborah S. Bernstein and Musia Lipman discuss the effect of a challenging existence on the female pioneers: "The loneliness was immense. . . . There was a preoccupation with suicide."[7] One thinks instantly of the connections between affect and sociopolitical phenomena: A particular weltanschauung collided with a certain utopian worldview—the result was melancholy.

The psychologist Donald Capps, citing Robert Burton's famous work of 1621, *The Anatomy of Melancholy,* identified the structure that ties melancholy to utopia.[8] Burton, Capps explained, "provides a description of his own utopia . . . and then declares, 'All the world is melancholy.'"[9] In Capps's view, "For the melancholic, there may be very little distinction to be made between reformists who seek to amend, and utopianists who seek to reconstruct, the world. . . . This may help to explain why utopian social programs are as likely to fail from internal conflicts among the members as from outside opposition, and why men despoil and wage war on mother earth."[10] For Capps it was imperative to "address this sense of lack."[11]

The interest of Toohey and Capps in the history of melancholy is grounded in cultural history, much like the works of Panofsky and Saxl or Jean Starobinsky. It compellingly explains the background for the phenomenology and affect of melancholy, but it cannot explain the political translation of melancholy in modern times nor its relation to a heterosexual, male, and universal worldview, as the sociologists and political theoreticians have done.

Recent political interpretations try to do precisely that: The historian Enzo Traverso attests to the growing relevance of "left-wing melancholia" and explores the roots of the present sense of melancholic defeat in political and social narratives that "are not revolutions of the future but the defeated revolutions of the past."[12] The urgent need to understand the collapse of past hopes and utopias inspires him, as it does Seth Mogeln, "to rethink Socialism in a time in which memory is lost, hidden, and forgotten and needs to be redeemed. This melancholia does not mean lamenting a lost utopia, but rather rethinking a revolutionary project in [a] nonrevolutionary age. This is a fruitful melancholia that, one could say with Judith Butler, implies the 'transformative effect of loss.'"[13] Traverso's method is similar to the one chosen in my book: He adapts Walter Benjamin's observations as an analytical tool in order to examine a series of cultural-historical phenomena that could contribute to the "transformative effect of loss." In contrast to what I have tried to point out with the help of Zarchi's narratives, however, Traverso attempts to transform Benjamin's own warning against left-wing melancholy and readapt it to Ernst Bloch's plea for "a concrete (and possible) utopia."[14] In the coming pages we examine the relation between melancholy and utopia with the help of Wolf Lepenies's classic text about the sociology of melancholy and utopia and Giorgio Agamben's stress on the shared "placeless place" of utopia and melancholy. The melancholic-utopian axis, we will see, is not only part and parcel of Western political imagination but also the very essence of its understanding of destruction and reconstruction.

2. The Placeless Place or the Utopia of Melancholy

In 1961 Wolf Lepenies (b. 1941) opened his acclaimed interpretation of melancholy, *Melancholy and Society*, with a dedication to his controversial teacher Jacob Taubes.[15] Lepenies extended Taubes's political-theological stress on modern politics and the position of the Jew as an exile by connecting melancholy and utopia: both the earlier "dis-order" of an individual mind and the later break with an existing order. More specifically, Lepenies adopted Robert Burton's conception of melancholy and saw it as "geared as it is to the difference between order and dis-order. . . . Burton calls his intermediate domain the 'state,' although the term 'society' would fit better."[16] Burton's discussion of melancholy served him "as a pretext for developing an anti-melancholic, utopian counterpart."[17] Developing melancholy as a limited case, separating and connecting the political and the theological, disorder and order, individual mind and collective action, imagination and institution, pushed Lepenies to adopt a powerful approach to melancholy as early as 1961. In later editions he explains that Carl Schmitt, Jacob Taubes, and Michel Foucault's stress on power makes it impossible to separate melancholy and utopia. Both are based on a deep sense of *ennui*, boredom, which "was the sign of a situation that relieved the person of all obligation."[18] In that context, "melancholy seized those who had attempted to change the relations of rulership, and had failed."[19] An eighteenth-century failure was represented later in the salon culture of the bourgeoisie and a growing separation between *l'homme intérieur* and *l'homme extérieur*, as seen clearly in Proust's literature.[20] The sociology of space, represented by Maurice Halbwachs and Georg Simmel's "intersection of social circles" and "the continuity of locality," missed the deeper sense that Freud and Foucault understood as a "loss of world" and "suspension of interest in the outside world."[21]

Giorgio Agamben's *Stanzas* (1992), published a few years before his acclaimed *Homo Sacer*, finds traces of melancholy at the center of the Western discussion of two seemingly unrelated issues: the psychology of the individual and the "placeless place" (u-topia) of the communal imagination.[22] He believed that the question "Where is the thing?" was linked tightly to "Where is the human?"—which led him to suggest that the loss of the object of mourning is a loss that becomes an obsession. Agamben quotes Justin Clemens while discussing how a pathology, a fetish, points to, as Clemens described, "a zone that is no longer objective or subjective, neither personal nor impersonal, neither material nor immaterial, but where we find ourselves suddenly facing these apparently so simple unknowns: the human, the thing."[23] Agamben adapts Clemens's discussion of u-topia into his work on the "zone of indistinction," a no-man's-land, the place of pure differentiation: "This utopian zone that the melancholic inhabits is unlivable and intolerable, a 'no-man's land,' at the very limits of human existence."[24] It is a zone that the melancholic in Agamben's view can escape only by creating and populating with new objects, emblematically, cultural objects such as art or literature. Agamben would later return to this zone, an affective no-man's-land, and recharge it with the political-legal structure; the "state of exception," as a zone of indistinction, is shared by democracies and totalitarian regimes.[25] In other words, Agamben's understanding of political melancholy in the postglobal age leads back, via Benjamin's, to the ancient melancholic civil war or what Toohey identifies as the "dissolution of the universe" or "the destruction of the state."[26] The philosophical zone of indistinction, the institutional no-man's land, an individual-psychological affect of melancholy, a political state of exception, is the starting point for true critical work.

What Agamben says about space, Toohey claims about time. According to Toohey, Lucan—Seneca's contemporary and nephew and the originator of a state of exception—wrote his ten-volume *Civil War* as a representative of "the revolt against the linearity of time" and the acknowledgment that in the civil war a series of suicides express that "there is little value in preserving a life that has become intolerable."[27] Toohey identifies Lucan's work as the poetic and political model for our time. Lucan's melancholic depiction of the fall of the Roman republic identifies it with the end of the world, or *ecpyrosis* [burning utterly], a primordial no-man's-land, which Agamben identifies, much like Lepenies and Toohey, with a "placeless place," or the point where utopia and melancholy meet.[28] How do these cultural histories and political or sociological theories—retrieving a Greek, Roman, or Christian past—help us understand the Zionist settlement, in general, and Zarchi's depiction of it, in particular?

Notes

1. Peter Toohey, *Melancholy, Love, and Time: Boundaries of the Self in Ancient Literature* (Ann Arbor: University of Michigan Press, 2004), 21.

2. Ibid., 26–28.

3. Ibid., 39.

4. Ibid., 149.

5. Ibid., 198.

6. Eran Rolnik, *Freud in Zion: Psychoanalysis and the Making of Modern Jewish Identity*, trans. Haim Watzman (London: Karnak, 2012), 45.

7. Deborah S. Bernstein and Musia Lipman, "Fragments of Life: From the Diaries of Two Young Women," in *Pioneers and Homemakers: Jewish Women in Pre-State Israel*, ed. Deborah S. Bernstein (Albany: State University of New York Press, 1992), 148.

8. Donald Capps, "Melancholia, Utopia, and the Psychoanalysis of Dreams," in *The Blackwell Companion to the Sociology of Religion*, ed. Richard K. Fenn (Malden, MA: Blackwell, 2001), 86.

9. Ibid.

10. Ibid., 95.

11. Ibid., 99. See also Ernst Bloch, "Something's Missing: A Discussion between Ernst Bloch and Theodor W. Adorno on the Contradictions of Utopian Longing," in *The Utopian Function of Art and Literature: Selected Essays*, trans. Jack Zipes and Frank Mechlenbourg (Cambridge, MA: MIT Press, 1988), 15.

12. Enzo Traverso, *Left-Wing Melancholia: Marxism, History, and Memory* (New York: Columbia University Press, 2016), 20.

13. Ibid. Traverso alludes here to Judith Butler, *Precarious Life: The Powers of Mourning and Violence* (London: Verso, 2004), 21.

14. Bloch is quoted in Traverso, *Left-Wing Melancholia*, 234.

15. The dedication was omitted in later editions and in the English translation. Wolf Lepenies, *Melancholie und Gesellschaft* (Frankfurt am Main: Suhrkamp Verlag, 1969), 1.

16. Wolf Lepenies, *Melancholy and Society*, trans. Jeremy Gaines and Doris Jones (Cambridge, MA: Harvard University Press, 1992), 19.

17. Ibid.

18. Ibid., 41.

19. Ibid., 52.

20. Ibid., 108.

21. Ibid., 121, 124.

22. Giorgio Agamben, *Stanzas: Word and Phantasm in Western Culture*, trans. Ronald L. Martinez (Minneapolis: University of Minnesota Press, 1993), 59. See also Justin Clemens, "The Abandonment of Sex: Giorgio Agamben, Psychoanalysis and Melancholia," *Theory & Event* 13, no. 1 (2010).

23. Ibid.

24. Ibid.

25. See Giorgio Agamben, *State of Exception*, trans. Kevin Attell (Chicago: Chicago University Press, 2005).

26. Toohey identifies it with Lucan, AD 39–65. See Toohey, *Melancholy, Love, and Time*, 216–17.

27. Ibid., 183.

28. Ibid., 217. See also Agamben, *Stanzas*, xix, 59.

7

THE REVIVAL OF HEBREW
Utopia, Indistinction, Recurrence

1. The Revival of Hebrew: Past as Future

Zarchi's melancholy exposes the Zionist condition, that is, that an absolute destruction or negation was the Zionist condition par excellence. For the Zionists, only the destruction of past worlds would open the possibility for revival. The cultural history of melancholy allows us to focus our attention on the "phantasmagorical" language of melancholy. As described earlier, the melancholic affect is the result of a double loss: the loss of an actual past (a home and family) and the loss of memory due to an ideological dictum. Sigmund Freud described the latter in 1917 as *a loss of the loss*. More recently, Judith Butler identified Freud's structure with the failure of the ego to find a substitution for the lost object (which it mourns).[1] Giorgio Agamben focused on the "placeless place" of melancholy and u-topia and described the relation as "the phantasmagorical reality of what is lost" and melancholy itself as what "opens a space for the existence of the unreal and marks out a scene in which the ego may enter into relation with it."[2] But how does this double loss or phantasmagorical relation work within a language that keeps referring to reality in utopian—albeit biblical—terms? The utopian revival of ancient Hebrew generally plays a central role in histories of early Zionism, and the messianic promise to return to Zion is never omitted.

In her *Recovered Roots: Collective Memory and the Making of Israeli National Tradition*, Yael Zerubavel talks about "the symbolic bridge that makes it possible to 'weave' the ancient past into the modern National Revival, skipping over the discredited exilic past."[3] The language of the settlers passively ignored or actively negated the actual reality of Jewish life in exile, in favor of a return to a mythic past. Phantasmagorical language was the traffic moving over this bridge of communal images. As I demonstrate below, for pioneers the notion of "home" became inseparable from terms of revival and images of phantasmagorical secular realization. Pioneers came to see Hebrew as a proof of the existence of redemption, fulfillment, self-realization. The double loss enabled them to preserve a sense of telos while forgetting the content or essence of movement. Because of the great symbolic charge of the revival of Hebrew, the literature that grew up around the revived language connected thinking, expression, and the territory itself. Zerubavel explains it thus: "In its bias toward social realism and efforts to present 'positive' heroes and 'constructive' themes, this Hebrew literature sought to heighten historical awareness and reinforce social commitment to the formation of a new society in ways reminiscent of Soviet literature."[4] In other words, a socialist utopia was built into every fictional narrative. Although the utopia guided the pioneers' gaze toward the future, the language that described the utopia avoided the loss, the home the pioneers had left behind. The new-old language was not adequate for the therapeutic work of mourning—yet that was its very purpose. The feelings of rage that escaped from this unrealizable project were channeled outside and used to occupy the land.

Could language truly change the conditions for comprehending and interacting with our social circle? Could the phantasmagorical language of melancholy change the ideological and political landscape in concrete terms? In *Hebrew and Zionism: A Discourse Analytic Cultural Study*, the historical linguist Ron Kuzar discusses the contours of this process, that is, the gradual revival and normalization of Hebrew. By the early 1920s the revival of the ancient language was transposed via powerful political channels into a clear territorial marker: the building of settlements. Language helped create a committed political subject: "The people who were involved in the process framed their own cultural experience as a 'revival,' a key term in the constitution of the subject position of 'the proud speaker of Hebrew' that Ben-Yehuda labored to establish. It was a militant, committed subject position that was solid enough to make people start speaking a language in almost all public contexts in a way they had never done before."[5]

Political Zionists promoted the view that, as Kuzar explains, "only a territorial national center can enhance the development of national culture and written language."[6] Their view imposed a barrier between medieval Hebrew, exilic and divine, and the new Hebrew, Zionist, anti-exilic, and secularized. Modernizing the ancient language, a project encouraged and advocated by both supporters and critics of territorial nationalism, not only unified the different factions within the Zionist movement, but it also made the Zionist weltanschauung more appealing to the gentiles. (As mentioned in chap. 2, right-wing supporters like Klausner and Greenberg and left-wing cultural Zionists such as Scholem, Bergman, and Zarchi all agreed on and advocated a fundamental revivalist position.) Historian Joseph Massad calls this situation "the revival of Hebrew geography," and other historians, specifically Tom Segev, agree with his assessment.[7]

Within the Zionist camp the revival of Hebrew served as a uniting force that transcended all political and discursive boundaries. Revisionists and peaceniks shared the same vocabulary and drive; since the early 1900s Gershom Scholem, Martin Buber, Yehuda Leib Magnes, Hugo Bergman, and others—cultural and political Zionists alike—had been pleading for a supra-ideological emphasis on Hebrew. "As Ahad Ha'am, the proponent of cultural Zionism, emphasized, only the Hebrew language could function as the tongue through which Jews could connect again with their national past."[8] Scholem and Bergman advocated the revival of Hebrew even while describing the dangers of this approach. Bergman, a radical advocate of Hebrew revivalism and a bitter opponent of political Zionism, protested against the chauvinism of the young Zionist pioneers: In his view, they would do better to focus on the "living word" than on a revived and fetishized language.[9] Scholem, tackling the same issue from the perspective of religious anarchism, wrote a famous letter to Franz Rosenzweig in which he warned, "The people certainly don't know what they are doing. They think they have secularized the Hebrew language, have done away with its apocalyptic point. But that, of course, is not true: The secularization of the language is no more than a *manner of speaking*, a ready-made expression. It is impossible to empty the words so bursting with meaning, unless one sacrifices the language itself."[10] Bergman's and Scholem's diaries are full of such critique, as well as recurrent references to Hebrew as, in Scholem's words, "the inner center of the soul."[11]

Among the leading objects of Scholem and Bergman's scorn was Joseph Klausner, who published a series of articles and essays in which he called for shrinking the revival to territorial and messianic terms, similarly to Eliezer Ben-Yehuda's prophetic position that attached the revived language to a political-theological position. Modernizing a biblical language transformed the political-theological legitimacy from the divine to the secular sovereign and settler. If this sounds like the kind of work only reactionary nationalists could do, the reality was that both conservative nationalists and progressive socialists contributed to its realization, and both perceived themselves as "revolutionaries" in very similar terms. As the political theorist Zeev Sternhell explains it, "The concept of the Zionist revolution as a personal revolution and a national revolution, but not as a universal social revolution, was passed on to the labor movement. . . . [This revolution] had two aspects: rebirth and a complete break with the exile on the one hand and an attachment to one's historical roots to the religious content of national life on the other."[12]

Klausner and cultural Zionists such as Scholem, Bergman, Buber, Greenberg, and Zarchi were worlds apart politically, but they shared the same position concerning the political-theological mission of the revived language and its contribution to the resettlement of the land. Kuzar explains that the revolutionary aspects of the revived language included the rechanneling of ancient material to modern sensibilities, yet the particular approaches taken by different groups also played a part. As Kuzar shows, the blurring of lines, both political and linguistic, go all the way back to the origin: Ben-Yehuda. For Ben-Yehuda, the revolutionary Russian world of the *Narodnik* was crucial.[13] His commitment to socialist revolution helped mobilize the second and third aliyot, most of which emigrated from eastern Europe. Kuzar explains, "The almost ascetic demands of self-realization here and now through total self-devotion and self-risking ring familiar to anybody acquainted with the Zionist ethos of *khalutziyut* 'pioneerism' in Palestine, which involved a totally uncompromised personal commitment to the Zionist socialist cause."[14]

It was only during his forties, Kuzar writes, that Ben-Yehuda started talking about the people as a nation. David Ben-Gurion and the leadership of the political Zionists ignored the revolutionary rhetoric of early Ben-Yehuda, enabling Ben-Gurion to declare during the early 1950s that "the revival period has ended" and that a new and modern Hebrew had been born.[15] With this reductive collectivizing and territorializing process, the Hebrew language—now committed to the Zionist narrative—narrowed every linguistic telos to the act of settlement, a fetish of massive and material construction: "Only a territorial national center," wrote Ben-Yehuda, "can enhance the development of national culture and written language."[16] This reduction created a political paradox: As Boaz Neumann expressed it, "Pioneer rebirth in the Land of Israel served as the most radical manifestation of the 'negation of exile' phenomenon."[17]

Ben-Yehuda's autobiography explains the Gordian knot between the revival of language and the revival of Jewish nationality in clear terms. Ben-Yehuda bears much of the responsibility for this development. He presented the political-theological view as the principle that guided both the Jewish enlightenment and the national revival in the land of Israel. Ben-Yehuda wished to produce a process of socialization and collective unification, effectively a "purification" of Hebrew that cast off its exilic attributes.[18] Kuzar identifies this course as an internal process of fetishization, concerned particularly with holy places and territorial markers.[19]

Like Kuzar, the professor of law Chaim Gans connects the revival of Hebrew with an attempt to reorganize the national narrative in an ahistorical fashion. According to Gans, the revival of Hebrew enabled a retroactive mythification of Jewish history: "When Zionism first appeared, the Jewish collective was a nation only in a partial sense of the word, and the fact that a minuscule portion of that collective had settled in the Land of Israel by the thirties. . . . The central Zionist faction established the position that the entire Jewish collective was a nation in every sense of the word, and that it had always been one."[20] Needless to say, the many factions and civil wars that pepper the pages of the Bible and Midrashic sources are absent from such mythical tales.

Michael Gluzman, a historian and theorist of Hebrew literature, examines the mechanism of revival in the context of both sovereignty and melancholy in post-1948 literature.[21] Presenting "the melancholy of sovereignty" as a "discursive transformation," Gluzman quotes from Ben-Gurion, "We shall have to forge a new Hebrew style that could not have existed in the Diaspora. We shall have to solidify our connection with our past, [while] also paving our way toward the messianic vision of peace on earth."[22] Gluzman asserts that the majority of the authors and scholars of the period felt "that it was incumbent upon them to 'go to the people,' in the Narodnik sense."[23]

The negation of exile marked the necessary and complementary aspect of a positive "pioneer desire for the land," as Neumann describes it, and my argument in this book—backed by Kuzar's and Gluzman's analyses—is that this desire was based on an aggressive, fetishistic identification, grounded in the temporality of revival and directed by the ideologues of Zionism for their own territorialist purposes.[24] In the following section I show that Zarchi chose to tackle both the negation of exile and the revival of Hebrew by retelling the myth about the ancient Jewish tribe coming from the east. In his tale the utopian dream about the reoccupation of the holy land and the revival of Hebrew shatters the sick and melancholic imagination of an Orthodox Jew.

2. "Sambatyon" (1947)

"Ben-Yehuda's Zionism was linguistic," Ilan Stavans writes. "You might almost say he wanted Jews to create their own country so that they could speak Hebrew in it. The land was a stepping-stone for linguistic redemption—a way of moving into the future and back."[25] Turning this characterization around, one could argue that Ben-Yehuda's Hebrew was Zionist, meaning a secularized form of redemption through language. The cost for this fusion of revivalist and secularized forms was high: The modern language lost much of the content and complexity that its ancient precursor had accrued over centuries. Gone were the legendary and the mythical, and gone was the messianic hope that Zionism claimed to realize. Myths that did not fit with the modern ethos of the occupying pioneer were erased or simply ignored.

One such lost story was the legend of the ten lost tribes and the great river Sambatyon, which separated the lost tribes from the rest of Israel and created a physical barrier between the two parts of the people—messianic times were conditioned on reuniting them.[26]

In his recent history of the legend of the ten lost tribes, Zvi Ben-Dor Benite explains that every child in the Jewish *cheder* knew the legend.[27] The mythic river Sambatyon marked the actual end of the known world and the end of time, defining the *oikumene*, the border of the inhabitable zone, beyond which lay only catastrophe and redemption.[28] The reappearance of the ten lost tribes—which had been lost beyond the Sambatyon—promises redemption: "Now it is the return of the 'three companies of exile'—the ten tribes—that will stir the return of the Jews to the Holy Land. In spatial terms, the messianic return begins with them."[29] The heart of the mythic story, however, is not a tale of happy return but rather a story about desultory wondering. The legend of the Sambatyon, Ben-Dor Benite shows, reflects the idea of "permanent exile" or "that the tribes are out there still, lost, wandering, and unknown."[30] Is it surprising that this "permanent exile" has been suppressed or even negated by the Zionist plea for return, in both biblical and modern terms? After all, "the lostness of the ten tribes is . . . both loaded with and derived from an acute theological anxiety."[31] The legendary story emphasized the melancholic search—and one of the principal activities of Israel Zarchi's protagonists.

In his retelling of this myth, Zarchi framed the hopeless call for unity in the context of two other Jewish symbols that carry a distinct melancholic tone: the Jewish mother who mourns her dead sons and the mysterious appearance of a black dog as a signifier of collective destruction. Zarchi wrote the short story "Sambatyon" in 1947, the last year of his life, and it carries his distinct poetic marks. A Haredi Jew abandons his community and sets off in search of the ten lost tribes. The protagonist, R' Moshe Yehoshua, is a melancholic mystic whose quest is inspired by a Yemenite rabbi's tale of encountering a remnant of the lost tribes. R' Yehoshua decides his mission is to bring the lost tribes back to Jerusalem. The themes explored in this story recall *And the Oil Flows*, as well as the impressions recorded in *Jerusalem's Ornaments*, discussed in chapter 4. Zarchi attaches a fantastic mythic past to the life story of an exceptional figure, R' Yehoshua, whom he describes as a failed dreamer who takes on the myth as his own personal vocation.

Long pages detail the poverty and gloom of Jerusalem: "A small, wretched town, a heap of demolished stones, its houses damaged, its alleyways in disarray, neglect and emptiness in all its courtyards. And a small number of Jews sitting hunched and crowded studying the Torah, constructing worlds in their imagination only to destroy them the very next moment" ("Sambatyon," 97). This description echoes Ecclesiastes. See the following reference of the midrash to the construction and destruction of worlds: "From this [we learn] that the Holy One, blessed be He, kept on constructing worlds and destroying them until he constructed the present one and said, 'This pleases me, the others did not.' R. Eleazar said: 'This is a door which is opened to the depths, as it is stated, "And God saw everything that He had made, and behold, it was very good."'"[32] The allusion creates an ironic analogy between the Jews and God, and opening "to the depths" goes further still: The word *tehom* means both abyss and nothingness. For R' Yehoshua, we learn, constructs castles in the air: His life is "nothing but a few hours of awakening, after which the sadness is greatly increased . . . a plant in a pot, whose root does not reach the soil" (99).

As in several of Zarchi's other stories, here the hostile force is not the "Ishmaelites" but apocalyptic Jews who "accelerate the end" by reviving the performance of sacred rituals: "If it becomes common knowledge, God forbid[o], this deed [of settling the land] will bring forth a great disaster for the people of Israel, in bondage to foreign powers and the bloodthirsty sword—it is not yet time" (100).

The other destructive force in this story is R' Yehoshua's own obsessive and narcissistic personality, fusing the religious and secular ideas of redemption. In line with Scholem's plea to avoid the secular nationalization of Hebrew, R' Yehoshua comes to see his own role in this world as the savior of the sacredness. However, the gap opens where Jewish culture and ritual meet with secular politics, that is, where R' Yehoshua meets the language of his admired Ben-Yehuda:

> Every page that he wrote in those holy characters he kept safe in his cabinet, even those that dealt with mundane matters. In recent years people have stopped being very strict with these matters. Every week the *Havatzelet* publishes a bulletin in the holy language, and Ben-Yehuda follows suit and publishes *HaZvi*. People read the bulletins and quickly scatter the pages, passing them along to cooks and druggists, as if they were devoted to mundane subjects. Their fragments are scattered in the courtyards, and the wind blows them from wall to wall. . . . From the window one can see the site of the temple; old cypresses stand perfectly still, their topmost branches unmoving; open gates await the redeemer, and the redeemer does not come. (103)

The act of collecting the pages with the Hebrew script on them fails to yield the hoped-for messianic effect or the success the protagonist is dreaming about, thus triggering his melancholy: "And he was still more saddened to see that nobody worried about salvation, nobody demanded and requested and asked, 'How shall we take the steps toward redemption?' and nobody pursued the traces of the Messiah. The few who reside in Zion and study the Torah before God think they have saved themselves, and they ignore that their redemption is no redemption at all. Quite the contrary: he, Rabbi Moshe Yehoshua, felt the bondage of foreign powers more keenly here in the holy city of Jerusalem than in Bialystok" (104). R' Yehoshua may be the paradigmatic protagonist of Zarchi's poetics: "The world seems pale, and he himself is but a broken vessel, and only sometimes, in despair and great misery, does he still believe that the day will come, that the moment will still come and someone will knock on his door and give him a great message, a sign of redemption, even the slightest hint" (104).

The topsy-turvy character of him who keeps faith after countless disappointments looks much like a manic-depressive. After he hears the myth of the Sambatyon from the Yemenite rabbi, R' Yehoshua declares, "The sorrow of the divine spirit is now greater than ever before; the gaze of the Jews is worn out, and they live out their exile in darkness. . . . The kingdom of his imagination, which he thought had perished, never to return, has once again awakened . . . and he is filled with much excitement. The flames are like those of the early days" (113). As in *Unsown Land* and *The Guesthouse*, Zarchi wraps the story of R' Yehoshua and the Yemenite myth of the return of the lost tribes in the warm blanket of the prophecy of destruction and the famous Jewish lamentation from Jeremiah 31:15: "A voice is heard in Ramah, lamentation and bitter weeping, Rachel weeping for her children. And hearing the terrible lamentation a sadness descends upon Jerusalem until the heart is broken. . . . And we, stricken with grief and anguish at the destruction of Jerusalem, our mind is lost, our heart floats, soars to the heavens, and plummets like a vessel in the midst of stormy seas" (122).[33]

Alluding to Jeremiah, Zarchi's narrator laments the lost sons of Israel, and moves on to recall the failure to bring home the fetishized tribes and to dwell on the strongest component of Jewish exile, namely, the ritual and poetics of lamentation over the destroyed Jerusalem. Thinking about the lost tribes does not help the protagonist; rather it entombs him under a mass of myths. When reality flickers and vanishes, Zarchi's protagonists escape to the world of fantasy, losing their last grip on the world.

Ben-Dor Benite traced the philological relation between the words *Sambatyon, sabbath,* and *Saturn,* connecting this relation to the messianic and anarchistic Sabbatean movement[34]: "The evidence connecting Saturn, the Sabbath, and the Jews in the Roman period is vast and well known. Saturn, the seventh planet . . . and a Greco-Roman god, was naturally perceived as governing the Sabbath, the seventh day."[35] At the center of the analysis is Ben-Dor Benite's concept of a "geographic theology" centered on nonexistent space, on a messianic promise that cannot be realized. Recalling Panofsky and Saxl, he points out that melancholic Saturn is both the farthest and the nearest star: It stands at a vast distance from Earth, yet it is the most concrete sign of "the spatial dimensions of God's works."[36]

Gershom Scholem wrote about Jewish Sabbatean apocalypse and messianism from a similar perspective, dwelling on the collapse of a united Jewish space, geographical and theological. That cataclysm occurred during a Jewish civil war that "cancelled all laws of nature," turning man, as the Mishnah said, into an animal: "A man's enemies are the men of his own house. The face of the generation is like the face of a dog."[37] With this historical reminder, Scholem was warning his readers not to lose the legendary contents of the ancient Hebrew language. As Todd Hasak-Lowy showed, S. Y. Agnon reacted to this warning in his *Only Yesterday* (1945) by "trac[ing] the gradual, steady conflation of referent and signifier, in which the dog (referent) upon whom it is written 'mad dog' (signifier) eventually becomes mad. . . . Here we find a rare bidirectional fit between words and world: the words not only match the state of the world . . . they make it so."[38] The identity of words and world represents a messianic unity of space and time, utterance and action. "Agnon seems to ask what may be lost by secularizing Hebrew and what is at risk in treating a sacred, mystical language as a mundane vernacular."[39] Agnon's protagonist, like the dog in the story, goes mad, apparently an analogy for the loss of the spoken Torah and Midrash: "And he too studied the Torah but when his soul was not sated with the bread of Torah he went to seek some secular bread. He left his city for another city and that other city for another city."[40] Agnon's warning is starker than Zarchi's: His protagonists lose touch with reality, go mad, and die a tragic death. But the story keeps a realistic tone and a limited perspective. Agnon's irony disables pathos and keeps the allegorical subtext in the background. In short, the implied author clarifies his distance from the protagonist's melancholy.

Like Agnon, Zarchi dwelt on the hostility between two characters: R' Yehoshua, the dreamer of myths of unity and coherence, and the yishuv. The conflict is unfolding as R' Yehoshua sinks in his illusions and is treated like a pariah dog, chased by children who throw stones at him and mockingly call him "Sambatyon."

For Zarchi's protagonist, much like Agnon's protagonist Isaac Kumer, there is no way back. But Zarchi's language, with its invocation of the legendary past, goes further to fuse words and world. Not only does his protagonist go insane and die, the whole land suffers. The story ends with a plague that—as in Camus's eponymous novel—kills thousands and fills the city with "black dogs covered with boils." Zarchi's dreamer, R' Yehoshua, becomes one of those who creep out at night to collect and burn the bodies of the dead. When he finally succumbs, "the grave they dug for him on the Mount of Olives was one of the last graves dug in the face of this calamity, for with him the plague ceased" (148).

"Sambatyon" exposes the political-theological structure of a linguistic Zionism. Toward the end of his life, R' Yehoshua obsessively collects the pages of the Hassidic and Sefardic *Havatzelet* as well as Ben-Yehuda's Zionist and Ashkenazi secular *HaZvi*. (While pious Jews would carefully bury every scrap because of the sanctity of printed Hebrew, secular Jews tossed the bulletin on the ground.) And then he fashioned from them a garment, or perhaps a shroud. One might say that he was eking out a weak messianic force from secularized Hebrew, extracting it through melancholy and fetishism. He had ceased to hope for full collective redemption—the coming of the messiah—but he retained his faith in a small fusion of words and world, space and time.

3. Saturn

In *The Political Philosophy of Zionism: Trading Jewish Words for a Hebraic Land*, Eyal Chowers reminds us of the god Kronos, whose children live inside of him after being swallowed. Kronos is a ruler less interested in territorial control than in symbolic power achieved in time: "Saturn (Kronos), who devours his children, is a symbol of the constant and unbeatable movement of time, the arrow is a symbol of linearity. The clock is a symbol of regularity and cyclicality, the hourglass is a symbol of time running out."[41]

When Julia Kristeva thought about the pre-Christian temporality of melancholy, she gave it the form of the self-devouring Bellerophon "because he was forsaken by the gods, exiled by divine decree . . . condemned to banishment, absence, void."[42] Chowers, by contrast, reads Saturn/Kronos as a linear temporality. Even where "regulation and circularity" rule the day, avers Chowers, time is running out. His reading of Saturn, contra Kristeva's Christian perspective and Ben-Dor Benite's stress on global and revolutionary Sabbateanism, presents it as a political force of occupation, normalization, and linguistic adaptation. Unlike Kristeva, Chowers and Benite look at Saturn from a Jewish, post-Zionist perspective: Zionism adopted the language of linear action and rejected a theological language. Both sound much like Gershom Scholem and Shai Agnon when they speak of the resultant dilution of Hebrew: "Zionism as it evolved in Palestine was also a repudiation of word-based communal life in the deepest sense. . . . It is somewhat overshadowed by the fact that Zionism championed the renewal of Hebrew as a language of everyday life."[43]

According to Chowers, the revival of modern Hebrew was marked by a strong interest in linearity. Modern Zionist nationalism, he argued, grew from G. W. F. Hegel's *Volksgeist*, a concept that united a conception of national language and a particular homeland. Both the centrist Zionists of Theodor Herzl and David Ben-Gurion's school and the reactionary revisionists of Ze'ev Zabotinsky's school grounded their understanding of the nation in that concept. Like Scholem, Chowers urges us to heed the suppression of ancient Hebrew's apocalyptic and messianic content. But while Scholem stuck to the throbbing heart of historical charge, Chowers looks consistently forward, hoping to shape "a democratic understanding" to link the ancient and the modern, the old understanding of essential value and the new democratic understanding of human rights and the separation of government into several independent branches.[44] In contrast to Walter Benjamin's antinomy, and the understandings of power offered by Michel Foucault, Wolf Lepenies, and Giorgio Agamben, Chowers proposes to transform a negative critical position into a positive, constructive politics. This proposal places him, of all the critics, closest to Kristeva's plea to transcend the negative aspects of melancholy.

Chowers permits us to read Zarchi backward, to see him anticipating the implications of his own poetics, the relation between an idealist language and its political-theological temporality. Zarchi's temporal order has nothing to do with those of either of his mentors, Joseph Klausner and Ahad Ha'am. Unlike the former, he chose a political position that was tolerant of the Arab population and resistant to the acceleration of history. Unlike the latter, he did not limit his investigation to the ideal-realization relation. In fact, in his late writing, about the mythic Sambatyon or about the Yemenite Jews of Jerusalem, he promoted a view of revival and return based not on Hebrew and territorial identity but on a mythic and exilic identity.

A darker apocalyptic register crept into Zarchi's late stories. Paradoxically, it was the gap between legend and reality that enabled him to maintain his commitment to reality. Realizing how the melancholic myth of the lost tribes serves the manic R' Yehoshua enables the reader to keep her distance from both R' Yehoshua and the secular Zionist indoctrination that surrounds him and that makes the Zionists see him as a freak. In contrast to the unconscious mythification of heroic Zionism, R' Yehoshua at least preserved the primordial force of the sacred language of prayer, never giving over to the hollow declarations of a secular language. His use of melancholy shows how words and world, sacred and profane, cyclical and linear connect. Zarchi the Sabbatean opened the door to religio-political anarchism, a treasonous theopolitics that exposes mistakes rather than hiding them. At the end of his life, Zarchi adopted a legendary mode as the only possible consolation left him.

4. Land of Our Fathers (1946)

Zarchi wrote his fifth novel, *Land of Our Fathers*, during the second half of 1944.[45] A short work, it was serialized during 1945 in *Meoznaim*, the literary magazine of the writers' union, and it appeared in book form in June 1946. For his subject, Zarchi returned once more to the lives of the early settlers, setting his tale among Jerusalem's poor. The novel follows three generations of Polish-Jewish immigrants, presenting the first as idealists who left their homeland for Palestine only to give up and return to Poland. When the grandsons, fleeing persecution in Poland, repeat the first voyage, Palestine is their last resort. The ironic story gives us the grandfather, Rabbi Yaakov, standing for what might be called secularized messianism. He buys a parcel of land on the outskirts of Jerusalem but cannot stand the harsh conditions and gives up. The grandson, called simply Yaakov, travels to Palestine only in order to sell the land, but he is forced, because of the advent of the Holocaust, to stay there. In other words, he is forced to realize the messianic promise of the grandfather against his will, and by the end of the story he comes to accept his fate.

Again Zarchi traces the recent history of Jerusalem, focusing here on two neighborhoods: Kerem Avraham and Me'a Shearim. Laid out chronologically, the two parts of the novel are titled "In Those Days" and "At This Season (Time)," echoing the Hanukkah blessing that reiterates the fulfillment of the divine promise and the existence of miracles.

Linear and circular axes control the content of each of the parts. The novel unpacks the different interpretations of an inheritance, considering ancient Jewish customs (a theological understanding), the practices of the Ottoman occupiers of the country (secular, legal, political), and Yaakov's emotional (psychological) understanding of his inheritance.

As in *The Guesthouse*, the ticking of a clock in the protagonist's living room bears a special meaning: It unites the individual story of immigration with the longue durée of Jewish life, on the one hand, and the coming destruction of European Jewry, on the other hand. Yet unlike other stories about this theme, *Land of Our Fathers* shows us something other than a land of milk and honey. Between the promise of the past and the destructive future, there is only a sad present: Not only is there no milk, there is also no water. Everyone is thirsty. The narrator links this suffering to the failure of the messiah to appear, much though he is expected.

Yaakov is assailed by melancholy when he encounters the dry, gray city, and when the news of the Holocaust sweeps into Palestine, he feels much worse. Yaakov realizes that all his work has been in vain; he collapses into an apathetic stupor. Two people try to console him. The first, a poor Yemenite laborer, is motivated by human compassion; the second, a close friend of Yaakov's grandfather, finds reaching out to his friend's grandson a means of reconnecting with the good old days: "And honestly, how grand was Jerusalem back then, when we were all still living in the city between the walls . . . one big ruin, a breached and abandoned stone wall, through whose cracks the wind wails. Not like today, knock wood—houses and streets and marketplaces, and rich Jews, a grand city of God. . . . And let me tell you, in the evil days of this war, this Armageddon, I sense the coming of the Messiah, the pangs of the Messiah . . . and the end must come" (113).

The messianic hope, the old man explains, is what keeps him alive. But for Yaakov, the secular youngster, these nostalgic reveries mean nothing. The short novel concludes with a minor vision of consolation, a romantic vision Yaakov experiences while strolling through the hills near the city. He has no interest in the Messiah; all he wants is some rest. And that he finds, as he comes to terms with his new life.

In his comments on the book, Dov Sadan, the editor of the book series and one of the best-known critics and scholars of Hebrew literature, speaks of "a boat heading toward the shores of a distant childhood. . . . And you go along with those seeking this distant childhood, that is, the waves of *Aliyah* of recent years."[46] Focusing on childhood and concrete historical phenomena for Sadan meant overlooking the book's messianic and apocalyptic elements, and he misses the point.

Zarchi's novel does not hide its contempt for nostalgia and distance from the early days of the settlement. The title, *Land of Our Fathers* (*Nachalat Avot* in the Hebrew), emphasizes the ambivalence of the act of return: The legacy in question is the plot of land traditionally passed down as a burial site. The word *nahalah* was formerly used to refer to the burial place of kings and prophets.[47] For thousands of years, this custom preserved continuity between the generations—land, lineage, and faith were one. During the exilic period, returning to the promised land meant returning to the dead, who would be revived after the end of days (*Ahrit Hayamim*). A long-lost past was one with the far future. But Zarchi's novel makes no explicit reference to the theological concept, and it resists the quick messianic shove toward the end of days; instead, it keeps returning to a melancholic "geographic theology," as Zvi Ben-Dor Benite calls it.

If Zarchi's "placeless space" extends the dualism of imagination (theology) and reality (geography), idealism and realization, of past dreams and future hopes, it does so while rejecting the idea of Hegelian syntheses. Zarchi, who was an admirer of Ahad Ha'am's cultural Zionism alludes to an article by Ahad Ha'am, entitled "Nachalat Avot," published in 1895. Ahad Ha'am criticized the nostalgic and mystical concept of return, which he contrasted with history itself and a Hegelian understanding of law:

> It is a great mistake to think that the wall of tradition can be knocked down today by the blast of a trumpet. We have to take into account the powerful feeling of respect for antiquity, which guards the wall like an armed battalion, and is only reinforced by the clarion. . . . The day will come when we feel a new kind of need, a need to understand the rise and fall of traditional practices as a natural process, when we have a new Maimonides, gifted with a historical sense, who will rearrange the whole Law, not in an artificial, logical order, but according to the historical evolution of each prescription, when in place of critics . . . we have commentators of a new kind, who seek the source of the Law in the mental life of the people, to show why and how it grew up from within. . . . On that day, but not before, will the link be sundered between reverence for antiquity and practical life.[48]

Ahad Ha'am was attacking Herzl's political Zionism and Baron von Rothschild's bureaucratic take on settlement, while advocating a revival of Hebrew and Jewish spirit (Geist) in a reterritorialized Zion. Zarchi's melancholic critique took a different turn.

5. *Shiloh Village*: Orientalism and a Mythical Alternative

Zarchi's last novel, the book he declared his best, was published posthumously.[49] It told the story of the small community of Yemenite Jews who settled in Siluan, in between the walls of the Old City of Jerusalem and the Mount of Olives. The Yemenite settlement started on a provisory basis during the 1880s, for the Jews had no money to purchase houses in the more affluent neighborhoods and settled first at the caves under the Mount of Olives. With the help and advocacy of Israel Frumkin (1850–1914), the owner of the monthly *Havatzelet*, they later built homes on the outskirts of the Arabic village Siluan and lived there peacefully until the rise of political Zionism in the area, during the early 1920s. Zarchi started researching the novel in 1944 and labored on it until his death, through a series of depressions and a final bout of cancer. In January 1945, when newspapers were filled with news about the Holocaust, he wrote a diary entry about a community that he had embraced:

> I am entirely immersed in studying the lives of the Yemenites and their ways. Sometimes I feel intoxicated by the sights and stories and the abundance of friendships suddenly bestowed upon me. . . . I do not know whether all the hard work I have put into this book will be recognized and whether its value

will be appreciated. This is different from the [socialist Russian-based Zionism of the] *Biluim*.[50] That book too is mostly based on authentic material, but most of the details about the *Biluim* and their first days on the land are well known. These nice Ashkenazis—they wrote so much, and so much was written about them, and is still written to this very day. Most of my work there was sorting through the materials and creating an artistic-literary dramatization of known events. . . . While here, with the Yemenites, everything about their first days on the land, filled with indescribable agony and replete with a pure and unique vision—all this is shrouded in fog. They are not men of letters, and their friends are not men of letters, and it is all about to sink into an endless sea of oblivion. And I have awakened at the final hour, the very final hour, and have started to put together mumbles and syllables and half-syllables and sighs and smiles commemorating the forgotten and all these whispers and all the faraway experiences have been brought back once again to the hearts of the elders of the community before they are lost forever. But even if others do not know, I know the measure of my work and the responsibility that comes with it, and may I do what my heart sees fit.[51]

One might compare those words to the declarations of the Orientalist who saw the people of the Middle East as, to quote Said, "a decrepit canvas awaiting his restorative efforts."[52] Zarchi's impulse to preserve an ideal image of the uncorrupted native of the Levant was full of admiration and sentimentality. In that respect, he was no different from other Zionists, from both liberal and conservative sides of the political spectrum. Zionist politicians had, since the early days of the *yishuv*, responded to the Yemenites with admiration and arrogance.[53] They cultivated this community as a replacement for Arab workers and—as Sami Shalom Chetrit demonstrated—for those Ashkenazi settlers who failed to internalize the image of the muscle Jew.[54]

In Zarchi's favor, we should note that he observed the community of Yemenites with honest admiration, admitting his own failure to assimilate to his new context. Unlike the Zionist establishment, his idealization did not serve the Orientalist's attempt to distance himself from the native via cultural segregation and economic discrimination, but protested against it. The Yemenites represented to Zarchi a community that could better bridge the gap between past and present, an alternative to Ahad Ha'am's plea for a new lawgiver. Their work, like his own, was ultimately connected with a mythical pre-Zionist world that they did not try to secularize or modernize. The Zionist narrative of Jewish history developed an opposition between West and East, Jews and Arabs, Ashkenazi Jews and Arab Jews, exilic past and heroic present.[55] It created a history that denied any possibility that Jews had a variety of experiences.[56] In contrast, Zarchi mimicked the language of the old Yemenites he interviewed. He chose the ancient alternative to a Zionist notion of Jewish history, or Walter Benjamin's characterization of the Social-Democrat: "Social-Democrats preferred to cast the working class in the role of a redeemer of future generations, in this way cutting the sinews of its greatest strength. This indoctrination made the working class forget both its hatred and its spirit of sacrifice."[57] In Zarchi's case, for "Social-Democrats" read "political Zionism" and Yemenite language its opposite.

Zarchi's insistence on authentic Yemenite discourse fostered an alternative, though it would be misguided to deny his orientalist and idealist proclivity. After all, identity is far more complex than white or black, right or wrong. As Yehouda Shenhav demonstrated, a European interpretation of Zionist history "was based on a temporal-territorial continuum 'in the region' and, as such, was polarized into a conception of continuity (of the negation of exile) as obliged by Zionist history. This approach has a triple expression: territory, history, and identity."[58] Zarchi's melancholic antiheroes, Ashkenazi or Yemenite, represent the opposite of this continuity.

Shiloh Village has only scant traces of a plot. We follow the emigration and settlement of several generations of Yemenite Jews from 1881 to the 1930s. The book presents a wide prism of multiple figures, voices, and perspectives, giving a textured portrait of the community. At the center of all these details is the growing gap between life in and around Jerusalem and the language of ideals and myths, important in the early Yemenite days. The closer the Yemenite settlers, both religious and Zionist, get to the Ashkenazi settlers and the Orthodox believers, the wider becomes the gap between those two communities. The two groups disagree about how to depict everyday life in Jerusalem. While the Ashkenazi settlers strive to develop a practical secular language, the Yemenite settlers build their world around ancient myths. An attempt to cooperate with the Ashkenazi Orthodox community culminates with a racist attack.

The narrator of *Shiloh Village* links the Yemenites to the ten lost tribes, turning them into a bridge between exile and redemption without resorting to the Zionist negation of exile. Their suffering is seen on their faces: "Exile has blackened their faces, which are like the edges of a pot, . . . for indeed their exile is dark and bitter—for many generations they have dwelt among evil people" (15).

In Jerusalem the Yemenites confront famine, hostile overlords—first the Ottomans, then the British—and a hostile Ashkenazi community, who are "astonished at the sight of these dark-skinned Jews" (16). Mediated from the eyes of Abraham Mahfoud, one of the key figures of Zarchi's narrative, the plot of the novel accentuates the fading of any messianic hope due to the ingrained racism of the Ashkenazi community:

> [Abraham] was amazed to see that everyone continued to look at the street, as if they had not seen him enter and complete their minyan. For a while he stood and waited patiently. . . . Then his anger exploded, his voice emerged as a furious high-pitched squeal, and he excoriated the group: "You are wretched and evil! You do not deserve to be setting foot on the soil of Jerusalem!" . . . He felt utterly abandoned, lonely, and desolate. He had come from so far away; he is a foreigner in this vast land, a tree severed from its roots, without father or friend; every person he meets is a malicious foe; he has nowhere to rest his head, and he has no hope of getting a loaf of bread for his children without anguish and insult. His pride had been crushed, and his soul was pulverized. (52–53)

The gaps between the communities stand in stark contrast to the messianic hope grounded in unity, as demonstrated by the recurring reference to the Yemenite myth of the lost ten tribes. Different characters in this novel wonder about the inability of European Jews to acknowledge their brethren as equal. The failure to reunite the ideal with reality threatens to leave both communities in a state of permanent exile: "Is this the Jerusalem that Jews were yearning for all these generations? Is this the redemption of the soul they were always hoping for? It is, after all, enslavement of the body pure and simple, much worse than things were in Yemen" (59). And further, "There, in Yemen, the Jew was like the son of a king in exile among the evil gentiles, enslaved on the outside and free on the inside, which gave him strength to endure the torments. . . . Here, by contrast, there is exile within His sacred Jerusalem, sorrow on the outside and torments and insults on the inside" (62).

The perspective of the novel remains close to that of the Yemenite protagonists. It enables Zarchi to adopt a mythic or "Sambatyonic" view, often at odds with reality. Zarchi situates the narrator's voice and perspective as far in the background as he can, allowing the many characters to take possession of the story for long stretches. The extraordinarily wide scope of his canvas allowed him to shape a polyphonic historical-anthropological narrative (for example, he worked hard to avoid the Eurocentric Ashkenazi dubbing of the Yemenite dialect), a narrative that depicts three generations who gradually come to terms with both the past and the present.

Yosef Tobi described the harsh conditions immigrants suffered in his history of the Yemenite culture.[59] During the first decades of Yemenite settlement in Palestine, natural demographic growth was negative. Those who chose to emigrate from Yemen began choosing Egypt and even India over Palestine, according to Tobi.[60] Tobi was deeply impressed by the accuracy of Zarchi's take on the Yemenite community, and the contemporary advertisement he quoted from *Havatzelet* sounds much like Zarchi's descriptions: "Having come from the city of Sana'a in Yemen, we . . . wander the streets and find ourselves barred from the marketplaces. No one has any compassion or mercy, no one helps or supports us, and no one takes us in."[61]

Shiloh Village won a little more attention than Zarchi's other novels, maybe because it touched on a sensitive issue in Israel, that is, the social and economic gaps between Ashkenazi and Mizrahi Jews. Critics read Zarchi's novel next to another novel of the early *yishuv*, Haim Hazaz's *Thou That Dwellest in the Garden* (*HaYoshevet BaGanim*, 1944), which traced three generations of Yemenite settlement in Jerusalem. Historian of literature Hillel Barzel described this novel as a "meta-realistic" work that fused "visions and naturalism," which for Barzel "fit the Yemenite's self-image in its traditional clothing, taking shape in protagonists whose spirits rise to the heavenly spheres despite being surrounded by vice and temptation."[62]

Thou That Dwellest in the Garden won a level of recognition that Zarchi never received, not even for *Shiloh Village*, possibly because Hazez's novel relied on a more conventional structure and set of narrative devices. Zarchi's radical documentary approach convinced Gershon Shaked that his literary skills were wanting; Shaked preferred Hazaz's "spatial and thematic motifs": "Zarchi took the peel from Hazaz and threw away the content. . . . He collected Yemenite material and studied the genealogy of the place very well, but did not leave his own mark on the material. . . . Much like the previous novel [*Unsown Land*], here the materials are left to their own devices."[63]

This very effect that Shaked deplored was one that Zarchi quite consciously sought. In November 1945 he wrote with undisguised pride about a conversation with Yehuda Ratzabi: "The knowledgeable Yemenite scholar told me that the whole book possesses an original Yemenite spirit, as if I was a Yemenite author."[64] Is it possible that many misinterpreted Zarchi's subversive documentary approach? Mordechai Robinson had accused Zarchi of "chronic psychological detachment, consisting of a certain degree of negation of sentiment."[65] Dov Sadan believed that the novel's depiction of Zionism amounted to a failure: "Many characters are portrayed in the story

Shiloh Village, but the storyteller succeeded in depicting the whole congregation of our Yemenite brethren only as 'a holy seed, an ancient race,' Jews 'who have escaped their bitter enemy and have managed to find themselves a path toward the redemption of Zion and the renewal of their lives in it— be the conditions as they may.'"[66]

Shiloh Village follows the conflict between Zionist settlers and "Ishmaelites" from an ambivalent perspective: The need for a Jewish homeland is accepted even as the price paid by the local population is acknowledged. The key is the way the Yemenite settlers see the conflict. On the one hand, they endorse the idea that settling the land is the fulfillment of a biblical promise. On the other hand, they never give up their messianic and mythic discourse, nor do they avert their eyes from their Arab neighbors. After experiencing many hardships, the Yemenites choose to found their settlement close to the Arab village Siluan, on the outskirts of Jerusalem. Ignoring the recurrent warnings of the Ashkenazi community, they succeed in forming an alliance with the local Arab leadership. The sheik of Siluan ensures that the settlement is protected even in 1929, when violent clashes break out between Jews and Arabs in the rest of the land. As we listen to the Yemenite settlers, the usual image of savage tribal violence never appears, and instead we are informed about the interests of the colonialist powers, described as "countries seeking revenge and inciting conflict between the two peoples of this land, secretly paying money and encouraging hate, preventing Israel from being redeemed" (285).

Can it be surprising that in the late 1940s and early 1950s so many Israeli readers rejected this message? Zarchi was wise enough to keep the critique hidden among dramatic sentences describing the "dark clouds" over the land and the Jewish settlers who "heroically and honorably defend their lives." But piercing accusations lash out: "The actions of the Jews, intensifying from one conflict to the next, provoked resentment among the Ishmaelites" (287).

In spite of the arrangement with the sheik, the Yemenite settlers sensed that "the time of [messianic] return seemed to move farther and farther away from them" (289). Indeed, in 1936 they were forced to leave their homes by Zionists who threatened to stop all of the support they'd provided up to that point.

Why did Zarchi choose the Yemenite community as the topic of his last work? Yosef Tobi argued that the book grew out of a series of conversations between Zarchi and his neighbor, Abraham Ovadia, a member of the vanished community of Shiloh. It was he, according to Tobi, who convinced Zarchi to write "a Yemenite *Unsown Land*."[67] It is equally possible that the inspiration was Zarchi's sudden comprehension, after years of conflicts and disappointments, that the only possible alternative to the Zionist national-ist narrative was the mythic narrative of the Yemenites. After all, it was the only *aliyah* that preceded the Ashkenazis' second *aliyah*.

But what of melancholy and fetishism? Zarchi saw a certain desire for pain in the Yemenite anecdotes, a masochistic impulse that lies at the heart of every fetishistic passion for the real. As he explained it, "All the tribes are drawn to Jerusalem, and they are all involved in settling it, but those who come from Yemen are more lovesick with the place than anyone else—they become attached to the pangs of their love, which give purpose to their lives" (327). Yemenite myths and folklore became the core of the language of affect that suited Zarchi and his protagonists. In contrast to the realistic-scientific-nationalistic Ashkenazi version of history, these myth-oriented stories opened up the possibility of what Judith Butler called "melancholic identification." This form of identification allows material objects to slip away because the ego preserves them by internalizing the objects, denying that the loss is complete.[68] The pleasure the individual psyche gets from the melancholic celebration of the loss turns this into a dialectical phe-nomenon: "Melancholy is both the refusal of grief and the incorporation of loss, a miming of the death it cannot mourn."[69] If we transform this theor-etical language to the more concrete language of working through histor-ical and political symbols, then a melancholic pleasure celebrating the loss of a mythic Jerusalem implies the loss of a mythic sign of wholeness and unity, real time and messianic time, time and space. Jerusalem itself be-longs to a theopolitical register that precedes political Zionism, and—as the Yemenite example demonstrates—supersedes it by detaching the allegory from the real city.

An examination of Zarchi's literary language reveals that discussing a melancholic alternative to the nostalgic and nationalistic is possible when one employs myth; this approach exposes the true distance between the promise and the realization, between the historical discourse of Zionism and its politics, the supposed utopian content and the politics that covers its own destructive apparatus with an idealistic language.

Shiloh Village does not end with redemption but with acceptance of suffering and pain as inevitable. If there is fetish in this, it functions largely to move the reader to reexamine his or her basic assumptions. In structural terms Zarchi radicalized both ends of the equation: He radicalized the idealistic language up to the point of collapse, but he also attached the idealistic discourse to a dark, mythic language of destruction and permanent exile, possibly exile inside Jerusalem. Then, at the very end, the Yemenites offered him a way out, a rejection of the Zionist demand for normalizing and secularizing Hebrew, sticking to the ancient theological root rather than building on the detached roots of a reinvented language.

Tobi mourned the sinking of Zarchi's novel into oblivion: It was eclipsed, he wrote, by contemporaneous works by Haim Hazaz and Mordechai Tabib. Haya Hoffmann also decried the novel's negative reviews; she praised *it* as a heroic effort to rescue from oblivion the Yemenites of Jerusalem. In her analysis of the book, she writes of Zarchi: "He also describes how they preceded their Ashkenazi counterparts as pioneers, but unfortunately no one remembers these acts, which were performed modestly, without publicity, and using meager means, and [therefore] the Ashkenazis became known as the founding pioneers."[70] Could Zarchi's use of language, melancholic and mythic, have been borrowed from Hazaz, who published *Hayoshevet Baganim* in 1944, while Zarchi was doing his research among the Yemenite elders? Such is Hoffmann's hypothesis, and she sees an influence of Arabic on Zarchi's style as well: "It is peppered with verses and passages from the sages, yet it remains original and independent."[71] For Hoffmann, the novel presented "the sublime, ideal, beautiful side of Yemenite life in the kibbutz," as the Yemenites "arrived in the land with their hearts full of the messianic idea, but when they stumbled upon earthly Jerusalem, everyday life, they postponed their dreams and devoted their efforts to a life of work and construction."[72] She relates the gap between ideals and reality to the pragmatic rhetoric she finds in Zarchi: "Zarchi's book indicates that in the land of Israel there is no place for dreams and fantasies."[73] For her, the structure of the novel is affirmative, leading from the first generation of Yemenite immigrants—"representing traditional, spiritual Judaism"—to the second generation—"the antithesis, the generation in thrall to the materialism of the world."[74]

In my view, Zarchi's last novel and his whole poetics rely on a set of very different assumptions. Instead of a story about Zionist realization and secular redemption, it is a story about a double loss—the loss of the Yemenite past, "devoured by the evening darkness," and the demand on the part of secular Ashkenazi Zionists that the lost past be suppressed. That loss notwithstanding, this book is a celebration of, among other things, a mythical past that keeps rising from the depths. Thinking about this structure in psychoanalytical terms, it is the reenactment of the trauma that triggers the appearance of the mythical past—the trauma is not the suffering of the immigrants but the Ashkenazi attempt to silence it.

Walter Benjamin and Gershom Scholem correctly identified the temporal order of melancholy and community. As Vivian Liska explains, Scholem, following Benjamin, recognized "the language of deferral that postpones accomplishment, resists change and progression, thwarts any message or conclusion, and ultimately refuses meaning altogether."[75] To fend off "left-wing melancholy," as Walter Benjamin called it, Scholem mentioned the lament, calling it "a deferral [that] is achieved in language, a language of endless recurrence ... where 'the dark and melancholic light' is brought to shine like Benjamin's messianic sparks in the night."[76] As Scholem showed in his classic essay on messianism, Judaism (after the destruction of the temple) always lived between three forces—the conservative, the restorative, and the utopian. For him, those three "aim at a state of things which has never yet existed."[77]

While lament reminds one of the lost exilic world that cannot be brought back to life, melancholy is future-oriented and has a clear utopian dimension. It is impossible to separate the double loss that traps it from the promise of future release, a doomed u-topia. Having discovered the worthlessness of the ideal, melancholy cannot detach from its potential. Even when it acknowledges the potential destructive force of this ideal, it cannot separate from its promise of redemption. A work about Zionism and melancholy exposes the internal temporal order of melancholy itself, especially in a theopolitical context; unlike mourning, and in contrast to Freud's early emphasis, it is obsessed with more than the past loss of an object—the future utopian community is also of interest. If mourning is oriented toward an overcoming of the past—understanding and separating from it—melancholy instrumentalizes it for the sake of a different future, for both the self and the community.

6. A Mizrahi Melancholy

One of the more interesting interpretations of the melancholic image, especially in the context of a Middle Eastern culture, is that of Yosef Raz, who studied queer Mizrahi cinema.[78] While Zionism drew on the negation of exile, recent Mizrahi authors and filmmakers "have been restaging their lost Arab-Jewish past and confronting the trauma of the immigration to Israel while critically exploring the traumatic construction of the Mizrahi gendered body under the Ashkenazi Orientalist gaze."[79] This Mizrahi identification was based on a notion of what he calls "ethnic melancholy."[80] The ethnic melancholy of the Mizrahi Jew is double: "The Mizrahi subject was not only required to negate and eradicate his Arab identity but also forced to re-identify with that loss, because the Mizrahi subject was prevented from fully participating in the Ashkenazi national ideal."[81] A Mizrahi protagonist and his or her reflections on this double loss are essential to any alternative to the normative discourse: "This discourse foreclosed any possibility of remembering and missing their Arab home and homeland. Such memories became taboo."[82] Following Freud's "Mourning and Melancholy" and Ella Shohat's "Taboo Memories and Diasporic Visions,"[83] Raz proposes a postcolonialist reading of this double loss as an act of political refusal to forget the diasporic life and decolonize (or depathologize) the ethnic melancholy of the Mizrahi protagonist.[84] Raz's argument is similar to a recent postcolonial theory written by a leading theoretician of melancholy, Ranjana Khanna. Her analysis starts by refusing the analytical tools of psychoanalysis, which she identifies with "coloniality" or what "brought into the world an idea of being that was dependent on colonial political and ontological relations, and through its disciplinary practices, formalized and perpetuated an idea of uncivilized, primitive, concealed, and timeless colonized peoples."[85] As Khanna points out, Freud worked within the confines of a Western understanding of dislocation—"Dislocation from political affiliation led Freud to a different conceptualization of the ego"—that unsurprisingly led to "Freud's own melancholic response to the loss of national affiliation, and thus also of power, [that] was eventually acted out in the form of a lament."[86]

Raz does not quote from Khanna, but his understanding of Mizrahi identity follows the same course from Freud's sense of dislocation to a postcolonial understanding of placeless and homeless melancholy: "Memory of the Mizrahi past is a place that cannot be revisited, even if one can travel to geographic territory that appears to be a place of 'origin.' 'Home' is a mythic place of desire in the imagination of the Mizrahi immigrant."[87] Acknowledging the past and its loss is the only way to overcome the traumatic unconscious repetition.

Zarchi's emphasis on the remythification of the Zionist ideal seems to follow the same logic of double refusal that Khanna and Raz describe.

I have argued that Zarchi's poetics—especially in his last stories and novel—reflects an attempt to depathologize the diasporic identity. Zarchi's documentary approach suggests the same investment in the psychological and imaginary structure of a lost-not-lost, which Judith Butler, with Raz following her, defines as the place of subversive possibility.[88] The process that led from the Ashkenazi mystic in "Sambatyon" to the Yemenite myth in *Shiloh Village* proves that Zarchi's poetics was built on this subversive possibility and a diasporic negation of negation.

Notes

1. Judith Butler, *The Psychic Life of Power: Theories in Subjection* (Stanford, CA: Stanford University Press, 1997), 169.

2. Giorgio Agamben, *Stanzas: Word and Phantasm in Western Culture*, trans. Ronald L. Martinez (Minneapolis: University of Minnesota Press, 1993), 20.

3. Yael Zerubavel, *Recovered Roots: Collective Memory and the Making of Israeli National Tradition* (Chicago: University of Chicago Press, 1995), 33.

4. Ibid., 83.

5. Ron Kuzar, *Hebrew and Zionism: A Discourse Analytic Cultural Study* (Berlin: Mouton de Gruyter, 2001), 132.

6. Ibid., 81.

7. Joseph Massad, *The Persistence of the Palestinian Question: Essays on Zionism and the Palestinians* (New York: Routledge, 2006), 38. See also Tom Segev, *One Palestine, Complete: Jews and Arabs under the British Mandate* (New York: Henry Holt, 2000).

8. Zerubavel, *Recovered Roots*, 30.

9. Hugo Bergman, "Torat Ahad Ha'am ve'hatfisa haproletarit" [The philosophy of Ahad Ha'am and proletarian perception], *Sheifoteinu* 3, no. 3 (1932): 85.

10. Gershom Scholem, "On Our Language: A Confession," trans. Ora Wiskind, *History and Memory* 2, no. 2 (1990): 97–99 (emphasis in original).

11. Entry from 11 October 1916, Gershom Scholem, *Lamentations of Youth: The Diaries of Gershom Scholem, 1913–1919*, trans. Antony David Skinner (Cambridge, MA: Harvard University Press, 2007), 143.

12. Zeev Sternhell, *The Founding Myths of Israel: Nationalism, Socialism, and the Making of Israel*, trans. David Maisel (Princeton, NJ: Princeton University Press, 1998), 72.

13. Ron Kuzar defines "Narodnik" as a "populist, romantic, and nihilistic view of revolutionary Russian critics of the regime." See Kuzar, *Hebrew and Zionism*, 49. Robert H. McNeal defined the name given to pre-Marxist revolutionaries and the socialist revolutionaries, in Robert H. McNeal, "Women in the Russian Radical Movement," *Journal of Social History* 5, no. 2 (Winter 1971–72): 145.

14. Kuzar, *Hebrew and Zionism*, 53. Kuzar quotes here from Michael Confino, *Misankt-peterburg leleningrad: Masot al Darka Hahistorit shel Rusya* [From St. Petersburg to Leningrad: Essays in Russian history] (Tel Aviv: Am Oved, 1993), 310.

15. Kuzar, *Hebrew and Zionism*, 63.

16. Quoted in ibid., 81.

17. Boaz Neumann, *Land and Desire in Early Zionism*, trans. Haim Watzman (Waltham, MA: Brandeis University Press, 2011), 45.

18. Kuzar, *Hebrew and Zionism*, 117.

19. Ibid., 143.

20. Chaim Gans, *Teoria Politit LaAm HaYehudi: Sholsha Narrativim Zioniim* [A Political theory for the Jewish people: Three Zionist narratives] (Tel Aviv: Yediot Ahronot, 2011), 51.

21. Michael Gluzman, "Sovereignty and Melancholia: Israeli Poetry after 1948," *Jewish Social Studies* 18, no. 3 (Spring/Summer 2012): 164–79.

22. Eliezer Ben-Yehuda, "Shituf Anshei ruah be-itsuv demutah shel ha-medinah" [Contribution of intellectuals in the shaping of the state] *Davar*, 28 March 1949, 1. Quoted and translated in Gluzman, "Sovereignty and Melancholia," 167.

23. Gluzman, "Sovereignty and Melancholia," 168.

24. Boaz Neumann, *Land and Desire in Early Zionism*, trans. Haim Watzman (Waltham, MA: Brandeis University Press, 2011), 82.

25. Ilan Stavans, *Resurrecting Hebrew* (New York: Random House, 2005), 35.

26. Israel Zarchi, "Sambatyon," in *Yalkut Sipurim* [A collection of stories] (Tel Aviv: Yachdav, 1983). Page numbers for subsequent quotes for "Sambatyon" follow this edition and will be given in line. All translations are mine.

27. Zvi Ben-Dor Benite, *The Ten Lost Tribes: A World History* (Oxford: Oxford University Press, 2009). Cheder, literally "room," is the early Jewish religious educational institution in Europe, beginning in the eighteenth century. It usually had small class sizes and took place at the teacher's house or in a specific room; students would learn Hebrew, Talmud, and the basics of Jewish law.

28. Ibid., 3, 83.

29. Ibid., 83.

30. Ibid., 17.

31. Ibid., 20.

32. *Midrash Rabbah: Ecclesiastes*, trans. A. Cohen (New York: Soncino, 1983), Parasha 3: 11.

33. In the King James translation: "Thus saith the Lord; A voice was heard in Ramah, lamentation, and bitter weeping; Rachel weeping for her children refused to be comforted for her children, because they were not." See www.biblegateway.com (last accessed June 16, 2016).

34. The best-known research of the Sabbatean movement is, of course, Gershom Scholem's book, *Sabbatai Sevi: The Mystical Messiah: 1626–1676*, trans. R. J. Zwi Werblowsky (Princeton, NJ: Princeton University Press, 1973).

35. Ben-Dor Benite, *Ten Lost Tribes*, 80.

36. Ibid., 83.

37. It is interesting to note that in the English translation of Scholem's text, the end of the sentence, "and a son will not feel ashamed before his father," is dropped. See Gershom Scholem, "Toward an Understanding of the Messianic Idea in Judaism," in *Toward an Understanding of the Messianic Idea in Judaism* (New York: Schocken, 1971), 12. The analogy between "the face of the generation" and "the face of a dog" appears also in S. Y. Agnon's *Only Yesterday*, with the addition "and not just an ordinary dog, but a crazy dog." See S. Y. Agnon, *Only Yesterday*, trans. Barbara Harshav (Princeton, NJ: Princeton University Press, 2000), 621.

38. Todd Hasak-Lowy, "A Mad Dog's Attack on Secularized Hebrew: Rethinking Agnon's Temol-Shilshom," *Prooftexts* 24, no. 2 (Spring 2004): 173.

39. Ibid., 172.

40. Agnon, *Only Yesterday*, 67.

41. Eyal Chowers, *The Political Philosophy of Zionism: Trading Jewish Words for a Hebraic Land* (Cambridge: Cambridge University Press, 2011), 23.

42. Julia Kristeva, *Black Sun: Depression and Melancholia*, trans. Leon S. Roudiez (New York: Columbia University Press, 1992), 7.

43. Chowers, *The Political Philosophy of Zionism*, 157.

44. Ibid., 168.

45. Israel Zarchi, *Nachalat Avot* [Land of our fathers] (Jerusalem: Reuven Mas, 1946). Page numbers for subsequent quotes for *Land of Our Fathers* follow this edition and will be given in line. All translations are mine.

46. Dov Sadan, *Ben Din LeHeshbon: Massot al Sofrim veSfarim* [Between judgments: Essays on authors and books] (Tel Aviv: Dvir, 1963), 281.

47. Meir Bar Ilan, "Ha'kvura beNahalat Avot ben Yehudim beEt HaAtika" [Patrimonial burial among the Jews in the ancient period], in *Kvarim veNohagei Kvura BeEretz Israel baEt HaAtika* [Graves and burial practices in Israel in the ancient period], ed. I. Singer (Jerusalem: Yad Ben-Zvi, 1994), 212–29.

48. Ahad Ha'am, "Ancestor Worship," *Selected Essays*, trans. Leon Simon (Philadelphia: Jewish Publication Society of America, 1912), 215–16.

49. Zarchi, *Kefar ha'Shiloah* [Shiloh Village] (Tel Aviv: Am Oved, 1948). Page numbers for subsequent quotes for *Shiloh Village* follow this edition and will be given in line. All translations are mine.

50. Bil'u (Bilu'im in plural) was a movement of young Russian Jewish socialists who fled Russia during the pogroms and antisemitic legislation of 1882. As described in the section dedicated to Zarchi's *Youth*, the members of the Bilu'im settled, with the help of the Baron Edmond de Rothschild, in Mikve Israel and G'dera. For more about this topic, see Ran Aaronsohn, *Rothschild and Early Jewish Colonization in Palestine* (New York: Rowman & Minefield, 2000).

51. Undated entry from January 1945. Diary, Israel Zarchi Archive, file 171, sig. K-3694, Gnazim Institute, Tel Aviv.

52. Edward W. Said, *Orientalism* (London: Penguin Books, 1995), 171.

53. "For European [Bilu'im] Zionists the Yemenite immigrants in Palestine resembled the pious communities who had dwelled in the holy cities for centuries. . . . [They] were frequently viewed by the ideologically motivated secular Zionist pioneers with the same suspicion they displayed towards the traditional, non-productive Jewish communities of the Arab ha-Aratzot. But in at least one respect the Yemenites were different. . . . They would help create a Jewish laboring proletariat in Palestine which was able to compete with Arab labour." Tudor Parfitt, *The Road to Redemption: The Jews of Yemen, 1900–1950* (Leiden: Brill, 1996), 52.

54. Sami Shalom Chetrit, *Intra-Jewish Conflict in Israel: White Jews, Black Jews* (New York: Routledge, 2010), 28.

55. Ella Shohat, "Rupture and Return: Zionist Discourse and the Study of Arab Jews," in *Social Text* 21, no. 2 (2003): 60. See also Ari Ariel's excellent discussion of this history and conceptualization in the introduction to his *Jewish-Muslim Relations and Migration from Yemen to Palestine in the Late Nineteenth and Twentieth Centuries* (Leiden: Brill, 2013).

56. Shohat, "Rupture and Return," 60.

57. Walter Benjamin, "On the Concept of History," in *Selected Writings*, ed. Howard Eiland and Michael W. Jennings (Cambridge, MA: Harvard University Press, 2003), 4: 394.

58. Yehouda Shenhav, *The Arab Jews: A Postcolonial Reading: Nationalism, Religion, and Ethnicity* (Stanford, CA: Stanford University Press, 2006), 149.

59. Yosef Tobi, *The Jews of Yemen: Studies in Their History and Culture* (Leiden: Brill, 1999), 95–103.

60. Ibid., 102.

61. Yosef Tobi, "Al Kfar Hashiloah ve'al Hasefer 'Kfar Hashiloah' Le'Israel Zarchi'" [About Kfar Hashiloah and about the book *Kfar Hashiloah* by Israel Zarchi], *Afikim* 127/128 (August 2006): 29.

62. Hillel Barzel, *HaMe'a HaChatzuya: MiModernism lePostmodernism* [The split century: From modernism to postmodernism] (Tel Aviv: Poalim, 2011), 476.

63. Gershon Shaked, "Meotam Sichim she'Biladeihem en Etzim: Al Yetzirato shel Israel Zarchi" [About those bushes without which there are no trees: About Israel Zarchi's literature], *Bitzron* 4, no. 15 (1982): 17.

64. Diary, 11 November 1945, Zarchi Archive.

65. Mordechai Robinson, "Motivim Yishuviim (Hatlishut shel Zarchi)" [Motifs of settlement: Zarchi's detachment], *Haaretz*, February 12, 1937. See also the discussion in Aviva Mahlo, *Ben Shnei Nofim* [Between two landscapes] (Jerusalem: Reuven Mas, 1991), 137.

66. Dov Stock (Sadan), "Ahrit Davar," Epilogue to Israel Zarchi, *Kfar Hashiloah* (Tel Aviv: Am Oved, 1948), 364.

67. Tobi, "Al Kfar Hashiloah," 33.

68. Butler, *Psychic Life*, 134.

69. Ibid., 142.

70. Haya Hoffmann, "Saga Teimanit al Olei TRMB" [A Yemenite saga about the immigration of 1881], in *S'ei Yona: Yehudei Teiman be'Israel* [Go, dove: Yemenite Jews in Israel], ed. Shalom Peri (Tel Aviv: Am Oved, 1983), 116. I would like to thank Avner Holtzman for this excellent reference.

71. Ibid., 116. See also Joseph Klausner, "Darkei Yetzirato" [His ways of creating], in *Iturim: Measef Sifruti Lezecher Israel Zarchi* [Ornaments: A literary collection to commemorate Israel Zarchi], ed. Haim Toren (Jerusalem: Achiasaf, 1949), 64. See also Hoffmann, "Saga," 116.

72. Hoffmann, "Saga," 120.

73. Ibid.

74. Ibid.

75. Vivian Liska, "Against Melancholy: On the Demonic in Gershom Scholem," in *Das Dämonische: Schicksale einer Kategorie der Zweideutigkeit nach Goethe*, ed. Lars Friedrich (Paderborn: Fink, 2014), 323.

76. Ibid., 324. Liska is analyzing here Scholem's own expressions.

77. Gershom Scholem, *"The Messianic Idea in Judaism" and Other Essays on Jewish Spirituality*, trans. Michael A. Meyer (New York: Schocken, 1972), 3.

78. Yosef Raz, *The Politics of Loss and Trauma in Contemporary Israeli Cinema* (New York: Routledge, 2011). Lital Levy explains the term *Mizrahi* thus: "Mizrahi (plural mizrahim), Hebrew for 'Easterner,' refers to a collective identity created in Israel to distinguish the totality of Asian, African, and Southeastern European Jews from the population of Eastern, Western, and Central European Jews, collectively referred to as 'Ashkenazim.'" Levy

contrasts this opposition with the much better concept Arab-Jew. See Lital Levy, *Poetic Trespasses: Writing between Hebrew and Arabic in Israel/Palestine* (Princeton, NJ: Princeton University Press, 2014), 6.

79. Ibid., 6.
80. Ibid., 70.
81. Ibid., 65.
82. Ibid., 63.
83. Ella Shohat, "Taboo Memories and Diasporic Visions: Columbus, Palestine, and the Arab-Jew," in *Performing Hybridity*, ed. May Joseph and Jennifer Natalya Fink (Minneapolis: University of Minnesota Press, 1999), 131–58.
84. Raz, *Politics of Loss and Trauma*, 83.
85. Ranjana Khanna, *Dark Continents: Psychoanalysis and Colonialism* (Durham, NC: Duke University Press, 2003), 6.
86. Ibid., 148.
87. Raz, *Politics of Loss and Trauma*, 67.
88. Yosef Raz, "Restaging the Primal Scene of Loss: Melancholia and Ethnicity in Israeli Cinema," *Third Text* 20, no. 314 (May/July 2006): 487–98. Raz quotes and analyzes Butler's observations in his text.

AFTERWORD

CANCER TOOK ISRAEL ZARCHI AT THE AGE OF thirty-eight. He asked his wife, Esther, to keep their two daughters away from his deathbed. As it turned out, he died on the operating table, after a final desperate surgical intervention, on July 24, 1947. Immediately before the operation, he wrote his wife a letter in which he explained his final thoughts, a literary and personal testimony: "I have lived a life of high spiritual intensity. I am happy for those hours when the revival of Zion gave me hope; without them I do not know how my heart could have survived the isolation of exilic life and its darkness."[1]

Those who came to mourn his passing were close friends and family. Shai Agnon read the kaddish, and both Joseph Klausner and Haim Toren delivered eulogies in which they noted that death had taken their friend at his artistic peak, after a crucial stylistic turn. Many felt that he had never found his proper place among the literati of the yishuv and that his style had impeded his message. In a later essay Klausner characterized his writing as "inflicted with *imperfectum*." The partial reality or imperfection that his former student found in his surroundings had become one with his writing, blocking readers' identification with his creations, "characters that appear to be deficient"; Zarchi, he said, "did not offer any corrections" to the aporias.[2] A failure to supply such instructive closure had to be, Klausner believed, an imperfection.

Toren described his friend's writing as "essentially negative" and "focusing mostly on the [disappointments related to the] land and [to a] woman."[3] Other friends talked about Zarchi's brief life as abundant with overflowing melancholy. They described a man who seemed disconnected but also warm and loving, full of ideas but unfocused and inclined to generalize.

A eulogy published the day after the funeral in *Davar*—a newspaper that served as the platform for the Labor movement and Ben-Gurion's party—said that as Zarchi grew older "he became more and more attached to the act of settling the land of Israel, and to that end he never missed an opportunity to resolve arguments between pioneers, to listen to their conversations, and to absorb a modicum of their existence."[4] This short and easy eulogy tried to do what Zionist rhetoric did best, which is to embrace its critics rather than listen to them.

I conclude with Zarchi's own literary testimony, connecting his idealism and melancholy—depicted in this book as a case of "left-wing melancholy"—to the political-theological context around him. As demonstrated above, I contend that his poetic drive was to extend literature itself from within, rather than from without, as a self-consciously "minor" writer: "My aim should be," he wrote in 1937, after completing *And the Oil Flows to the Mediterranean*, "the extension of the Hebraic novel. I know that this is strange, foreign, even to the best among the readers of Hebrew. But I say that it is possible to write a good novel *inside* Eretz Israel and not necessarily *about* Eretz Israel."[5] Indeed, a cypher and a symptom simultaneously.

Zarchi's symptomatic testimony cannot be considered complete without the work of his daughter, the poet and author Nurit Zarchi. In her novel *Games of Loneliness* (*Mishakey B'didut*, 1999), a character asks: "How can I let go of this sense of responsibility for his death, either because I caused it or because I did not prevent it? Somehow we believe, deep inside, that love permits us to thwart death, so each death is perceived as a failure of love's ability to do so. Do words sketch or constitute a situation? Do they know, or suggestively incite? Fair is foul, and foul is fair, so whisper the witches."[6] Nurit Zarchi has offered another way to depathologize the past, her own and ours: She broke out of left-wing melancholy by thematizing it. Her journey into the heart of her childhood, overlapping with some of her father's darkest times, exposes a moment that can shape a melancholy quite different from the one that developed after his death. Admitting the fusion of evil and good, foul and fair, is a good place to start.

As Wendy Brown shows, when she explains what "left-wing melancholy" is, the best intentions often lead to the worst results.[7] A language of nostalgic idealism is often nothing more than a conservative cover for a language of norms and control. As an alternative to the social-democrat language of governmentality, Brown and Nurit Zarchi propose to reexamine the language of affect that favors a left-wing analysis and its progressive self-destruction.[8] Such an examination was the purpose of these pages.

Notes

1. Diary, 7 June 1947, Israel Zarchi Archive, file 171, K-3700a, Gnazim Institute, Tel Aviv.

2. Joseph Klausner, "Darkei Yetzirato" [His method of writing], in *Iturim: Neasef Sifruti Lezecher Israel Zarchi*, ed. Haim Toren (Jerusalem: Achiasaf, 1948), 59.

3. Haim Toren, "Introduction," in *Iturim: Neasef Sifruti Lezecher Israel Zarchi*, 74.

4. "Ha'sofer Israel Zarchi" [The author Israel Zarchi], *Davar*, Nekrolog supplement, 25 July 1947. Unidentified author.

5. Diary, 9 May 1937, Zarchi Archive, file 171, K-3694.

6. Nurit Zarchi, *Mishakey B'didut* [Games of loneliness] (Tel Aviv: Yediot Ahronot, 1999), 24.

7. Wendy Brown explains how a "left-wing melancholy" turned—in spite of its high ideals—to "a mournful conservative, backward-looking attachment to a feeling, analysis, or relationship that has been rendered thinglike and frozen in the heart of the putative leftist." Wendy Brown, "Resisting Left Melancholy," *Boundary* 26, no. 3 (1999), 22.

8. Ibid., 27. As Brown writes, emotions—"including those of sorrow, rage, and anxiety about broken promises and lost compasses—that sustain our attachments to left analyses and left projects ought to be examined for what they create in the way of potentially conservative and even self-destructive undersides of putatively progressive political aims."

SELECTED BIBLIOGRAPHY

Aaronsohn, Ran. *Rothschild and Early Jewish Colonization in Palestine*. New York: Rowman & Minefield, 2000.

Adorno, Theodor. "Heine the Wound." In *Notes to Literature*, edited by Peter Uwe Hohendahl and Sander Gilman, 80–85. Lincoln: University of Nebraska Press, 1991.

Agamben, Giorgio. *Stanzas: Word and Phantasm in Western Culture*. Translated by Ronald L. Martinez. Minneapolis: University of Minnesota Press, 1993.

———. *State of Exception*. Translated by Kevin Attell. Chicago: Chicago University Press, 2005.

Agnon, S. Y. *Only Yesterday*. Translated by Barbara Harshav. Princeton, NJ: Princeton University Press, 2000.

Almog, Oz. *The Sabra: The Creation of the New Jew*. Translated by Haim Watzman. Berkeley: University of California Press, 2000.

Anderson, Benedict. *Imagined Communities: Reflections on the Origin and Spread of Nationalism*. London: Verso, 2006.

Anidjar, Gil. *The Jew, the Arab: A History of the Enemy*. Stanford, CA: Stanford University Press, 2003.

Antebi, Elizabeth. "Baron Edmond de Rothschild (1845–1934): From HaNadiv (The Benefactor) to HaNassi (The Prince)." In *Jewish Studies at the Turn of the 20th Century*. Vol. 2: *Judaism from the Renaissance to Modern Times*, edited by Judit Targarona Borras and Angel Saenz-Badillos, 251–56. Leiden: Brill, 1999.

Ariel, Ari. *Jewish-Muslim Relations and Migration from Yemen to Palestine in the Late Nineteenth and Twentieth Centuries*. Leiden: Brill, 2013.

Aurbach, Efraim E. "Yerushalaim shel Mata vi'Yerushalaim shel Ma'la." In *Yerhushalaim Le'Doroteeiah*, edited by Efraim Aurbach, 156–71. Jerusalem: Magnes, 1968.

Avineri, Shlomo. *The Making of Modern Zionism: Intellectual Origins of the Jewish State*. New York: Basic Books, 1981.

Band, Arnold. *Studies in Modern Jewish Literature*. Philadelphia: Jewish Publication Society, 2003.

Barzel, Hillel. *HaMe'a HaChatzuya: MiModernism lePostmodernism*. Tel Aviv: Poalim, 2011.

Beer, Haim. *Gam Ahavatam, Gam Sin'atam*. Tel Aviv: Am Oved, 2006.

Benbenisti, Meron. *Halom haTzabar haLavan: Autobiographia shel Hitpakchut*. Jerusalem: Keter, 2010.

Benite, Zvi Ben-Dor. *The Ten Lost Tribes: A World History*. Oxford: Oxford University Press, 2009.

Benjamin, Andrew, ed. *Walter Benjamin and History*. London: Continuum, 2005.

Benjamin, Walter. *Gesammelte Schriften* I. Frankfurt am Main: Suhrkamp Verlag, 1991.

———. *The Origins of German Tragic Drama*. Translated by John Osborne. London: Verso, 1998.

———. *Selected Writings*. Vol. 2: *1927–1934*. Edited by Michael W. Jennings, Howard Eiland, and Gary Smith. Cambridge, MA: Harvard University Press, 1999.

———. *Selected Writings*. Vol. 4: *1938–1940*. Edited by Howard Eiland and Michael W. Jennings. Translated by Edmund Jephcott et al. Cambridge, MA: Harvard University Press, 2003.

Benjamin, Walter, and Gershom Scholem. *The Correspondence of Walter Benjamin and Gershom Scholem, 1932–1940*. Translated by Gary Smith and Andrew Lefevre. New York: Schocken, 1989.

Bergman, Hugo. "Torat Ahad Ha'am ve'hatfisa haproletarit." *Sheifoteinu* 3, no. 3 (1932): 85.

Bernstein, Deborah S., and Musia Lipman. "Fragments of Life: From the Diaries of Two Young Women." In *Pioneers and Homemakers: Jewish Women in Pre-State Israel*, edited by Deborah S. Bernstein, 145–64. Albany: State University of New York Press, 1992.

Bertram, Ernst. *Nietzsche: Attempt at a Mythology*. Translated by Robert E. Norton. Urbana: University of Illinois Press, 2009.

Biale, David. *Eros and the Jews: From Biblical Israel to Contemporary America*. Berkeley: University of California Press, 1997.

Bloch, Ernst. "Something's Missing: A Discussion between Ernst Bloch and Theodor W. Adorno on the Contradictions of Utopian Longing." In *The Utopian Function of Art and Literature: Selected Essays*, translated by Jack Zipes and Frank Mechlenbourg, 1–15. Cambridge, MA: MIT Press, 1988.

Blumenberg, Hans. *Shipwreck with Spectator: Paradigm of a Metaphor for Existence*. Translated by Steven Rendall. Cambridge: MIT Press, 1997.

Brooke, George J. *Intertextual Studies in Ben Sira and Tobit, Essays in Honor of Alexander A. Di Lella*. Washington: Catholic Biblical Association of America, 2005.

Brown, Wendy. "Resisting Left Melancholy." *Boundary* 26, no. 3 (1999): 19–27.

Bruggemann, Walter. *A Commentary on Jeremiah: Exile and Homecoming*. Grand Rapids, SD: William B. Eerdman, 1998.

Buber, Martin. *Torat ha'Neviim*. Jerusalem: Mossad Bialik, 1975.

Burton, Robert. *The Anatomy of Melancholy*. Edited by Thomas C. Faulkner, Nicolas K. Kiessling, and Rhonda L. Blair. Oxford: Clarendon Press, 1989.

Butler, Judith. *Precarious Life: The Powers of Mourning and Violence*. London: Verso, 2004.

———. *The Psychic Life of Power: Theories in Subjection*. Stanford, CA: Stanford University Press, 1997.

Capps, Donald. "Melancholia, Utopia, and the Psychoanalysis of Dreams." In *The Blackwell Companion to the Sociology of Religion*, edited by Richard K. Fenn, 84–105. Malden, MA: Blackwell, 2001.

Chetrit, Sami Shalom. *Intra-Jewish Conflict in Israel: White Jews, Black Jews*. New York: Routledge, 2010.

Chowers, Eyal. *The Political Philosophy of Zionism: Trading Jewish Words for a Hebraic Land*. Cambridge: Cambridge University Press, 2011.

Clemens, Justin. "The Abandonment of Sex: Giorgio Agamben, Psychoanalysis and Melancholia." *Theory & Event* 13, no. 1 (2010).

Cohen, Hillel. *Year Zero of the Arab-Israeli Conflict, 1929*. Waltham: Brandeis University Press, 2015.

Confino, Michael. *Misankt-peterburg leleningrad: Masot al Darka Hahistorit shel Rusya*. Tel Aviv: Am Oved, 1993.

Dekel, Mikhal. *Oedipus beKoshinev: Zionut, Sifrut, Tragedia*. Translated by Tal Hever-Hibovsky. Jerusalem: Mossad Bialik, 2014.

Deleuze, Gilles, and Félix Guattari. *Kafka: Toward a Minor Literature*. Translated by Dana Polan. Minneapolis: University of Minnesota Press, 1986.

———. *A Thousand Plateaus: Capitalism and Schizophrenia*. Translated by Brian Massumi. Minneapolis: University of Minnesota Press, 1987.

Esposito, Roberto. "Community and Nihilism." In *The Italian Difference*, edited by Lorenzo Chiesa and Alberto Toscano, 37–54. Melbourne: re.press, 2009.

———. *Terms of the Political: Community, Immunity, Biopolitics*. Translated by Rhiannon Noel Welch. New York: Fordham University Press, 2013.

Ferber, Ilit. *Philosophy and Melancholy: Benjamin's Early Reflections on Theater and Language*. Stanford, CA: Stanford University Press, 2013.

Fieldhouse, D. K. *Western Imperialism in the Middle East, 1914–1958*. Oxford: Oxford University Press, 2006.

Finke, Ulrich. "Dürer and Thomas Mann." In *Essays on Dürer*, edited by C. R. Dodwell, 121–46. Manchester, England: Manchester University Press, 1973.

Freud, Sigmund. *The Standard Edition of the Complete Psychological Works of Sigmund Freud*. Vol. 14. Translated by James Strachey. London: Hogarth Press, 1957.

Gailus, Andreas. *Passions of the Sign: Revolution and Language in Kant, Goethe, and Kleist*. Baltimore, MD: Johns Hopkins University Press, 2006.

Gan, Alon. "Ha'sufim ba'zariach ve'siach lochamim ke'zirei zehut mitpazlim." *Israel* 13 (2008): 267–96.

Gans, Chaim. *Teoria Politit LaAm HaYehudi: Sholsha Narrativim Zioniim*. Tel Aviv: Yediot Ahronot, 2011.

Gertz, Nurit. *Al Daat Atzmo: Arba'a Pirkei Haim Shel Amos Kenan*. Tel Aviv: Am Oved, 2010.

Gilman, Sander L. *Franz Kafka, the Jewish Patient*. New York: Routledge, 1995.

Ginsburg, Shai. *Rhetoric and Nation: The Formation of Hebrew National Culture, 1880–1990*. Syracuse, NY: Syracuse University Press, 2014.

Gluzman, Michael. "Sovereignty and Melancholia: Israeli Poetry after 1948." *Jewish Social Studies* 18, no. 3 (Spring/Summer 2012): 164–79.

Goethe, Johann Wolfgang von. *Faust: The First Part of the Tragedy*. Translated by David Constantine. London: Penguin, 2005.

Govrin, Nurit. "Ha-Nistarot ba-niglot: 'Al ha-shirah veha-prosah shel Asher Barash." In *Keri'at ha-dorot: Sifrut 'ivrit be-ma'aglehah*. Vol. 1. Tel Aviv: Gvanim and Tel Aviv University Press, 2002.

———. "Ledaber al ha'Kotel." *Gag: KeTav Et LeSifrut* no. 5 (Winter 2001): 103.

———. "Naftulei Yetzira: Hamishim Shana Le'ftirato shel S. Ben Zion." *Siman Kria'a: Rivon Meorav LeSifrut* 16/17 (April 1983): 578–92.

Grumberg, Karen. *Place and Ideology in Contemporary Hebrew Literature*. Syracuse, NY: Syracuse University Press, 2011.

Ha'am, Ahad. "Ancestor Worship." In *Selected Essays*, translated by Leon Simon, 205–16. Philadelphia: Jewish Publication Society of America, 1912.

Halper, Jeff. *Between Redemption and Revival: The Jewish Yishuv of Jerusalem in the Nineteenth Century*. Boulder, CO: Westview Press, 1991.

Harshav, Benjamin. *Language in Time of Revolution*. Stanford, CA: Stanford University Press, 1993.

Hasak-Lowy, Todd. "A Mad Dog's Attack on Secularized Hebrew: Rethinking Agnon's *Temol shilshom*." *Prooftexts* 24, no. 2 (2004): 167–98.

Heine, Heinrich. "A Topsy-Turvy World." In *Poems of Heinrich Heine*, translated by Louis Untermeyer, 260. New York: Henry Holt, 1917.

Hever, Hannan. *Lareshet et Haaretz, Lichbosh et haMerchav*. Jerusalem: Mossad Bialik, 2015.

———. *Moledet Ha'mavet Yafah*. Tel Aviv: Am Oved, 2004.

———. *Payetanim u'Viryonim: Tsemihat haShir haPoliti haIvri beErets Israel*. Jerusalem: Mossad Bialik, 1994.

Hobsbawm, Eric. *The Age of Extremes: The Short Twentieth Century, 1914–1991*. London: Vintage Books 1996.

Hobsbawm, Eric, and Terence Ranger, eds. *The Invention of Tradition*. Cambridge: Cambridge University Press, 2012.

Hoffmann, Haya. "Saga Teimanit al Olei TRMB." In *S'ei Yona: Yehudei Teiman be'Israel*, edited by Shalom Seri, 115–31. Tel Aviv: Am Oved, 1983.

Holtzman, Avner. "Yerushalaim HaMandatorit baSifrut HaIvrit." In *Yerushalaim biTkufat HaMandat: Ha'Asiyah ve'Hamoreshet*, edited by Yehoshua ben Arie, 370–92. Jerusalem: Yad Itzhak Ben Tzvi, 2003.

Ilan, Meir Bar. "Ha'kvura beNahalat Avot ben Yehudim beEt HaAtika." In *Kvarim veNohagei Kvura BeEretz Israel baEt HaAtika*, edited by I. Singer, 212–29. Jerusalem: Yad Ben-Zvi, 1994.

Jayne, Edward. *Negative Poetics*. Iowa City: University of Iowa Press, 1992.

Kaplan, Eran. *The Jewish Radical Right: Revisionist Zionism and Its Ideological Legacy*. Madison: University of Wisconsin Press, 2005.

Khanna, Ranjana. *Dark Continents: Psychoanalysis and Colonialism*. Durham, NC: Duke University Press, 2003.

Klausner, Joseph. *The Messianic Idea in Israel*. Translated by W. F. Stinespring. New York: Macmillan, 1955.

———. *MiYeshu Ad Paulus*. Vol. 2. Tel Aviv: Mada, 1940.

Kleist, Heinrich von. *Michael Kohlhaas*. Translated by Martin Greenberg. New York: Melville House, 1960.

———. *Shalosh Novellot*. Translated by Israel Zarchi and Mordechai Temkin. Tel Aviv: Am Oved, 1982.

Klibansky, Raymond, Erwin Panofsky, and Fritz Saxl. *Saturn and Melancholy: Studies in the History of Natural Philosophy, Religion, and Art*. London: Nelson, 1964.

Kristeva, Julia. *Black Sun: Depression and Melancholia*. Translated by Leon S. Roudiez. New York: Columbia University Press, 1992.

Kuzar, Ron. *Hebrew and Zionism: A Discourse Analytic Cultural Study*. Berlin: Mouton de Gruyter, 2001.

Laor, Dan. *Alterman: Biographia*. Tel Aviv: Am Oved, 2013.

———. *Shaye Agnon: Biyograpfyah*. Tel Aviv: Shocken, 1998.

Laor, Yitzhak. *Anu kotvim otach moledet*. Tel Aviv: Hakibbutz Hameuchad, 1995.

———. "Sipur al Ahava veChoschech: Taamula, Narkicism veHamaarav." *Mitaam* 7 (September 2006): 67–90.

Lebovic, Nitzan. "The Jerusalem School: The Theopolitical Hour." *New German Critique* 35, no. 3 (2008): 97–120.

———. "Nihilism as Stasis." In *The Politics of Nihilism: From the Nineteenth Century to Contemporary Israel*, edited by Roy Ben-Shai and Nitzan Lebovic, 13–33. London: Bloomsbury, 2014.

Lepenies, Wolf. *Melancholie und Gesselschaft*. Frankfurt am Main: Suhrkamp, 1969.

Levine, Emily. *Dreamland of Humanists: Warburg, Cassirer, Panofsky, and the Hamburg School*. Chicago: Chicago University Press, 2015.

Levy, Lital. *Poetic Trespasses: Writing between Hebrew and Arabic in Israel/Palestine*. Princeton, NJ: Princeton University Press, 2014.

Liska, Vivian. "Against Melancholy: On the Demonic in Gershom Scholem." In *Das Dämonische: Schicksale einer Kategorie der Zweideutigkeit nach Goethe*, edited by Lars Friedrich, 311–25. Paderborn: Fink, 2014.

———. *When Kafka Says We*. Bloomington: Indiana University Press, 2009.

Mahlo, Aviva. *Ben Shnei Nofim*. Jerusalem: Reuven Mas, 1991.

Maimonides. *Mishneh Torah*. Translated by Eliyahu Touger. Chabad-Lubabitch. http://www.chabad.org/library/article_cdo/aid/910346/jewish/Deot-Chapter-Six.htm (accessed March 13, 2015).

Massad, Joseph. *The Persistence of the Palestinian Question: Essays on Zionism and the Palestinians*. New York: Routledge, 2006.

McNeal, Robert H. "Women in the Russian Radical Movement." *Journal of Social History* 5, no. 2 (Winter 1971–72): 143–63.

Mendes-Flohr, Paul and Jehuda Reinhartz, eds. *The Jew in the Modern World: A Documentary History*. Oxford: Oxford University Press, 1995.

Miron, Dan. *From Continuity to Contiguity: Toward a New Jewish Literary Thinking*. Stanford, CA: Stanford University Press, 2010.

———. *The Prophetic Mode in Modern Hebrew Poetry*. Milford, CT: Toby, 2010.

Moglen, Seth. *Mourning Modernity: Literary Modernism and the Injuries of American Capitalism*. Stanford, CA: Stanford University Press, 2007.

Myers, David N. *Between Jew and Arab: The Lost Voice of Simon Rawidowicz*. Hanover, NH: Brandeis University Press, 2008.

Naftali, Michal ben. *Al Ha'Prishut*. Tel Aviv: Resling, 2009.

Naveh, Hannah. "Al ha'ovdan, al ha'shchol, ve'al ha'evel ba'havaya ha'Israelit." *Alpaim* 16 (1998): 85–120.

Neumann, Boaz. *Land and Desire in Early Zionism*. Translated by Haim Watzman. Waltham, MA: Brandeis University Press, 2011.

Nietzsche, Friedrich. *Beyond Good and Evil*. Translated by Judith Norman. Cambridge: Cambridge University Press, 2002.

———. *Thus Spoke Zarathustra: A Book for Everyone and Nobody*. Translated by Graham Parkes. Oxford: Oxford University Press, 2005.

Nir, Oded. *Signatures of Struggle: The Figuration of Collectivity in Israeli Fiction*. Albany: State University of New York Press, 2018.

Nordau, Max. *The Conventional Lies of Our Civilization*. Chicago: L. Shick, 1884.

Noy, Amos. "Al ha'poschim, yehandes lo lishkoach? Iyyun be'mila ahat shel avot yeshurun." *Teoria U'vikoret* 41 (2013): 199–221.

Orland, Yaakov. *Mivhar Ketavim*. Vol. 3. Jerusalem: Mossad Bialik, 1997.

Oz, Amos. *A Tale of Love and Darkness*. Translated by Nicholas de Lange. New York: Harvest, 2005.

Pardes, Ilana. *Agnon's Moonstruck Lovers: The Song of Songs in Israeli Culture*. Seattle: University of Washington Press, 2014.

Parfitt, Tudor. *The Road to Redemption: The Jews of Yemen, 1900–1950*. Leiden: Brill, 1996.

Patton, Paul. *Deleuze and the Political.* London: Routledge, 2000.

Pensky, Max. *Melancholy Dialectics: Walter Benjamin and the Play of Mourning.* Amherst: University of Massachusetts Press, 1993.

Penslar, Derek J. *Zionism and Technocracy: The Engineering of Jewish Settlement in Palestine, 1870–1918.* Bloomington: Indiana University Press, 1991.

Pinsker, Leon. *Auto-Emancipation.* Translated by D. S. Blodheim. New York: Maccabean, 1906.

Radden, Jennifer, ed. *The Nature of Melancholy from Aristotle to Kristeva.* Oxford: Oxford University Press, 2000.

Raz, Yosef. *The Politics of Loss and Trauma in Contemporary Israeli Cinema.* New York: Routledge, 2011.

———. "Restaging the Primal Scene of Loss: Melancholia and Ethnicity in Israeli Cinema." *Third Text* 20, no. 314 (May/July 2006): 487–98.

Raz-Krakotzkin, Amnon. "Jewish Memory between Exile and History." *Jewish Quarterly Review* 97, no. 4 (2007): 530–43.

Rilke, Rainer Maria. *Translations from the Poetry of Rainer Maria Rilke.* New York: Norton, 1993.

Rodrian, Fred. "Notizen zu Erich Kästners Kinderbüchern." *Neue deutsche Literatur* 8–9 (1960): 117–29.

Rokem, Na'ama. *Prosaic Conditions: Heinrich Heine and the Spaces of Zionist Literature.* Evanston, IL: Northwestern University Press, 2013.

Rolnik, Eran. *Freud in Zion: Psychoanalysis and the Making of Modern Jewish Identity.* Translated by Haim Watzman. London: Karnak, 2012.

Rose, Jacqueline. *The Question of Zion.* Princeton, NJ: Princeton University Press, 2005.

Sadan, Dov. *Ben Din LeHeshbon: Massot al Sofrim veSfarim.* Tel Aviv: Dvir, 1963.

Said, Edward W. *Orientalism.* London: Penguin Books, 1995.

Salzberger, Eli M., and Fania Oz-Salzberger. "The Secret German Sources of the Israeli Supreme Court." *Israel Studies* 3, no. 2 (Fall 1998): 159–92.

Sammons, Jeffrey L. *Heinrich Heine: Alternative Perspectives, 1985–2005.* Würzburg: Königshausen and Neumann, 2006.

Santner, Eric. *On Creaturely Life: Rilke, Benjamin, Sebald.* Chicago: Chicago University Press, 2006.

Scholem, Gershom. *Dvarim Be'go.* Vol. 1. Tel Aviv: Am Oved, 1976.

———. *Lamentations of Youth: The Diaries of Gershom Scholem, 1913–1919.* Translated by Antony David Skinner. Cambridge, MA: Harvard University Press, 2007.

———. *"The Messianic Idea in Judaism" and Other Essays on Jewish Spirituality.* Translated by Michael A. Meyer. New York: Schocken, 1972.

———. "On Our Language: A Confession." Translated by Ora Wiskind. *History and Memory* 2, no. 2 (1990): 97–99.

———. *Sabbatai Sevi: The Mystical Messiah: 1626–1676.* Translated by R. J. Zwi Werblowsky. Princeton, NJ: Princeton University Press, 1973.

———. "Toward an Understanding of the Messianic Idea in Judaism." In *The Messianic Idea in Judaism and Other Essays on Jewish Spirituality,* 1–36. New York: Schocken, 1971.

Segev, Tom. *One Palestine, Complete: Jews and Arabs under the British Mandate.* Translated by Haim Watzman. New York: Henry Holt, 2000.

Sela-Sheffy, Rakefet. "HaYekim BiSde HaMishpat veDfusim shel Tarbut Burganit BiTkufat HaMandat." *Iyunim BiTkumat Israel* 13 (2003): 295–322.

Shaked, Gershon. "Meotam Hasichim She'biladehem ein Etzim: Al Yetzirato shel Israel Zarchi." *Bitzron: Rivon Le'sifrut, Hagut U'mechkar* 4, no. 15 (1982):11–19.

Shapira, Anita. *Ha'alicha al kav ha'ofek*. Tel Aviv: Am Oved, 1997.

———. *Land and Power: The Zionist Resort to Force, 1881–1948*. Stanford, CA: Stanford University Press, 1992.

———. *Yosef Haim Brenner: A Life*. Translated by Anthony Berris. Stanford, CA: Stanford University Press, 2015.

———. "Zionism and Political Messianism, Comments on Israel Kolatt's Paper." In *Totalitarian Democracy and After*, edited by Yehoshua Arieli and Nathan Rottenstreich, 354–61. New York: Routledge, 2002.

Shenhav, Yehouda. *The Arab Jews: A Postcolonial Reading of Nationalism, Religion, and Ethnicity*. Stanford, CA: Stanford University Press, 2006.

Shohat, Ella. "Rupture and Return: Zionist Discourse and the Study of Arab Jews." *Social Text* 21, no. 2 (2003): 49–74.

———. "Taboo Memories and Diasporic Visions: Columbus, Palestine, and the Arab-Jew." In *Performing Hybridity*, edited by May Joseph and Jennifer Natalya Fink, 131–58. Minneapolis: University of Minnesota Press, 1999.

Soffer, Sasson. *Zionism and the Foundations of Israeli Diplomacy*. Cambridge: Cambridge University Press, 1998.

Starobinski, Jean. "L'encre de la melancolie." *La nouvelle revue française* 123 (January 3, 1963): 410–23.

———. *Melancholie: Genie und Wahnsinn in der Kunst*, edited by Jean Clair. Berlin: Staatliche Museen, 2006.

Stauber, Roni. *The Holocaust in Israeli Public Debates in the 1950s*. Edgware, Middlesex: Vallentine Mitchell, 2007.

Stavans, Ilan. *Resurrecting Hebrew*. New York: Random House, 2005.

Sternhell, Zeev. *The Founding Myths of Israel: Nationalism, Socialism, and the Making of Israel*. Translated by David Maisel. Princeton, NJ: Princeton University Press, 1998.

Tobi, Yosef. *The Jews of Yemen: Studies in Their History and Culture*. Leiden: Brill, 1999.

———. "Al Kfar Hashiloah ve'al Hasefer 'Kfar Hashiloah' Le'Israel Zarchi.'" *Afikim* 127/128 (August 2006): 29–35.

Toohey, Peter. *Melancholy, Love, and Time: Boundaries of the Self in Ancient Literature*. Ann Arbor: University of Michigan Press, 2004.

Toren, Haim. *Israel Zarchi: ha'hof hanichsaf: spiurim*. Jerusalem: Eruven Mass, 1950.

———. "Israel Zarchi." *Moznaim: Journal of the Hebrew Writers Association in Israel* 1, no. 7 (December 25, 1947): 153–58.

———. *Iturim: Measef Sifruti Lezecher Israel Zarchi*. Jerusalem: Achiasaf, 1948.

Traverso, Enzo. *Left-Wing Melancholia: Marxism, History, and Memory*. New York: Columbia University Press, 2016.

Wedepohl, Claudia. "Warburg, Saxl, Panofsky, and Dürer's *Melencolia I*." *Schifanoia: A Cura dell'Instituto di Studi Rinascimentali di Ferrara* 48–49 (2015): 27–44.

Yahalo, Joseph. *Yehuda Halevi: Poetry and Pilgrimage*. Jerusalem: Hebrew University Press, 2009.

Zalashik, Rakefet. "Psychiatry, Ethnicity, and Migration: The Case of Palestine, 1920–1948." *Dynamis* 25 (2005): 403–22.

Zarchi, Israel. *Alumim*. Tel Aviv: Mitzpe, 1933.

———. *Bet Savta Shecharav: Sipurim*. Tel Aviv: Misrad Habitachon, 1988.

———. *Eretz lo Zru'a.* Tel Aviv: Am Oved, 1947.

———. *Har HaTzofim.* Jerusalem: Ahiasaf, 1940.

———. *Ha'Neft Zorem La'Yam Ha'Tikhon.* Jerusalem: Israeli Publishing, 1937.

———. *Israel Zarchi: Yalkut Sipurim.* Tel Aviv: Yachdav, 1983.

———. *Iturei Yerushalaim, shvilim ba'Ir Ha'atika.* Jerusalem: Weinfeld, 1942.

———. *Kefar ha'Shiloah.* Tel Aviv: Am Oved, 1948.

———. *Massa Le'Lo Tz'ror.* Jerusalem: Hotza'at Ha'Sfarim Ha'Eretz-Israelit, 1939.

———. *Nachalat Avot.* Jerusalem: Reuven Mas, 1946.

———. "Sambatyon." In *Yalkut sipurim,* edited by Avinoam Barshai, 96–148. Tel Aviv: Yachdav, 1983.

———. *Yamim yechefim.* Tel Aviv: Mitzpe, 1935.

Zarchi, Nurit. *Be-tsel gevirtenu.* Tel Aviv: Yedi'ot Aḥaronot: Sifre Hemed, 2013.

———. *Mischakei B'didut.* Tel Aviv: Yediot Ahronot, 1999.

Zertal, Idith. *Israel's Holocaust and the Politics of Nationhood.* Cambridge: Cambridge University Press, 2005.

Zerubavel, Yael. *Recovered Roots: Collective Memory and the Making of Israeli National Tradition.* Chicago: Chicago University Press, 1995.

INDEX

NITZAN LEBOVIC is Associate Professor of History and Apter Chair of Holocaust Studies and Ethical Values at Lehigh University. He is author of *The Philosophy of Life and Death: Ludwig Klages and the Rise of a Nazi Biopolitics*, editor (with Roy Ben-Shai) of *The Politics of Nihilism: From the Nineteenth Century to Contemporary Israel*, and editor (with Andreas Killen) of *Catastrophes: A History of an Operative Concept.*

9 780253 041821